MODERN POETRY

AND THE

CHRISTIAN TRADITION

AWARDED THE DECENNIAL BROSS PRIZE

MODERN POETRY
AND THE
CHRISTIAN TRADITION:

A STUDY IN THE RELATION
OF
CHRISTIANITY TO CULTURE

AMOS N. WILDER

Test the spirits whether they are of God
                    I JOHN *iv, i*

WIPF & STOCK · Eugene, Oregon

Wipf and Stock Publishers
199 W 8th Ave, Suite 3
Eugene, OR 97401

Modern Poetry and the Christian Tradition
A Study in the Relation of Christianity to Culture
By Wilder, Amos and Hawkins, Peter S.
Copyright©1952 by Wilder, Amos
ISBN 13: 978-1-62564-506-7
Publication date 1/3/2014
Previously published by Charles Scribner, 1952

TO
WARD DIX KERLIN
IN MEMORIAM
AND
JENNEY GILBERT KERLIN

SERIES FOREWORD TO THE AMOS N. WILDER LIBRARY

GIVEN THE SUPERFLUITY OF books in the world, there has to be a compelling reason to reissue those that have gone out of print. Most often a curious reader can rely successfully on interlibrary loan or Google Books to gain access to what the publishing world has otherwise let drop. But this piecemeal retrieval is not sufficient when an author, rather than a single volume, warrants being brought back into circulation; when there is a whole body of work deserving of a fresh audience. Such is the case with Amos Niven Wilder (1895–1993), whose prodigious writing, spanning the better part of a century, claims our attention with its extraordinary variety of genres (poetry, essay, and memoir) and disciplines (biblical study, literary criticism, theology).

First, the man behind the publications. A gift for writing and a passion for literature were very much in the family's DNA. Named for his newspaper-publisher father, Amos was the eldest of five, four of whom distinguished them as writers. Most famous of them was his only brother, the playwright and novelist Thornton Wilder, about whom he wrote "Thornton Wilder and His Public" in 1980. Educated at Yale University, from which he eventually received four degrees, he also undertook biblical and theological studies in France and Belgium but most importantly at Mansfield College, Oxford, where he encountered the likes of Albert Schweitzer (*The Quest of the Historical Jesus*) and C.H. Dodd (renown for the notion of "realized eschatology," wherein the end is not near but now). These years of schooling launched his career as a distinguished New Testament scholar at Andover-Newton Theological Seminary, the Chicago Theological Seminary and the University of Chicago, and finally at Harvard Divinity School. Yet perhaps more crucial to his personal development than this academic training was his service in World War I, during which time he served as a volunteer ambulance driver in France and Macedonia (receiving the *Croix de guerre*) and later saw significant action as a corporal with the U.S. Army field artillery in France. That the "Great War" shaped his life and career is suggested by the works that bracket his publications: his first book, a collection of poems, *Battle Retrospect* (1923), and his very last, *Armageddon Revisited: A World War I Journal* (1994). Both bear witness to a traumatic wartime experience that neither destroyed him nor ever let him go.

For many, the trenches marked the end of faith, but not for Wilder. Upon his discharge he went to Yale Divinity School, was ordained in the Congregational Church, and served briefly as a parish minister in New Hampshire. By the end of the 1920s, however, he was back at Yale to do doctoral work in the New Testament. Impelled by a fascination with eschatology, that branch of theology concerned with "last things," he focused research and imagination on traditional themes: death, the end of the world, and the ultimate destiny of humanity. But this was no antiquarian theological interest; it was his way into a deeper understanding of the Gospel and the times in which he lived. It is not difficult to connect the academic study that culminated in *Eschatology and Ethics in the Teaching of Jesus* (1939, 1950, 1978) with the trauma of World War I; it is even easier to understand why throughout his career he was drawn to the apocalyptic literature of both Jews and Christians. In France he had been inside an apocalypse, had felt the earth reel and rock, had seen the foundations of the world laid bare (2 Sam. 22: 8, 16). It would not do to dismiss these biblical visions, as many did at the time, as surreal and grotesque fantasy; they were, he would argue, grounded in an actual Armageddon he had witnessed firsthand. "Reality" as it had been known before the world had been torn open for judgment. It was time for revelation.

The correspondence Wilder saw between ancient apocalyptic and the experience of his own generation—between notions of biblical crisis and the revolutions of the twentieth century—inspired an already established biblical scholar to become a literary critic as well. Turning to texts sacred and secular, ancient and modern, he discovered in them a common situation, what in a 1971 essay he called "nakedness to Being," an "immediacy to the dynamics of existence." When you live in a ruined world, you must study the ruins. Literature was a place to begin.

He began, in fact, with the particular literature of biblical writers: parable, myth, apocalypse, and Christian rhetoric in all its forms. Moreover, rather than travel the well-worn, dusty paths of the New Testament academy, Wilder invested himself in an exploration of biblical imagination at a time (unlike the present day) when few were doing so. What precisely was the world the Scriptures asked us to enter, and how did language bring it to life? Parable and apocalyptic were especially compelling to him as they emerged, he argued, from "a crucible where the world is made and unmade."

Wilder did not approach the Bible "as literature," but rather as the Word of God articulated in a variety of literary forms. He welcomed the new attention being paid by literary scholars to the Scriptures—Northrop Frye, Robert Alter, Frank Kermode—and was grateful that windows had been opened "in an ancient library long obscured by stained glass and cobwebs" (as he wrote in an endorsement of Alter and Kermode's *Literary Guide to the Bible*). Yet he was not uncritical of what they found on the sacred page, nor did his interest in literary theory prevent him from arguing against the Deconstructionist notion that biblical narrative (*pace* Kermode's *The Genesis of Secrecy*) was finally indeterminate and open-ended. For Wilder, the Gospel of Mark, for instance, was "too urgent for puzzles and mystification"; it was not a cryptogram but an "opening and crowning disclosure" of glory.

In a daring move for a "guild" scholar, even one long drawn to questions of biblical interpretation, Wilder also opened his readers to the poetry, fiction, and drama of the twentieth century. An early foray into this career-long exploration was *The Spiritual Aspects of Modern Poetry* in 1940; a decade later came the decennial Bross Prize-winning *Modern Poetry and the Christian Tradition* (1952), *Theology and Modern*

Literature (1958), and then *The New Voice: Religion, Literature, and Hermeneutics* (1969), where he touches on novelists (Proust, Gide, Sartre) and poets (Eliot, Robert Lowell, David Jones). These books invite the theological reader to be at once nourished and challenged by twentieth-century literature. However, the were written not only to expand the horizons of biblical scholars, but also to develop an interest in religion among those not inclined to seek it out. Still more ambitious is Wilder's 1976 book, *Theopoetic*, with its call for a renewal of biblical religion itself through the cultivation of the imagination. This required the risk of the new, stepping beyond the safety of the familiar and time-worn to explore deeper waters: "Old words do not reach across the new gulfs, and it is only in vision and oracle that we can chart the unknown and new-name the creatures." Before the message, came the vision; before the sermon, the hymn; before the prose, the poem. (He began his life as a writer in 1923, after all, as a Yale Younger Poet.)

Wilder's *The Bible and the Literary Critic*, published in 1991—just two years before his death in his 98th year—offers his own retrospection on a life's work spent on a border between Scripture and literature, proclamation and critique, God's Word and the poet's new account of everything old. Thanks to Wipf & Stock's republication of his works in "The Amos N. Wilder Library," we now have a chance not merely to look back on an extraordinarily varied creative life but to realize anew what it stands to offer our future explorations of the Bible and its literary afterlife.

Peter S. Hawkins
Professor of Religion and Literature
Yale Divinity School
New Haven, CT
October 2013

ACKNOWLEDGMENTS

The author acknowledges with thanks his debt to the individuals, periodicals and publishing houses listed below for permission to use copyrighted material.

Harper and Brothers for use of selections from A STREET IN BRONZEVILLE by Gwendolyn Brooks, copyright, 1945 by Gwendolyn Brooks Blakely; and for material from SPIRITUAL ASPECTS OF NEW POETRY by Amos N. Wilder.

Harcourt, Brace and Company, Inc. for use of material from ESSAY ON RIME, copyright, 1945, by Karl Shapiro. Reprinted by permission of Harcourt, Brace and Company, Inc. For material from FOUR QUARTETS, copyright, 1943, by T. S. Eliot. Reprinted by permission of Harcourt, Brace and Company, Inc. From THE FAMILY REUNION, copyright, 1939, by T. S. Eliot. Reprinted by permission of Harcourt, Brace and Company, Inc. From THE COCKTAIL PARTY, copyright, 1950, by T. S. Eliot. Reprinted by permission of Harcourt, Brace and Company, Inc. For selections from the poem "The First Sunday In Lent," from LORD WEARY'S CASTLE, copyright, 1944, 1946, by Robert Lowell. Reprinted by permission of Harcourt, Brace and Company, Inc. And for selections from the poem "Conversation Overheard in the Subway" from AFTERNOON OF A PAWNBROKER AND OTHER POEMS, copyright, 1943, by Kenneth Fearing. Reprinted by permission of Harcourt, Brace and Company, Inc.

Vanguard Press, Inc. for use of the poem "Still Falls the Rain" reprinted by permission of Vanguard Press, Inc. from THE CANTICLE OF THE ROSE: POEMS 1917-1949 by Edith Sitwell. Copyright 1949 by Edith Sitwell.

Oxford University Press for the use of eight selections from POEMS OF GERARD MANLEY HOPKINS, copyright 1930; and for material from THE CORRESPONDENCE OF GERARD MANLEY HOPKINS AND RICHARD WATSON DIXON by C. C. Abbot, copyright 1935.

Charles Scribner's Sons for use of selections from the poem "Tetelestai" by Conrad Aiken which appears in his SELECTED POEMS, copyright 1933; and for selections from the poems "The Last Days of Alice," "Sonnets At Christmas," and "More Sonnets At Christmas" by Allen Tate, all of which are reprinted from POEMS: 1922-1947 by Allen Tate, copyright 1932, 1937, 1948 by Charles Scribner's Sons; used by permission of the publishers.

Pantheon Books, Inc. for use of selections from three poems in EXILE AND OTHER POEMS by St.-John Perse, copyright 1949; for material from CHARLES PÉGUY: MEN AND SAINTS by Julian Green, copyright 1944; and from MYSTÈRE DES SAINTS-INNOCENTS by Charles Péguy, translated by Julian Green.

The Macmillan Company for use of selections from the poems "Vacillation" and "The Second Coming" from COLLECTED POEMS OF WILLIAM BUTLER YEATS, copyright 1950 by Macmillan; "In Distrust of Merits" from NEVERTHELESS by Marianne Moore, copyright 1944; and for material from CHRISTIAN DISCRIMINATION by Brother George Every.

Sheed and Ward, Inc. for use of material from JACOB'S NIGHT by Wallace Fowlie, copyright Sheed and Ward, Inc., New York, 1947.

ACKNOWLEDGMENTS

Columbia University Press for use of material from Vol. I, copyright 1939, and Vol. III, copyright 1949, of RELIGIOUS TRENDS IN ENGLISH POETRY by Hoxie N. Fairchild.

Cambridge University Press for use of material from THE POETRY OF GERARD MANLEY HOPKINS by E. E. Phare.

Random House, Inc. for use of selections from ROAN STALLION, TAMAR AND OTHER POEMS by Robinson Jeffers; of selections and six poems from THE COLLECTED POETRY OF W. H. AUDEN, copyright 1945; and from the poem "Prayer in Mid-Passage" from SPRINGBOARD by Louis MacNeice, copyright 1945; from THE AGE OF ANXIETY, copyright 1947; for selections from the poem "A Christmas Oratorio" from FOR THE TIME BEING, copyright 1944, both by W. H. Auden.

The Dial Press for use of selections from LITTLE FRIEND, LITTLE FRIEND by Randal Jarrell, copyright 1945; and for the poems "Poetry" and "Roses Only" from OBSERVATIONS by Marianne Moore, copyright 1924.

Abingdon-Cokesbury Press for use of material from "T. S. Eliot's *The Cocktail Party*: Of Redemption and Vocation" by Nathan A. Scott, Jr. which appeared in *Religion In Life*, Vol. XX, No. 2, Spring, 1951.

New Directions Press, 333 Sixth Avenue, New York City, for use of the poem "In the Ruins of New York" from FIGURES FOR AN APOCALYPSE, copyright 1947; and for selections from A MAN IN THE DIVIDED SEA, copyright 1946; from THE TEARS OF THE BLIND LION, copyright 1949, all by Thomas Merton; from IN THE DREAMS BEGIN RESPONSIBILITIES, by Delmore Schwartz, copyright 1938; and for the poem "Especially When the October Wind" from SELECTED WRITINGS, copyright 1947; for material from THE WORLD I BREATHE, copyright 1939, both by Dylan Thomas; and for use of the poem "Blandula, Tenulla, Vagula," from THE SELECTED POEMS OF EZRA POUND.

The Harvard University Press for use of material from "The Drift to Liberalism in the Eighteenth Century" by Howard Mumford Jones, which appeared in AUTHORITY AND THE INDIVIDUAL, published in 1937.

Martin Secker & Warberg, Ltd. for use of material from THE DOUBLE IMAGE: MUTATIONS OF CHRISTIAN MYTHOLOGY IN THE WORK OF FOUR FRENCH CATHOLIC WRITERS OF TODAY by Reynal Heppenstall, copyright 1947.

Longmans, Green & Co., Inc. for use of material from PÉGUY AND LES CAHIERS DE LA QUINZAINE by Daniel Halevy.

The John Rylands Library for use of material from "Some Approaches to Religion Through Poetry During the Past Two Generations" by C. H. Herford, which appeared in the *Bulletin*, Vol. VII, No. 1, July, 1922.

Poetry, A Magazine of Verse for use of selections from "Poem" by Anne Ridley, which appeared in the June 1949 issue, page 141.

Christianity and Crisis for use of material from "Secularism in Church and Synagogue" by Will Herberg, which appeared in Vol. X, No. 8, May 15, 1950.

The Partisan Review for use of material from "T. S. Eliot as the International Hero" by Delmore Schwartz, which appeared in Vol. XII, No. 2, Spring, 1945.

Marion Saunders Literary Agency for use of selections from the poem "Thomas Gray In Patterdale," from ROCK FACE by Norman Nicholson, published by Faber and Faber, copyright 1948.

Mr. Selden Rodman for use of material from his review "Poems from a Boston Jeremiah" which appeared in the *New York Times Book Review* section of November 3, 1946.

The Rev. Terence L. Connolly for use of three selections from POEMS OF FRANCIS THOMPSON, edited by Father Connolly and published by Appleton-Century-Crofts, copyright 1941.

Miss Victoria Sackville-West for use of selections from her book THE LAND, published by William Heinemann, copyright 1927.

ACKNOWLEDGMENTS

Mr. Alexander Koyré for use of material from his book ENTRETIENS SUR DESCARTES, published by Brentanos, Inc., copyright 1944.

Mr. Delmore Schwartz and *The Kenyon Review* for use of selections from "Starlight Like Intuition Pierced the Twelve" by Delmore Schwartz, which appeared in *The Kenyon Review*, VI, 3, Summer, 1944.

Mr. Wallace Stevens, Alfred A. Knopf, Inc., and *The Kenyon Review* for use of selections from "The Auroras of Autumn" by Wallace Stevens, which first appeared in *The Kenyon Review*, X, 1, Winter, 1948 and later in the book THE AURORAS OF AUTUMN, published by Alfred A. Knopf.

The author acknowledges with thanks permission to use here with some revision material of his own previously published.

To Harper and Brothers for the use in Chapter III of his chapter, "The Spirit of Our Culture" in THE CHALLENGE OF OUR CULTURE (Interseminary Series, Vol. I), 1946; for the use in Chapter II of several pages from his chapter, "Literary Sources" in FOUNDATIONS OF DEMOCRACY, 1947 (an address given under the auspices of the Institute for Religious and Social Studies—to which acknowledgment is likewise made); for the use also in Chapter II of several pages from his chapter "The Christian Tradition in Modern Culture" in THE VITALITY OF THE CHRISTIAN TRADITION, 1944.

Chapters IX and X represent revision and amplification of two lectures given at the Andover Newton Theological School in 1949 on the Stephen Greene Foundation, the first of which was published in the Andover Newton *Bulletin*, February 1950. The second is to be published by Harper and Brothers in a forthcoming volume edited by Dr. Stanley Hopper for the Institute of Religious and Social Studies entitled, CONTEMPORARY SPIRITUAL PROBLEMS AS REFLECTED IN CONTEMPORARY LITERATURE. Permission to use these two lectures is gratefully acknowledged.

In Chapter VIII a section is taken over with thanks from the author's article, "The Protestant Witness in Contemporary Poetry," in *Theology Today*, Vol. VI, No. 2, July, 1949.

The author wishes to record his special appreciation to the Edward W. Hazen Foundation and Haddam House, for whom the volume was first planned, for their generosity in permitting him to submit the manuscript for the Bross Prize.

PREFACE

IT should not be necessary today to justify close attention on the part of Christians to the artistic movements of our time. We are no longer satisfied with the view that art is a kind of decoration on the surface of life, or that poetry is a kind of marginal luxury, a form of escapism that may be tolerantly indulged. We recognize rather that the creative, imaginative expressions of culture are often our best clues to the diagnosis of men's hearts and the deeper movements of the age.

Theological study and discussion give good heed today to contemporary movements in philosophy and science. They likewise concern themselves with the social phenomena of the time. But any true understanding of the modern situation requires similar attention to the deeper cultural factors as they reveal themselves in the arts and in related symbolic expression. This is evidently not just a matter of studying the uses of the arts in the church: church music, church architecture, sacred poetry and hymnology, and religious drama. It is rather a matter of observing and interpreting the modern arts generally: poetry, fiction, drama, criticism, painting, music, etc., viewed as indices of the modern crisis and of the spiritual alternatives and trends of the time.

The scriptural figure of the faithful as God's watchmen is suggestive here. The eyes of the Lord are upon the transactions of men. The eyes of the church must be constantly directed to the deeper hungers and dilemmas of men, testing the spirits, noting the emergence of new insights, and ready also to learn from new and often magnificent creations prompted by the secret working of the Spirit. Ezekiel's symbolism for the activity of God among men is relevant here, that of the chariot, the wheels and the cherubim, "full of eyes round about," suggesting as it does God's omniscient scrutiny of man's life.

The character of our culture makes such scrutiny of the arts specially imperative today. The alienation of large elements of society from the religious institutions, their partial alienation, indeed, from the Christian tradition itself, has resulted in a remarkable situation. If this alienation were complete, if we had to do actually with a "post-Christian" epoch, the problem would be clearer. But the situation is a complex one. Large strata and movements in the western world are outside the church. But the religious tradition operates in them still in an indirect and disguised way. The river has gone underground; it has not ceased to flow. .The faith has taken on ambiguous expressions in a wide gamut running from mild to acute secularization. The historical background of this situation must be studied if we are to assess the present situation justly. The issues here are so profound and delicate that a scrutiny of the arts becomes mandatory for any adequate appraisal.

The most remarkable feature of this situation is that the custody and future of the Christian tradition has to a considerable degree passed over into the keeping of non-ecclesiastical and even secular groups. The fateful issues of the Christian faith are often wrestled with more profoundly outside the church than within. The crisis of modern culture has in many respects taken the church by surprise; that is, the deeper movements of the age have outrun the church and left much of its experience, formulation, apologetic behind for the time being. There has been an exceptional widening of the gulf between the religious institutions and Christendom itself, leaving the

PREFACE   XIII

church and its immediate constituency in relative isolation. The terms in which the church continues to bear its historic and pure witness are too often unmeaningful even to those secularized groups in which the tradition is still powerful. The message lacks relevance because its expression has not been shaped in adequate awareness of the modern experience. The church, moreover, is itself to such a degree under judgment that its conscious authority is shaken, the power of the keys undermined.

Therefore large elements in Christendom have perforce had to deal with religious and theological issues on their own terms. The Spirit has continued to operate on the hearts of men outside the churches as well as within, through uncanonical as well as canonical channels. In a period of cultural crisis like ours with its accompanying costs and anguish, the secular world has been constrained for its very life to identify the spiritual resources needed for survival, and to come to terms in its own way with the moral and religious traditions of the West. It is not surprising, therefore, that the major works of contemporary literature are undeniably theological in character. The period is one of spiritual gestation. We are confronted on all sides with a spiritual ferment, an existential wrestling, an exploration of ultimate issues. Much of this moves on the margin at least of the biblical view of man and history. Striking instances appear of secular or uncanonical witness to Christian faith, besides actual conversions or returns to Christian confession and practice.

More significant, however, than the evidences of actual return to the church is the process of reconception of the faith which is going on both within and outside the institutions. The modern situation, both in its external aspects of wars and economic insecurity, and in its deeper aspects of dehumanization and "lostness," serves as a crucible for the reformulation of Christian faith and community. Contribution to this development comes both from outside and inside the religious institutions today, both from Christendom in the wider sense and from the churches themselves. But the contribution of those outside, of "the outriders of the tradition," is often the most significant just because these witnesses speak out of immediate initiation into the stresses of the age.

In these circumstances it is evident that wide opportunities are open for new forms of apologetic and defense of the faith. Secular literature moves toward theological and Christian themes. Christian writers move toward a presentation of the faith in terms of the modern experience. That "cultural vanguard" in the church which Paul Tillich sees as necessary for spiritual reconstruction is more and more active. In the last decade or two an increasing number of Christian writers, baptized into the modern experience and sensibility and at home in the modern arts, have entered this field. Much of the most significant work in literary criticism in our time, moreover, inevitably passes over into what can only be called a theological level. This has been inevitable since the creative writers at the forefront of attention today among those concerned with world literature and the humanities cannot be dealt with in strictly esthetic terms. All in all, a powerful movement of theological inquiry, assessment of the Christian tradition in the West, and apologetic has emerged in connection with modern imaginative literature and criticism. The ground upon which such discussion moves and the outcomes may often fall short of what might be desired in the way of traditional commitment and orthodox formulation. Here is where the obligation to test the spirits becomes imperative. But it is just because such formulation today calls for restatement and because the meaning of orthodoxy requires clarification that all such reassessment is important.

The plan of the present volume follows from these considerations. Our final interest is in the vitality and operation of the Christian tradition, the work of the Holy Spirit, in our contemporary world, especially in its secularized aspects. Thus our particular topic is set in the larger frame of the relation of the church to contemporary culture. The field of observation we choose is that of modern poetry, the poetry, that is, which reflects our modern crisis. This field is enlarged occasionally by reference to imaginative literature generally and to contemporary criticism. The implications of the discussion often involve all the modern arts. Our first task is, then, to give attention to representative poets of our time, to note the wider implications of their work, and so to "test the spirits" and assess the impulses and trends of our age. Such a scrutiny evidently also offers us opportunity for further acquaintance with the artistic achievement of various gifted poets of our time whose work is first of all to be recognized as art in its own right.

An accompanying aim in these chapters has been to interpret the significance of modern poetry, in the sense in which it is used here, and to justify the importance we assign to it. There are many readers today for whom the new poetry is still an undiscovered country or for whom its features are occasion of demurral if not scandal. We have therefore devoted chapters IV, V and VI to discussion of the relation of "traditional" to "modern" poetry, availing ourselves of the opportunity to continue our introduction of the work of non-traditional writers.

We desire to lay emphasis on the importance of the cultural and social context of our discussion. Interpretation of the modern arts is deprived of the major part of its significance if their interrelations with the situation of modern society are overlooked. But here some historical setting is indispensable. Chapters II and III present this cultural context essential for understanding either the arts or the spiritual issues of our century.

Finally, we have been concerned to distinguish the poetry

of Catholic, Anglican and Protestant background and inspiration in assessing the artistic fertility of the Christian tradition today. The special resources or limitations of each community in the faith, the flexibility of Christian symbolism in its encounter with a new world, these are significant factors in assessing the modern relevance of the Christian faith. Here too the basic question of the relation of poetry to religion is involved and to this we devote our first chapter.

CONTENTS

		PAGE
PREFACE		XI
I.	POETRY AND RELIGION	1
	1. THE ORIGINS OF POETRY	4
	2. POETRY IN THE BIBLE AND THE CHRISTIAN FAITH	6
	3. DISPARAGEMENT OF THE POET'S FUNCTION ON RELIGIOUS GROUNDS	10
	4. THE AUTONOMY OF POETRY	15
II.	THE BACKGROUND: A CULTURAL RETROSPECT	21
	1. THE CHRISTIAN "MYTH" AND THE NEW FORCES	23
	2. THE CHRISTIAN TRADITION AND THE ROMANTIC MOVEMENT	28
	3. PURITANISM AND AMERICAN CULTURE	31
	4. A DIVERGENT CULTURAL ANALYSIS	38
III.	CULTURAL CRISIS AND THE CONFUSION OF TONGUES	44
	1. DISINTEGRATION: RECENT BACKGROUND	46
	2. DISINTEGRATION: THE CONTEMPORARY PICTURE	50
	3. REINTEGRATION: NEW ORDERS AND NEW CULTS	59
IV.	RE-ASSESSING "TRADITIONAL" POETRY	69
	1. "TRADITIONAL" POETRY AS A CULTURAL SURVIVAL	71
	2. HANDICAPS OF THE "TRADITIONAL" POET	76
V.	NATURE IN TRADITIONAL AND MODERN POETRY	87
	1. *THE LAND*, BY V. SACKVILLE-WEST	89
	2. NATURE IN APOCALYPSE: NORMAN NICHOLSON	97
	3. MAN AND NATURE IN DYLAN THOMAS	100
	4. NATURE AND THE IMMACULATE WORD IN ST.-JOHN PERSE	103
VI.	THE RENEWAL OF CATHOLIC DEVOTIONAL POETRY	112
	1. FRANCIS THOMPSON'S "FROM THE NIGHT OF FORE-BEING"	114
	2. THE DILEMMA OF CATHOLIC SYMBOLISM	126

	3. PÉGUY: POET OF CHRISTIAN FRANCE	130
	4. CONTEMPORARY CATHOLIC POETRY	137
VII.	*GERARD MANLEY HOPKINS: THE PRIEST AS POET*	148
	1. *AMA NESCIRI*	148
	2. "STRUNG BY DUTY AND STRAINED BY BEAUTY"	152
	3. LINEAGE AND MODERN RELEVANCE	156
	4. THE TERRIBLE CRYSTAL	161
	5. ART AND RELIGIOUS VOCATION	167
VIII.	*SECULAR INVOLVEMENT: POETRY OF PROTESTANT AND ANGLICAN BACKGROUND*	176
	1. THE CHRISTIAN ARTIST AND THE WORLD: THE THREE ALTERNATIVES	178
	2. ACUTE SECULARIZATION	182
	3. THE LIVING TRADITION	187
	4. ART AND THE PROTESTANT PRINCIPLE	190
	5. MR. W. H. AUDEN: TOWARDS A NEW CHRISTIAN SYNTHESIS	196
IX.	*THE SHAKING OF THE FOUNDATIONS*	205
	1. THE NEW APOCALYPSE	207
	2. THE VISION OF EVIL	216
	3. THE THEME OF PURGATION: MR. ELIOT'S *THE FAMILY REUNION*	223
X.	*VICISSITUDES OF CHRISTIAN BELIEF*	231
	1. THE DILEMMA OF FAITH	231
	2. MR. ALLEN TATE'S "SONNETS AT CHRISTMAS"	236
	3. MR. WALLACE STEVENS' "SUNDAY MORNING"	239
	4. THE OUTRIDERS AND THE TRADITION	242
	5. THE LATER STEVENS: "CREDENCES" AND "FICTIONS"	245
	6. RECOVERY OF THE TRADITION: MR AUDEN'S "CHRISTMAS ORATORIO"	251
XI.	*THE SURPRISES OF GRACE*	257
	1. SECULAR THEOLOGY AND WITNESS	259
	2. THE DARK DOVE: GRACE IN CATASTROPHE	269
	3. GRACE AND DISPOSSESSION IN ELIOT'S *FOUR QUARTETS*	274
THE BROSS FOUNDATION		281
INDEX		285

The rediscovery of a Christian heritage in the revolution of our time remains the most important gain that has been made in these last years for the conscience of our generation.

IGNAZIO SILONE

And He shall convict Israel through the chosen ones of the Gentiles,
Even as He reproved Esau through the Midianites . . .
Becoming therefore children in the portion of them that fear the Lord.

TESTAMENT OF BENJAMIN
X, 10

I
POETRY AND RELIGION

THE relation of poetry to religion, more particularly of poetic to religious experience, is a perennial question. We are obliged to come to terms with it as best we can for the purposes of this study. We meet head on here the whole problem of the esthetic life. It is presupposed throughout our examination of modern poetry that esthetic expression has bearings that are more than esthetic in the narrow sense. We believe that the experience of the artist and of those that encounter the work of art, of the poet and the reader of poetry, partakes of the character of religious experience and of religious vision. But many qualifications are in order here. Perhaps the best service our present chapter can render is to present the many-sidedness of the matter and so forestall oversimplification.

Popular misconceptions as to the relation of poetry and religion fall commonly into two types. There is the mystical or spiritualist view that all poetry is religious and religious in much the same way though, indeed, varying in quality. It is "inspiring," it quickens emotion and imagination, it adds intensity to experience: therefore it is "religious." The difficulty with such a view is that significant religion is too easily confused with partial or shallow levels of experience; often with thrills, gratifications, moods which do not claim the deeper personal life. In the second place, there is the moralizing or didactic view that poetry is religious when it deals explicitly with God, Christ, Scripture, ideals or conduct, and that all other poetry is merely secular, pretty, frivolous or even immoral. Such popular misconceptions rest as much upon erroneous views of religion as of poetry. They reappear in more learned versions. For example, on the basis of a systematic distinction between the natural order and the order of revelation, poetry like all the arts, may be assigned to the former and its exercise viewed therefore as relatively unimportant for religion.

To define the relation between poetry and religion is, indeed, a hazardous task. Age-old cruxes in esthetic theory are involved as well as the most recent critical discussion. Anyone who proposes to deal with these problems must walk circumspectly for fear of running afoul either of those who have special views as to religion, or those who have special views as to esthetics. He has to thread his way delicately between Plato and Aristotle, between Thomist and romantic, between those contemporary critics who assert the autonomy of poetry, and those modern poets who, like many older poets, see themselves as seers and prophets.

We shall not here add one more definition of poetry to the many that exist. The inadequacy of some views will appear in the course of our discussion. It is more to the point here to urge that austere standards be maintained in consideration of the art, that we keep constantly in mind its greater possibilities and achievements. Great poetry is priceless and achieved at inestimable cost. It comes by a kind of miracle through the convergence of innumerable favoring circumstances. What we have constitutes an incomparable and many-sided revelation of man. In it man comes to consciousness of himself, his scope and faculties and the terms of his lot. It is with poetry of this stature that men should always be primarily concerned. In the light of it the limitations of lesser poetry, whether "traditional" or modern, should always be recognized.

Such due recognition, however, of the august character of the greatest poetry does not mean indifference to other and lesser kinds. It rather confers an honor upon all poetry and should make us appreciative of the innumerable more modest forms which spring up perpetually in the varied circumstances of man's life past and present.

For a working definition of religion we shall have in mind our relation to the "unconditioned" or ultimate, or that which has unconditional obligation for us, together with our response to it. Such a definition is, indeed, very general and highly abstract. Ordinarily we shall be concerned with the relations of poetry to our western religious tradition. But even in this generalized form the basic relation of poetry to religion suggests itself. Certainly the poetic experience like religious experience involves a relation with the "unconditioned."

> Poetry is ontology, truly; it is even theology, in accordance with the great saying of Boccacio. But in the sense that it takes its birth at the mysterious sources of being and after its own fashion reveals them by its own creative movement.[1]

But if poetry coincides with religion in this respect, as an art it takes its own direction. The religious life involves our total response to the unconditioned. The esthetic life moves toward the shaping of the work of art. But of all the arts poetry, since it is an art of language, of the word, will often retain and sustain a varied relation to religion.

We may here forecast two main theses and this will serve as a guide in what follows:

(1) Poetry and religion, the poetic and the religious experience, are profoundly and intimately related to each other if not consubstantial, and religion requires poetry in its discourse.

(2) In certain recurrent phases of culture poetry rightly

---

[1] *Situation de la Poésie*, by Jacques et Raissa Maritain (Paris: Desclée de Broumer, 1938), p. 117. Santayana's way of saying this is that poetry and religion are identical in essence, though they relate themselves differently to practical life: poetry by a dramatic presentation of values and religion by precepts and code.

tends to assert its own autonomy over against religion, but it still remains deeply religious in character.

The validity and meaning of these theses will best appear if we examine successively a number of instances and testimonies bearing on the matter in different periods and circumstances. We shall give attention: (1) to the origins of poetry; (2) to the place of poetry in the Bible and in the Christian faith; (3) to a number of instances in which for one reason or another the function of the poet has been disparaged on moral and religious grounds; and finally, (4) to contemporary claims made for the autonomy of poetry.

1. THE ORIGINS OF POETRY

We must reckon with the fact that in their beginnings poetry and religion are indistinguishable and consubstantial. The tribal soothsayer is the first poet, and his oracle or incantation or curse is proffered in rhythmic verse or chant. We may take our example from ancient Arabia where, says D. B. MacDonald, "poetry is magical utterance, inspired by powers from the unseen, and the poet is, in part an adviser and admonisher, and in part a hurler of magical formulae against his enemies."[1] The utterance of the Arabic diviners of the better type was cast in that primitive verse which was called Saj^c, literally "pigeon-cooing." This, continues MacDonald, became later the normal rhetorical form of language in Islam and consisted essentially of a series of short phrases in prose—it may be with rhythm—all rhyming together. Mohammed was "a poet of the old Arab type, without skill of verse, and with all his being given to the prophetic side of verse."[2] In early Hebrew vaticination and poetry we have an analogous story. The "wizards, that chirp and mutter" (Is. 8:19) correspond to the Arabic diviners and the Hebrew term corresponds. This pattern of utterance evolved into the literary form of Hebrew poetry. Thus the poet

---

[1] *Religious Attitude and Life in Islam* (Chicago: 1909), pp. 16, 17.
[2] *Op. cit.*, pp. 16, 17.

was originally a *vates* and his chant a *carmen* (charm) to use the corresponding Latin terms.

Recurrent impulses in recent poetry and its precursors have exalted this idea of the poet as magical sayer and of poetry as incantation. A French tradition from Rimbaud to St.-John Perse with its influence on an American poet like Hart Crane, gives illustration. Such poetry is oracular, Dionysiac and has a religious character even though devoid of any but the most indeterminate theological reference. To this we shall return later.

MacDonald's characterization of what he calls "the first feeling out of verse" in the lower cultural levels is connected with the practical tribal role of the shaman. We may, however, take a cue from the insight that "poetry is praise" and propose that the original urge of song was spontaneous celebration and lyric impulse. We have here the alternative which reappears in theories of primitive art and cave painting. On the one hand there is the instrumentalist view that early man designed art forms to offer himself the relative security of his own created order in a mysterious environment full of menace and arbitrariness. Indeed, there is also the related view that the cave paintings were magical charms against the malevolent powers. But the alternative view is that he wrought in the spirit of free play and delight in celebration of existence: art is praise.

Such a view of art and song can be carried back into the sub-human creation. Richard Cabot used to tell of an experience in the Adirondacks that drove this home upon him. Awaking on an open porch in the woods in the earliest dawn he heard the songs of countless birds, but also from a neighboring cottage the dove-like cooing and prattle of an infant that had awaked before its parents. In both he recognized the canticle of the creatures and perceived an impulse that was not different even when articulated and orchestrated in the most complex media of the modern arts.

2. POETRY IN THE BIBLE AND THE CHRISTIAN FAITH

Let us now bring into our picture of the relations of poetry and religion the prominent place that poetry occupies in the Jewish and Christian Scriptures and in the liturgy and piety of Christianity.

In the earlier strata of the Old Testament we find a continuation of the older Semitic poetry. The advance of the Hebrews, whether in poetic skill or in religious conceptions, does not mean that the religious character of their verse is lost. Thus it is true that the Song of Deborah is an epic lyric, an ode of triumph (to use classical categories) but it is the triumph of Jahweh that is celebrated and the verse patterns are in the tradition of the primitive Semitic soothsayer, as is even more clear in the ancient oracles of Balaam, where the magical character of the utterance is self-evident.

Not only the Psalter but the larger part of the prophetic and wisdom books of the Old Testament are poetry in the formal sense. Archeological evidence, moreover, has made it clear that not only the basic pattern of the poetic couplet but also the formal features of various types of Psalms, with their functions, have their antecedents in the earlier cultic poems of pre-Israelite Canaan. The primary role of poetry in the religion of Israel is, however, attested not only by the number of pages it occupies in the Scripture but by the peculiar fact that the prose sections of the Old Testament—especially the great historical sections—really depend upon the poetic core or foundation.[1] The prose of religion is a secondary stage. The nearest thing that we have to a non-religious poetry in the Old Testament is the wisdom writing in those sections that have a largely humanistic perspective especially in parts of Proverbs and in the much later skeptical core of Ecclesiastes. We see here an example already of how poetry at certain stages of cultural

---

[1] This observation I owe to Professor J. C. Rylaarsdam.

advance and under the spur of special religious conditions takes on an autonomous character.

The role of poetry in the formal sense in the New Testament is also extraordinarily important and interesting. Since we have the sayings of Jesus only in translation and with the modifications imposed upon them by tradition, we cannot be sure as to the particular rhetorical pattern they had in Aramaic. Scholarly discussion of the matter is still in process. It is at least clear that much of his teaching—apart from the parables, the briefer aphoristic pronouncements and certain sayings in the tradition of the scribes—had a parallelistic rhetorical character closely related to the forms of Hebrew poetry and frequently a strophic character, such that a large body of his most significant utterance must assuredly be classified as poetry in the formal sense. It supports the view that Jesus belonged to the "charismatic" type of the Near East whose insights and utterance often came, if not in ecstatic or near-ecstatic states, at least in that kind of heightened and visionary immediacy which inevitably took rhythmic expression. The oral transmission, translation into Greek, and later editing have added to or transformed the rhetorical patterns in various ways as can be seen sometimes by the comparison of the sayings in Matthew and Luke.

In the Fourth Gospel, on the other hand, we have prosodic forms, notably in the Prologue but also in the discourse assigned to Jesus, which proceed out of Hellenistic rhetorical patterns of a different character. The epistles of the New Testament are sprinkled with quotations of early Christian doxologies and liturgical poetry and allusions to "psalms and hymns and spiritual songs" current in the church, of which the most notable preserved to us are the canticles of Luke. Thus the New Testament too offers its evidence of the inseparable connection of religion with poetry.

This exhibit of the relation of poetry and religion in the Christian tradition must include in summary fashion a reminder of the inexhaustible poetic productivity of the faith through the centuries. Of poetry that may be called explicitly Christian in its theme and use in the church it is useful to distinguish several categories. Sacred or ecclesiastical poetry would include such as has been taken up into the actual offices or liturgy of the church, whether such ancient elements as the Te Deum or Hora Novissima, or the modern Protestant hymn. To be distinguished from this is the "devotional poem": i.e., St. Francis' "Canticle of the Creatures," John Donne's "Divine Poems," Keble's *Christian Year,* and certain of Gerard Manley Hopkins' sonnets. In such works we see the poet engaged in the actual exercise of religious devotion, though apart from the formal ritual of the church.

Professor Kenneth B. Murdock in speaking of this kind of poetry and its role in seventeenth century New England writes: "Many a New Englander would have agreed with Richard Baxter's assertion that 'there is somewhat of Heaven in Holy Poetry.' It charmeth souls into loving harmony and concord." New Englanders read George Herbert, in spite of his Anglicanism, because he concentrated his work on what was for the Puritan the core of religious life—the direct relation of the individual to God. Baxter said that Herbert "speaks to God like one that really believeth a God, and whose business in this world is most with God. Heart-work and Heaven-work make up his books." [2]

There is, in the third place, the vast body of poetry which takes its themes from the Bible, the Gospel, the faith and the Christian life; whether great epics like those of Dante and Milton, or shorter poems or poetic dramas. The variety here can be suggested by recalling such works as Racine's *Esther,* Blake's "Jerusalem," Browning's "Saul," T. S. Eliot's "Journey of the Magi," and W. H. Auden's "Christmas Oratorio." The

---

[2] *Literature and Theology in Colonial New England* (Cambridge, Mass.: Harvard University Press, 1949), p. 149. The citations from Baxter are from the *Poetical Fragments* (London: 1821), pp. iv, v.

penetration of literature in various degrees with Christian motifs would offer infinite ramifications. Shakespeare's *Measure for Measure* is in many respects a Christian parable of the king in incognito. The basic myths or saga of the Fall, of Joseph, of the Wandering Jew, of the Judgment, are taken up and utilized in direct and indirect ways in modern literature. Finally a fourth category of religious poetry can well be distinguished, that of mystical or Christian mystical verse as we find it in *The Oxford Book of Mystical Verse*, in Robert Bridges' anthology, *The Spirit of Man*, and many similar collections.

This brief review will suggest to us not only the interconnections of Christianity and poetry, but the nature of religion as requiring mythopoetic expression. Illustration of the same could be given in other faiths.

We have before us, then, a body of evidence supporting the idea that poetry and religion are inextricably related, that the poetic experience itself is basically akin to religious experience, and that religion necessarily expresses itself in poetry. "In great measure the inspiration of art has been religious ecstasy," says John Livingston Lowes, and quotes a declaration that "art is a form of worship."[3] The poet invokes Apollo and the Muses, or the Holy Spirit (or both, as Milton does). He invokes the divine afflatus, or the Wisdom and Spirit of the Universe (Wordsworth), or the Over-Soul, or Beauty, or the "womb-fire" or "unknown God" of D. H. Lawrence, or the "self-begotten" of Yeats. Surely the constant view of the poet, the orthodox view, we may say, through the centuries, has been that of one who delivers oracles under the inspiration of the gods, though the inspiring powers have been understood in different ways.

[3] Cited by Murdock, *op. cit.*, p. 9, from an address by Lowes made in 1926 at a symposium on religion and the arts, and printed in the *Harvard Alumni Bulletin*, XXIX (Jan. 13, 1927), pp. 409-413.

3. DISPARAGEMENT OF THE POET'S FUNCTION ON RELIGIOUS GROUNDS

For all that has been said, it still remains true that poetry, even if it be viewed as religious in its ultimate nature, is sometimes disparaged as dangerous or subversive of true religion or morality. Examples of this attitude which is both old and new must be considered, since it bears closely on our assessment of contemporary poetry.

It is certainly relevant here that Plato banishes most poets from his ideal republic. On the one hand poetry is seen as enervating the heroic temper of the citizen. On the other hand it compromises the ideal of serenity of the philosopher, allegedly a principle of disorder. We may connect these disparagements on the one hand with the precarious political situation of Athens at the time and with the particular philosophical ideal that obtained. Miss Dorothy Sayers has pointed out in connection with the somewhat contradictory judgments of Plato with regard to all the arts and the more positive views of Aristotle, that the Greeks in their own way recognized the same dangers in art that we do in two respects. (1) Art can be demoralizing when it ministers to unhealthy forms of fantasy and escape. (2) Art as propaganda or social control can, in this respect also, subvert personal responsibility through the ease with which spell-binding suggestion can be exerted on the populace or the masses. Lenin's definition of art as a *weapon* fits in here. Miss Sayers notes that the Greeks in defining art in a somewhat analogous way as *techne* could not assign the fully positive role to art (and poetry) that is possible with a Christian metaphysic.[1] But the attitude of Plato points us to forms of poetry that must be suspect from the point of view of sound religion.

---

[1] "Towards a Christian Aesthetic" in *Unpopular Opinions: Twenty-One Essays* (New York: Harcourt, Brace, 1947).

We may turn now for another instance to the current tendency to rebuke the religious pretensions of modern poetry. Just as romantic poets thought of themselves often as prophets, so poets in the modern symbolist tradition have conceived their work as oracular in character. It will be recalled that Matthew Arnold encouraged the view that poetry could take the place of religion in a significant degree for modern disbelief. With the loss of the biblical faith and other supporting traditions, the modern artist is thrown upon his own psychic resources, and poetry then offers itself as a substitute for or a form of religion. Thus in various forms of mysticism and surrealism, poets elaborate their private mythologies. They exploit the irrational as a means to power. But herein they falsify both poetry and religion. In any case they render poetry suspect and critics are led today to deny or circumscribe closely the religious character of poetry properly understood.

In a lecture on "poetic experience" delivered in 1944 at the University of Chicago, Jacques Maritain pointed out that the modern poetry movement from Baudelaire and Rimbaud on, in its exploration of the "unconscious," of dreams and other sources of symbolic expression, has added a new and significant area of poetic resource. But, he noted, the poets involved have been tempted to make a religion of their fruitful contact with the dynamics of the inner life. In this case they cannot but mislead themselves and others.[2]

Maritain here is saying in his own way what runs as a main theme through the Abbé Bremond's volume, *Prière et Poésie:* "The poet whose specifically poetic activity sought to identify itself with specifically mystical activity, would be violating the order of things: a lame man cannot walk straight."[3] It is

---

[2] Cf. *Situation de la Poésie*, pp. 79-159. See also "A Note on Hart Crane as Discussed by Yvor Winters and Allen Tate," in A. N. Wilder, *The Spiritual Aspects of the New Poetry* (New York: Harpers, 1940), pp. 122-130. Also Karl Shapiro, section, "The Confusion of Belief" in his *Essay on Rime* in which he canvasses the pseudo-religious mythologies of Crane and other poets of a recent period (Ch. X below).

[3] Paris: Grasset (1926), p. 209.

Bremond's theme that poetry is allied to mysticism (in the sense of the experience of the true contemplative) and stands to it in the relation of the sketch to final work of art. Both the poet and the mystic are united to God who is the reality of realities. But God so possessed can only be called by his name by the mystic, not by the poet.[4]

Mr. W. H. Auden has been particularly concerned to delimit the role of the poet and to deny him the role of seer and prophet. All such poetry easily takes on the character of an inebriated mysticism or even totalitarian spell-binding. He has in mind presumably certain neo-pagan ingredients in the work of various poets of the romantic movement who in effect were "false prophets" contributory to later Nazism, imperialism and disorder. He also has in view those utopian *mystiques* which flatter men's sense of power and obscure their limitations.

A further instance indicating suspicion of poetry for a religious motive is in some ways a special case, but nevertheless suggestive. We have in mind the attitude of the superb poet, Gerard Manley Hopkins, to his gift and to the practice of poetry. We shall give a fuller account of this nineteenth-century poet below (Ch. VII). It is enough to mention here that after his vocation as priest and Jesuit had declared itself, he abstained from writing poetry for seven years. Even after he had been encouraged to resume writing by his superiors he exercised infinite scruple about both composition and publication, viewed as distractions from his religious calling. Posterity came very close to never knowing anything of his priceless art. His correspondence with Bridges, Dixon and others on the relation of poetry to religion as it touched his own problem offers a remarkable document on the relation of the esthetic to the religious life. Like Kierkegaard's analysis of the realm of the esthetic, it reminds us that we should not too easily confuse poetry and religion.

[4] *Ibid.*, p. 216.

In this connection we have, moreover, the testimony of a contemporary American poet, also a religious—namely, Thomas Merton, a Trappist monk. As a supplement to his volume of poems, *Figures for an Apocalypse*,[5] Merton presents an essay, "Poetry and the Contemplative Life" in which he states the relation of the esthetic experience to contemplation, in its strict sense, and discusses the role of the Christian poet. On the one hand "contemplation has much to offer poetry." "No Christian poetry worthy of the name has been written by anyone who was not in some degree a contemplative."[6] "Genuine esthetic experience is something which transcends not only the sensible order (in which, however, it has its beginning) but also that of reason itself. It is a supra-rational intuition of the latent perfection of things . . . In the natural order, as Jacques Maritain has often insisted, it is analogue of the mystical experience which it resembles and imitates from afar."[7]

Thus the esthetic instinct, on Merton's view, can introduce us to the "superior soul," it can free even the unbeliever from lower desires, bad taste, emotional vulgarity (which often indeed afflicts believers, in their devotional practice). But the esthetic experience when it passes to performance then arrests the possible full experience of union with God. Our attention is turned to our "work," to what we bring back. In such a case there is "only one course for the poet to take for his own individual sanctification: *the ruthless and complete sacrifice of his art.*"[8] One complication is, however, added here. The poet may become convinced that God wills him to continue writing; God may perhaps signify it to him through his religious superiors, to the end of "some good purpose like the good of souls." In this case the poet will receive consolation

---

[5] Norfolk, Conn.: New Directions Press (1947).
[6] *Ibid.*, p. 99.
[7] *Ibid.*, pp. 101, 102.
[8] *Ibid.*, pp. 109, 110.

himself "that it is more meritorious to share the fruits of contemplation than it is merely to enjoy them ourselves." [9]

Finally we cite a striking opinion of Samuel Johnson who, in effect, puts the religious life proper out of bounds for the poet:

> "Poetical devotion," says Dr. Johnson in his *Life of Waller*, "cannot often please . . . The doctrines of religion may, indeed, be defended in a didactic poem, and he who has the happy power of arguing in verse, will not lose it because his subject is sacred. A poet may describe the beauty and the grandeur of Nature . . . and praise the Maker for His works, in lines which no reader can lay aside. The subject of the disputation is not piety, but the motives to piety: that of the description is not God, but the works of God.
>
> "But contemplative piety, or the intercourse between God and the human soul, cannot be poetical. Man, admitted to implore the mercy of his Creator, and plead the merits of his Redeemer, is already in a higher state than poetry can confer.
>
> "The essence of poetry is invention: such invention, as by producing something unexpected, surprises and delights. The topics of devotion are few, and being few are universally known; but few as they are, they can be made no more: they can receive no grace from novelty of sentiment and very little from novelty of expression." [10]

After quoting this in his study of Hopkins, E. E. Phare adds:

> I should imagine that, as a rule, those who know what contemplative piety is would feel that they were in a higher state than poetry could confer: but evidently there are exceptions. The existence of two such poets as Hop-

---

[9] *Ibid.*, p. 111.
[10] Cited by E. E. Phare, *The Poetry of Gerard Manley Hopkins* (Cambridge, England: The University Press, 1933), pp. 106, 107.

kins and Herbert proves that poetry and contemplative piety can be reconciled: though it is perhaps true that the kind of person usually described as a saint would lose all sense of poetic values in his sense of the religious.

With regard to Samuel Johnson's statement we ourselves may add the following observation. As in the case of Plato the disparagement of poetry is here relative to contemporary factors. The eighteenth century looked on poetry on the whole as a skill, a *techne,* an art or accomplishment in the narrow sense. It therefore appeared incongruous to Johnson that a poet should pray in rhyme. We may suppose that Johnson never thought of the Psalms as poetry or if he did he set them in a special category of inspired and revealed sacred rhetoric. We, of course, know that the Psalms were in the first instance personal poetry of devotion before they took on public cultic use as many did, and can recognize in them a highly sophisticated literary art. The general observation here is that each age has its own reasons for acknowledging or restricting the religious function of poetry. In our own day when poetry has taken on an ambiguously irrational character in many quarters and when the defense of culture has been identified with recovery of the religious traditions or with empirical rationalism, there is a powerful tendency to deny the religious character of poetry. Poetry that assumes an oracular character is characterized as pseudo-religion or magic.

4. THE AUTONOMY OF POETRY

A fourth and final type of evidence bearing upon the relation of poetry to religion is found in the recurrent tendency of the artist and the poet to declare the autonomy of the esthetic experience and activity. Far from claiming to be a seer or to deliver oracles, here the poet sees himself solely as a craftsman. Though as a man he may know religious experience and engage in moral activity, he would not confuse esthetic activity with either of these. The special gift and function of the artist must not be enslaved to public demands. The poet is not to be conscripted by society or the state in the interest of propaganda or encouraged to spell-binding in the interests of parties or sects. He is not even to be viewed as a teacher in any usual sense: that can be left to prose. Thus one aim of many modern artists has been to "purify the medium," and this has often led to an excessive divorce of art values from human values.[1]

We can find one expression of this conviction in the idea of a "pure poetry" as it was discussed some years ago especially in France.[2] The poetry of Poe and Mallarmé, of Keats and Valéry, was taken as normative, a poetry in which the element of communication of ideas was largely subordinated to other elements in the poem: phonetic, incantatory, symbolic. Paul Valéry in some of his criticism defined the poem as a calculated compounding of subtle devices and resources. A mysterious, powerful impact of the poem was sought—the inducing of an intense and rare "state of consciousness." This could be understood in altogether naturalistic terms. A psychological school of criticism, indeed, has sought to explain poetry as consisting of interrelated stimuli acting on the ocular nerves, the semi-circular canals of the ear and the digestive organs. But theory in the symbolist and surrealist movements commonly assigns a religious character to poetry, even where the idea of a pure poetry is maintained.

Mr. Auden in his fear of magic and of prophetic pretension on the part of the poet reduces his activity sometimes to a kind of game or higher artifice.

> Art in intention is mimesis
> But, realized, the resemblance ceases;
> Art is not life and cannot be
> A midwife to society.
> For art is a *fait accompli.*

[1] Cf. William Van O'Connor, *Sense and Sensibility in Modern Poetry* (Chicago: University of Chicago Press, 1948), Ch. 3, "The Break with Verism."

[2] See Henri Bremond, *La Poésie pure* (Paris: Grasset, 1926).

The great artists pursued and harassed by life, were, in fact,

> Hunted out of life to play
> At living in another way;
> Yet the live quarry all the same
> Were changed to huntsmen in the game,
> And the wild furies of the past,
> Tracked to their origins at last,
> Trapped in a medium's artifice,
> To charity, delight, increase.[3]

That is, the poet converts experience into an "artifice" that has a more modest role than prophecy. Yet he agrees that the dead poets "challenge, warn and witness."

In a Lyman Beecher lecture entitled, "The Things that are Caesar's," prepared for the Yale Divinity School convocation and read on April 19, 1950 Mr. Auden made a systematic distinction between the "frivolous" character of the work of the layman, including here the artist, as against the intrinsically "serious" character of the work of the priest. This "frivolous" character inheres in the peculiar occupations, crafts and talents of the "layman" generally as one whose activity is identified with the natural and historical order, with "the things that are Caesar's" in a good sense. The point at which seriousness comes into the work of the artist or layman is in what concerns his use of his free will over against the will of God, but this does not involve his technical work as artist. It is in this framework that Mr. Auden assigns a modest and non-religious role to poetry. We can appreciate his motive here and disagree with his categories. As a matter of fact, one has only to read much of his poetry to recognize immediately that practice belies theory. The poems, for all that they are not didactic prose, carry urgent theological and moral implications as most of the great poetry of the ages has done. Whether he likes it or not the poet finds himself in the role of seer and teacher and must

[3] "New Year Letter," from *The Collected Poetry of W. H. Auden* (New York: Random House, 1945), pp. 267-268.

acknowledge the great responsibilities and "seriousness" that this involves.

Further evidence could be given of the tendency of poetry in our period to dissociate itself from religion and ethics and to liberate itself from moralistic, romantic or idealistic "impurities." This impulse is a defensible one for two reasons. In the first place, whenever man in different cultures becomes particularly sophisticated and self-conscious with regard to "the works of the mind" he inevitably discriminates among them. He distinguishes, for example, the moral, the rational, the esthetic. This is all to the good: esthetic activity is pursued all the more effectively if its special resources and means are clearly grasped and studied in a specialized way. We have not, of course, had to wait until our time for this. The Greeks, the Renaissance, the Enlightenment, and, indeed, medieval esthetic theory, sought to distinguish the artist and his function.

But this tendency is defensible in another respect. When the religious tradition, the religious ethos in a culture becomes narrow, stifling or tyrannical, the artist must dissociate himself and his art from it. Such art then takes on an anti-dogmatic, a humanistic and often a "secular" character and defines itself in naturalistic terms. So we hear of "art for art's sake," of "pure poetry," of the "ivory tower," and charges are made against the artist that he is pagan, Bohemian, anarchistic. Such claims to autonomy on the part of the artist arise not only out of reaction to religion but also social pressures and dogmatism. Among contemporary poets we shall find those whose understanding of poetry and whose method is in this sense apparently purely "esthetic" just as we find an analogous criticism today. Close study will reveal often that such poets while they exclude on principle any immixture of religious and moral elements in the ordinary sense in their work, nevertheless, in the ultimate experience that animates the poem find themselves on religious ground—and this may well manifest itself in somewhat specific ways in their work. Indeed, the artist in dissociating himself from a decadent or coercive religious tradition serves a religious function. Of course, he may, as we have seen, take on the role of a false prophet or "magician." Poetry is a potent and dangerous vehicle just because it is always and inevitably religious in its ultimate nature.

We conclude, then, that the frequent disjunction today between poetry and religion, or poetry and our religious tradition, is due to special circumstances. This gulf between poetry and religion cannot be taken as normal. The curious thing is that the modern artist in declaring the autonomy of the esthetic experience is conditioned by special factors. This situation cannot be used as an argument against what we have called the consubstantiality of the two. The striking thing is that the so-called secular or iconoclastic artist or "pure poet" today is in effect calling the attention of religion to its own distortions and reminding it of its lost scope.

Thus James Joyce in repudiating his inherited faith, in saying *Non Serviam*—"I will not serve"—to his own church and in setting forth, breaking all his bonds with family, country and religion, to "forge the uncreated conscience of the race," can be looked on as an artist who by a long banishment and detour was carrying out a religious vocation. Similarly with writers like André Gide rebelling against Protestant traditions.

Thus we should look on the naturalistic esthetic of Valéry and others as a legitimate attempt to defend the autonomy of poetry and to analyze exhaustively its proper resources. Such critics only err if they finally cut the roots of poetry in religion. Correspondingly the position over against the religious tradition of poets like D. H. Lawrence and Yeats represents, with whatever excesses, a necessary criticism of that tradition, a criticism ultimately grounded in religion itself.

As a matter of fact, we have only to read a poem of Valéry like his "Cimitière Marin" or his *Charmes* generally to recognize that the works of such critics often belie their esthetic.[4] Such poems take on a religious dimension, even those in which didacticism or statement are most conspicuously absent.

In concluding that poetic and religious experience are so basically akin, we should recognize what this involves. In theological terms it implies a natural or universal revelation which has its expression in either art or religion. Religion must therefore include the witness of poetry among its evidences. This has a special value in that it acts as a check upon either moralistic or rationalistic one-sidedness in religion. The imagination comes into its full rights. This also is a safeguard in what concerns dogma. For it insists that dogma be understood as mythopoetic symbol and take its place with ritual and religious art. The Christian faith must not, indeed, be dissolved into "myth" or into "poetry." It rests on unrepeatable and decisive historical events and its formulations include an essential intellectual content. But dogma is always mythopoetic and not discursive.

If we are clear that a true poet is necessarily one in whom, among other things, is to be found a powerful operation of intelligence, we may go on to say, by way of parable, that the Deity is a poet rather than a mathematician. His dealing with the world is an epic poem as his redemption action is a drama. And man's primary response is a psalm, a lyric, a doxology.

---

[4] Compare Henri Bremond's phrase for Valéry: *le poète malgré lui*, the poet in spite of himself (*La Poésie pure*, pp. 60-68). Bremond begins his volume *Prière et Poésie* with the words: "A purely rational or non-mystical philosophy of poetry—whether true or false is not here the question—is an accident, a comet, throughout the whole history of esthetics: *Prolem sine matrem creatam*," p. 1.

II

THE BACKGROUND:
A CULTURAL RETROSPECT

ANY study of the religious bearings of the arts would be deprived of a major part of its significance if the cultural setting were ignored. We are particularly concerned in this volume with modern poetry as an index of our cultural situation, and as a means by which we can diagnose the spiritual dilemmas and trends of the age. The relation of poetry to society is a complex one. The poet is not at all necessarily concerned with the public demands or events of his day. Yet significant poetry and art are conditioned by the prevailing cultural situation and illuminate it. They also modify it. But the relation of poetry to culture must be viewed in a historical setting. The critic T. E. Hulme advised his readers to carry a library of a thousand years in mind as a balancing pole against the prejudice of the contemporary. This counsel holds in ways that go beyond narrowly esthetic considerations.

The spiritual-moral issues of our society take us back especially to the English Reformation. The evolving relations of English poetry to culture can well be referred back to the time of Milton in which the Renaissance, the Reformation and the rise of modern science are all present. Incidentally, it has this advantage that in Milton we have the supreme instance of a Protestant Christian poet, one whose work was inextricably related to public issues and events, and in whom the forces and factors that have conditioned the modern world were already at work. But our concern with background can only be illustrative and, as it were, cartographic. We desire only to sketch in the mountain range of faith that overlooks our later story, and trace the streams of cultural energies that flow thence to our time. Coming down from the seventeenth century we can single out the significant legacies and note how they have related themselves to successive later situations and influences, especially the romantic movement.

History is self-knowledge, the autobiography of culture. In evoking typical supreme expressions of the past we uncover our own continuing or suppressed habits of mind and heart. We bring to light the wells and springs of cultural vitality as well as the antecedents of our own dilemmas. For in our past there were conflicts as well as solutions, ancient meagreness and deprivation as well as power, expense of spirit and social traumas which have left their fateful blights on the present. All such legacies and forces come to expression in poetry in changing ways through the generations. The history of a man or a family as of a people or a culture is a compound of gifts and defects, of blessings and judgments, and all is pertinent to present self-knowledge and to assessment of present possibilities and choices. Much contemporary imaginative literature is a re-presentation and cogitation of these hitherto sunken levels; and the poet is engaged in

> Musing upon the King my brother's wreck
> And on the King my father's death before him.[1]

And much is a feeling out of the futures still left open to us, a selection and working of our available past, an identification of the directions in which the streams still run and in which the spirit may direct us.

Hence the necessity of retrospect and survey. Our past is our present in what concerns the relation of poetry, culture and religion. And this retrospect is all the more necessary because

[1] T. S. Eliot, *The Waste Land*, lines 191, 192. Cf. also Eliot's poem "Gerontion" viewed as it can be in part as a cultural retrospect and meditation.

different views are held as to what is important and unimportant, what is healthful and harmful, what is Christian and un-Christian, in the tangled skein of cultural traditions. For behind the vehement literary controversies of today—notably with regard to contemporary poetry—lie differing judgments as to the true spiritual heritage of the West and especially as to the Christian tradition in our English-speaking lands. Thus different values can be assigned to such main factors as Catholic order, the Protestant revolution, scientific empiricism, all of which have had their changing roles through the centuries and which have entered into special combinations with more recent phases of culture such as the romantic movement and recent industrialized society.

1. THE CHRISTIAN "MYTH" AND THE NEW FORCES

The cultural disintegration of our western life is commonly traced back to the close of the medieval period. The new learning, the new and powerful social forms, the explorations, brought about a growing revolt against the static patterns of life and thought that had so long given a degree of unity and order to the West. Spiritual and cultural authorities were undermined and the ruling symbols dethroned. This carried with it increasingly the dissolution of both religious traditions and religious institutions. The Renaissance meant

> the rebirth of a world forgotten and the birth of a new world. But also: criticism, undermining and finally dissolution and even destruction and progressive death of older beliefs, older conceptions, older tradition of truths that gave man certainty in knowledge and security in action. . . . A heap of treasures and a heap of ruins: such is the result of this fertile and confusing activity which demolished everything and could construct nothing or at least bring nothing to completion. Thus, deprived of his traditional norms of judgment and choice, man felt himself

lost in a world grown uncertain. A world where nothing is sure. And where everything is possible.[1]

In the centuries that have since elapsed the process has continued. It has been rendered complex by the emergence of successive new but unstable patterns of order and loyalty. In these the traditions of the older world have reasserted themselves in combination with modern forces and movements such as nationalism and Marxism, or (in the more specifically cultural area) the Enlightenment and romanticism.

The most fundamental feature of the Renaissance was that men passed from a finite into an infinite world. The medieval man's world had limits, whether as regards time and space or as regards the spiritual environment. This meant security, and therewith a kind of personal and social health. His demons were objectified, external and well under control. But modern man lives in an infinite world. The heavenly spaces terrify him. Science finds no limits whether it looks within or without, whether it looks backward or forward. Psychologically, modern man looks into himself and sees no bottom. He has "the sense of the abyss." He has moved from a world of Being into a world of Becoming. The change of outlook no doubt made for exhilaration but it also made for vertigo and even terror.

> What properties define our person since
> This massive vagueness moved in on our lives,
> What laws require our substance to exist?
> Our strands of private order are dissolved
> And lost our routes to self-inheritance,
> Position and Relation are dismissed,
> An epoch's Providence is quite worn out,
> The lion of Nothing chases us about.[2]

---

[1] Alexandre Koyré, *Entretiens sur Descartes* (New York: Brentano, 1944), pp. 34, 35. Translation mine.

[2] W. H. Auden, "Christmas 1940," from *The Collected Poetry of W. H. Auden* (New York: Random House, 1945), p. 119.

Erich Fromm has shown that freedom is an ambiguous gift. The opening up of infinite possibilities induces disquietude and a constant apprehension, since man misses the former limits and authorities. He is thrust into a period of lostness. The new emancipation is bought at the price of profound psychological tensions. Moreover, with new liberations come new possibilities of enslavement. Remove the older religious or moral restraints on freedom of action, and men proceed to act in such ways as to deprive others of their freedom. The abuse of economic power was soon to illustrate this.

It is a commonplace of criticism today to recognize that literature of any universality employs the "machinery" or the "mythology" of some widely accepted body of symbol, rich in imaginative association and thus capable of giving to a work coherence, depth and resonance. The effectiveness of such a mythology for art or literature requires that it continue to have prestige for faith and to be accepted as living and potent. Once the Greek myths, for instance, become unreal and incapable of winning imaginative assent, they forfeit any power to serve the writer other than as a passing ornament. So it could be with the biblical material.

The situation today of the biblical symbolism in this regard is fully clarified only when we return at least to the time of Milton and trace the factors which since his day have led to its diminishing place in literature. The scientific movement which was destined to shake the hold of the Christian worldview had found powerful expression already before Milton's time, particularly in the work of Bacon. As time passed, the seventeenth century gave itself with increasing zest to the new "mechanical philosophy," which promised to liberate the minds of men and to bring in the dawn of a new day. Yet it was still possible for John Milton in this period to use the biblical scheme of redemption as the basis of his heroic epic with full conviction himself and, what is more, in anticipation of a reading public prepared to accept this biblical foundation as not merely convenient or decorative but as real and living.

Milton was himself to a great degree a child of the Renaissance and a humanist. His own rationalization of the Scriptures had gone far, and it was no simple matter for him to marry his bold conceptions to the pictorial material of the Bible. Yet the massiveness and ardor, the granite and fire, of his Puritan faith lent coherence to the whole. The sublimity of the biblical conceptions found a voice and a language worthy of it, and the resulting work went forth to a generation still close enough to the ages of faith, to the Reformation, and especially to the puritan preachers, to hear and to understand. The whole cosmic scheme, the Genesis narrative, Satan and the fall, the angels and the devils, the redemption to come, all these had meaning and authority for Milton's time. He could utilize them. This mythology had not been exploded. The life currents of the age still ran through this body of conception, if not as unconsciously and inevitably as in the time of Dante, yet in some respects with more meaning because of the acute religious throes of the period. The alternative mythology of science, while it had had its unsettling influence on many, as on John Donne, had not yet supplanted it. And Milton's particular power in evoking the Christian metaphysics lay partly in the fact that he had not, like Donne, laid himself open to all the subtle impulses of the new age that was dawning.

As the century wore on, however, the new scientific philosophy took more and more possession not only of men's minds but of their imaginations. The impulses of the Renaissance came into their own and the war upon scholasticism went on apace. This carried with it the supplanting at length not only of the Catholic but also of the Reformation form of the Christian world-assumptions and not only of the Christian imagery but also of that classical imagery which had meant so much to the early Renaissance. For a time men were content with a divorce of reason and faith, but this segregation of religion meant its ultimate withering away before the exuberance of reason. So we are brought to a time in which the poets are permitted little use of the elder world's mythologies save as decoration and ornament.

The relation of Protestantism to Anglo-Saxon culture shows two chief phases, and each of them has a special relation to our literary heritage. Primary Protestantism, that of the sixteenth and early seventeenth century, was concerned with time and eternity, with the perpendicular dimension, with transcendental freedom. It interpreted life in terms of pilgrimage, spiritual warfare, and the biblical drama. When it found expression in literature, as it did, for instance, in Bunyan, it had a great world-picture and body of symbol to work with, and a great dynamic for its conception of the soul. But it was when it entered into fruitful union with the humanism of the Renaissance, as it did in the case of Milton, that we find its supreme literary expression. The gravity and dimensions of *Paradise Lost* spring out of the moods of primary Protestantism with its fresh sense of the august issues that gather about the human soul and the human lot.

In the latter seventeenth and especially in the eighteenth century it is "secondary" Protestantism which makes its impact on culture and is affected by it. This type, which includes pietism, is marked by a present realization of grace and present personal fulfillment, and is therefore inclined to world-affirmation and to mystical and ethical rather than metaphysical issues. The accent falls on the subjective experience, emotional release, and encourages individualism and sectarian groups. This type of Protestantism was able to marry itself in complex ways with eighteenth-century rationalism and subsequently with German idealism and romanticism, and thus to leaven these movements and be influenced by them. Thence come the most interesting literary productions of this type of Protestantism. But secondary Protestantism had unfortunate offshoots of eccentricity and emotionalism. Such phenomena hastened the divorce of significant elements of the modern world from the Christian tradition, and many romantic writers like Blake and Shelley are found in strong reaction against it. Meanwhile, the increasing prestige of science and rationalism had disallowed the authority of the biblical faith and "myth" for many.

2. THE CHRISTIAN TRADITION AND THE ROMANTIC MOVEMENT

We may take the situation of Wordsworth at the end of the eighteenth-century Age of Reason as instructive. For it was the altogether unprecedented task of Wordsworth to have to read significance into man and the world by the sole power of his own vision, without the resources, hitherto indispensable to poetry, of either the classic or the Christian symbolism. He was, as he says, "left alone, seeking the visible world."

> "To animize the 'real world,' the 'universe of death' that the 'mechanical' system of philosophy had produced, but to do so without using an exploded myth or fabricating a new one, this was the special task and mission of Wordsworth." [1]

In his origin among the independent freeholder population of the Lake District, Wordsworth is a good representative of the type produced by secondary Protestantism, a type which in this period had entered into fruitful if secularizing combination with eighteenth-century influences and romanticism. Nevertheless, the basic Christian cast and temper is there in its English Protestant form, manifesting itself in a dynamic personalism and a kind of stubborn critical or prophetic independence in dealing with experience. No doubt the special form that his early experience with nature took and his consequent romantic view of the soul, evidence influences which in many men of this period led to pagan extremes. But such

[1] Basil Willey, *The Seventeenth Century Background* (London: 1942), pp. 298, 299.

outcomes in him were checked by his Christian heritage. Thus when in his youth he was exposed to the full force of the ideas and emotions of the French Revolution, he was powerfully swayed and his period of disillusion was a dangerous one. But he found his balance, and in his creative period he wrote poetry dealing with moral issues that stands with the greatest. The sonnets dedicated to national independence and liberty and the sections of the *Prelude* that touch on the same themes rise above the work of Shelley or Byron or Heine or Victor Hugo or Swinburne in considerable part because they have a further dimension given to them by his latent Christianity. It is to this he appeals,

> our fearful innocence,
> And pure religion breathing household laws.

He speaks to those who

> the faith and morals hold
> Which Milton held.

Robert Will wrote of the Reformation that it gave to the aspirations of the Renaissance and of Humanism a breath, as it were, of eternity. We may transpose this and apply it to Wordsworth and say that Wordsworth's however diffused Protestant heritage gave to the aspirations in him of the romantic movement a breath of eternity, and thus deepened and generalized the purport of his themes.

Oversimplification is avoided in picturing the situation at the close of the eighteenth century if we make the following observations. For one thing William Blake's procedure shows us that it was possible then for a poet to draw on biblical doctrine and unite it with esoteric elements to raise a powerful voice against the dominant outlook, though one with a limited echo. Shelley's solution was to construct a personal mythology with the incorporation of eclectic elements from new and old.

In the case of Wordsworth himself one should by no means overlook the latent, and in his later period overt, influences of the Christian tradition. It is true that two prominent features in his work came from the world-view of his time: the sacred quality ascribed to the physical creation, and the romantic view of man. But disguised in his work is a nonconformist heritage, working through the handicaps of his situation and acting as a check upon the romantic pantheism then taking its rise.

What has been said about Wordsworth bears also on the cases of Emerson and Walt Whitman in this country later. In Hawthorne we recognize the last important figure here to do his work as one freely at home in the Hebraic-Christian tradition. Melville illustrates the acute and agonizing stage of the transition and partly for that reason is the most revealing and significant figure of the period. But with the work of Emerson and Whitman the Hebraic-Christian tradition goes underground, expressing itself only indirectly thereafter though still powerfully.

For the eighteenth-century rationalism and classicism had weakened the Christian symbolism, but not necessarily its deeper assumptions. One way of stating this as regards America may be put in the following words of Howard Mumford Jones:

> The story of eighteenth-century American development is the story of the slow fusion of a culture founded in Protestant dissent with certain of the secular ideas of classicism . . . the result was, on the whole, a secular but not a sceptical victory—that is to say, the transfer of the problem of universal order from the theological to the moral sphere.

I suggest that the central problem in American thought, at least until late in the nineteenth century, is the problem of the moral order of the universe—a problem so primary as on the whole to subordinate almost all other philosophical and aesthetic considerations to this central question.[2]

Thus we are pointed again to the continuing if disguised operation of the Hebraic-Christian tradition in its Protestant form in American culture.

3. PURITANISM AND AMERICAN CULTURE

We may well pause over this basic question as to the role of the religious heritage in American culture as it is illuminated by attention to the eighteenth and nineteenth centuries. What the American faith is and the part that the churches have had in shaping and sustaining it are matters that have been well clarified in recent historical studies.[1] The democratic faith represents an inextricable compound of elements drawn from Puritanism and from the Enlightenment. By these two chief sources plus the special influences of this new continent, our culture and our institutions have been shaped. The time is now gone by fortunately when Puritanism could be ridiculed and travestied, and (as Ralph Barton Perry's *Puritanism and Democracy* shows) we are disposed to recognize that this tradition has been the most significant of the influences that have made us what we are. This theme recurs in the judgment of an outsider, André Siegfried, who has again been quoted recently in this connection by Willard L. Sperry in his book, *Religion in America:*

---

[2] "The Drift to Liberalism in the Eighteenth Century," from *Authority and the Individual* (Cambridge: 1937), pp. 333, 336.

[1] Among other works we mention: Merle Curti, *The Growth of American Thought* (New York: 1943); Ralph Gabriel, *The Course of American Democratic Thought* (New York: 1940); Howard Mumford Jones, *Ideas in America* (Cambridge: 1944); F. O. Matthiessen, *American Renaissance* (New York: 1941); Perry Miller, *The New England Mind* (New York: 1939), and *Orthodoxy in Massachusetts, 1630-1650, a Genetic Study* (New York: 1933); Ralph Barton Perry, *Puritanism and Democracy* (New York: 1944).

> If we wish to understand the real success of American inspiration, we must go back to the English Puritanism of the seventeenth century, for the civilization of the United States is essentially Protestant. . . . We must go even farther, and realize that America is not only Protestant in her religious and social development, but essentially Calvinistic.²

The dynamic faith drawn from the English Reformation shaped us decisively, despite all later tributary elements, made us the mold and cast of man we are, gave us our primordial baptism, has been the ultimate if disguised force in our national ideals and decisions, and fostered our educational beginnings. This tradition later joined that of the Enlightenment in a fertile marriage. The later history of our culture is that of the vicissitudes of these fundamental faiths, the impact upon them of new forces, and their common and fateful struggle against the chief foes of the modern world.

In the course of the eighteenth century our basic Puritan heritage was transformed, notably by influences from the Enlightenment, and its essential insights were obscured, but there was no decisive revolution in our spiritual culture. While Puritanism was fighting a losing battle in the eighteenth century, yet, says Perry:

> A leaven working within itself conspired with external forces to bring about a gradual transition rather than an abrupt reversal. . . . The development was not so much a repudiation of Calvinism as the flowering of a certain strain which these clergymen recognized as their religious inheritance.³

This agrees with the view just cited of Howard Mumford Jones. It is the thesis of the latter writer that there never was

---

² *America Comes of Age* (New York: 1927), pp. 33, 34; cited by Sperry in the work named, p. 150.
³ *Puritanism and Democracy*, pp. 192, 200.

on this continent a dominant neo-classical age. Influences of the Enlightenment penetrated too slowly, the temper of the colonists resisted them; the ancient tongues were not widely enough cultivated; but above all, Jonathan Edwards and others made terms with the new ideas and new forces, whether speculative or emotional, in such a way as to turn the edge of their appeal for many.

Moreover, even where the Enlightenment took hold in a secularizing sense on this side of the water it had taken up into itself much of the Christian outlook or it proceeded to do so. Despite obvious disagreements there was much in common between the two streams of social and spiritual faith. John Locke has been called "a descendant of Calvin" and "a carrier of Calvinism from the Reformation to the revolutions of 1688 and 1776."[4] All in all, American culture viewed at all deeply had not become radically de-Christianized at the end of the century. Furthermore, the Calvinist heritage in its fuller range continued to operate under the surface of the prevailing forms of rationalism to appear in countless ways in nineteenth-century movements and writers.

This being the situation, any manifestations of the romantic movement in this country would have a quite different character from those in Europe. There it was largely "a liberalizing force directed against decadent classicism." In America there was no classical period to overthrow.[5] The Christian theological tradition was stronger here. This fact throws a great deal of light upon the writers of our great period whose work is so important still for the diagnosis of our culture. Just as our Puritan heritage was not dissipated by the rationalism of the eighteenth century, so it asserted itself strongly against the solvent effects of romanticism and transcendentalism. But distinctions have to be made.

In his massive work, *American Renaissance*, F. O. Matthies-

[4] Cited from H. D. Foster in Perry, *op. cit.*, p. 197.
[5] H. M. Jones, *Ideas in America*, p. 335.

sen has argued that from the vantage point of the present we can now recognize that Herman Melville is the most significant of the writers of that period if we judge in terms of the depth and lucidity with which man and society are interpreted. In both Melville and Hawthorne the insights of primary Protestantism are asserted against the shallower elations or intoxications of the time in a way we can now properly evaluate. The secondary Protestantism of the later seventeenth and eighteenth centuries had accommodated itself usefully to prevailing moods, to a this-worldly emphasis and a moral-psychological concern. But the resulting humanitarianism and emphasis on sentiment, though it furnished dynamic for reform and missions, was too easily exposed to neo-pagan impulses and to an excessive individualism. Thus we note the pertinence of Matthiessen's tribute to Hawthorne:

> He sensed that Emerson's exaltation of the divinity in man had obliterated the distinction between man and God, between time and eternity. Although no theologian, Hawthorne did not relax his grip on the Christian conception of time. This had been obscured by Thoreau and Whitman no less than by Emerson in their exhilaration over the fullness of the moment.[6]

Thus Hawthorne safeguarded the sense of man's limitations as a creature in time and the consequent tragic character of life. For him, man's eternal relationships were better understood because he had not lost sight of man's temporal realities. Matthiessen grants that Whitman and Thoreau offer a more compelling image of the rising common man than Hawthorne, but Whitman's romantic view of the poet as his own Messiah and Thoreau's occasional sour or self-confident individualism both show the dangerous slope on which these writers lived. In fact the individualism of an Emerson, a Thoreau, and a Whitman can lead on insensibly to that of a Nietzsche of the

---

[6] *American Renaissance*, p. 652.

first phase, and that to the Messianic complex of a Nietzsche of the last phase; eventually the irrationalism of the prophet can become the irrationalism of the Führer.[7] The "green wine" of Emerson and the Messianism of Whitman—like that of D. H. Lawrence—illustrate the ambiguous forms that the love of freedom can take when it gets away from the restraints of religious insight. And woe be to such modern prophets if some pseudo-religion, some idolatry of instinct or power or reason, flatters our antinomianism rather than restrains it.

In no person more than in Emerson do the contradictions of these varying sanctions and inspirations appear. There were naïve and dangerous aspects even of his mature thought, and there were deep sympathies and wise and prophetic discernments for which he was ready to pay a high price of devotion. Some of the criticism of Emerson by his contemporaries, gathered by Matthiessen, serves to localize the most suspect areas of his outlook. Father Taylor said: "Mr. Emerson is one of the sweetest creatures God ever made; there is a screw loose somewhere in the machinery, yet I cannot tell where it is, for I never heard it jar. . . . He knows no more of the religion of the New Testament than Balaam's ass did of the principles of the Hebrew grammar." Charles Eliot Norton wrote: "His optimism becomes a bigotry, and, though of a nobler type than the common American conceit of the preeminent excellence of American things as they are, has hardly less the quality of fatalism. . . . He refuses to believe in disorder or evil." Apropos of Emerson's view of evil as merely the deprivation of good, Herman Melville made a marginal notation: "To annihilate all this nonsense read the Sermon on the Mount, and consider what it implies." And the statement that "the first lesson of history is the good of evil" Melville derided: "He still bethinks himself of his optimism—he must make that good somehow against the eternal hell itself."

However unjust it is to marshal these adverse judgments,

[7] *Ibid.*, pp. 367, 368, 546.

they do, nevertheless, suggest where Emerson's thought was weakest. Concepts like that of the "infinitude of the private man" (compare: "the divine pride of man in himself"—Whitman) are disturbing. They can lead on to pretension, intoxication, and anarchy. Like other forms of mysticism, transcendentalism is "numb to the intricacies of human feeling," to use a phrase of Mr. Yvor Winters spoken apropos of the mysticism of some recent poets. Disregard of the biblical realism leaves all such immanentists with an insufficient sense of the tragic in life. And such immanentism invaded American thought in many forms in the period we are considering, and it still continues.

But there was another and magnificent side to Emerson and we presume to assign credit for it to the Puritan tradition behind him. He represents the human type, the cast of man produced by secondary Protestantism, and this appears in him. The specific Puritan strain is no doubt compounded with the cultural influences of the time but it cannot be silenced. It appears particularly in the insistence on autonomy, however confused; in the quest for present fulfillment and emotional release, indeed for ecstasy—and it was here that the temptation to an irrational romanticism was so strong in all Protestantism of this period; and in the aggressive moralism and the moral-prophetic vocation.

Stuart P. Sherman, in an essay on Emerson that today appears curiously dated,[8] well says that the new movement of the young American idealists led by Emerson was "genuinely Puritan by its inwardness, by its earnest passion for cleansing the inside of the cup, by its protest against external powers which thwarted or retarded the efforts of the individual soul to move forward and upward by light from within." His chief theme is that Emerson transmits in new and revitalized form

[8] "The Emersonian Liberation," Ch. IV in *Americans* (New York: Scribners, 1922).

"the vital forces of the great moral traditions while at the same time he emancipates them from the dead hand of the past." We have in him "a fresh flowering of the ancient passion for self-perfection." Sherman rightly identifies the Puritan lineage in Emerson, however obscured, and it is to this that we assign his best service. It appears in the radical protestantism of his discounting of old authorities and his readiness to question and revise all existing valuations, in his essentially moral concern with life, in his sound instincts and courage in the matter of the abolition movement, in his freedom from contamination by prevailing false values, and in his dedication to the disinterested life of thinker, poet, and artist. His witness falls short of the fundamental character of Melville's or the whole-souled immediacy of Walt Whitman. But in varying ways, all these men, together with Thoreau, gave to America the initial formulation of its democratic symbols, its master-myths, its heroes, fables and demi-gods. As Newton Arvin says of Whitman: he was "something more than the orator or lyrist of democracy"; he was "its biographer, its image maker."

Brief attention to Whitman will clarify further some of the issues raised above. The following lines from *By Blue Ontario's Shore* will introduce our observations.

Are you he that would assume a place to teach or be a poet here in the States?
The place is august, the terms obdurate . . .
. . . Are you really of the whole People?
Are you not of some coterie? Some school or mere religion?
Are you done with reviews and criticisms of life? animating now to life itself?
Have you vivified yourself from the maternity of these States?

Here the poet is imperiously summoning the poets of the future, the poets of democracy, and indicates to them their curriculum. Like himself they are to make America their study: its origins, its people, their livelihood, the war between the states, its mountains, and its rivers. They are to vivify themselves from "the maternity of these States." They are to become aware of that which alone "holds men together," "which aggregates all in a living principle"; they are to become prophets of "the great idea, the idea of perfect and free individuals," by this kind of initiation. And in contrast he repudiates those who would aspire to such a role who may be of some coterie, indeed of some school or "mere religion."

Whitman writes out of a passionate vision, a secular revelation, whose overwhelming force for him and his disciples can only be compared to that with which the early impulses of the French Revolution and the Bolshevist Revolution gripped their adherents. This is nothing less in his case than a magnificent irrationalism such as history occasionally brings forth under propitious circumstances—if not a religion, yet like a religion. And, though we may term it irrational, it is not therefore to be wholly depreciated, however much we may wish to scrutinize and to assess it. For such formidable waves of faith, whether they grip an individual chiefly or a school or a people, must have some real relevance to reality, must have partial validity, must be grounded in real needs and real satisfactions, however much they outrun their due limits.

We have dwelt on the ambiguities of the Protestant heritage in these writers in some detail because the whole matter has an immediate bearing on our understanding of more recent poetry. We are concerned to identify the continuing operation of the biblical and Christian tradition in its obscure disguises in modern movements.

4. A DIVERGENT CULTURAL ANALYSIS

Much can justifiably be said from a Christian point of view in disparagement of the trends of modern culture since the Reformation. The most elaborate case that has been worked out along these lines in connection with poetry is that of Professor Hoxie N. Fairchild in his three-volume work, *Religious*

*Trends in English Poetry.*¹ Professor Fairchild examines closely the expression and temper of poetry from 1700-1830 with a glimpse ahead into our period. He notes that there is a rather steady loss of any vital Christian stamp on even the religious poetry of the period. When he comes to the main romantic poets he finds in effect expressions of a rival religion to Christianity. For the romantic movement is involved in pride, individualism, humanism, intoxication with man's inner life or "genius," and represents a religion of self-esteem and deification of man. It is then quite understandable that the author sees disorders of our contemporary culture as traceable to romanticism. But what is most grave, in our view, is that the whole declension is related to an original principle of pride and disorder in Protestantism. For all such self-sufficiency is connected with

> a pantheistic mingling of God, man and nature in a universal harmony of beauty, truth and love. This form of religion may exist in a Catholic setting, but it can receive no positive support from orthodox Catholicism. Protestantism, however, not only allows it freedom to develop but lends it strong encouragement.²

Hence, not only is Calvinism "the ancestor of sentimentalism," but,

> the romanticism of the 1780-1830 period is simply Protestant Christianity in a more or less delightfully phosphorescent state of decay.³

Again:

> Hence the beginning and the end of romantic religion is what all old-fashioned folk call pride. All the loveliness

---

¹ New York: Columbia University Press, Vol. I, 1939: Vol. II, 1942; Vol. III, 1949. See also his pamphlet, *Religious Perspectives of College Teaching: In English Literature,* The Edward W. Hazen Foundation, 400 Prospect St., New Haven, Connecticut (1950).

² *Op. cit.,* Vol. I, p. 571.

³ *Ibid.,* p. 538.

that lies between results from the endeavour to impart some sort of numinous sanction to the craving for independent power. Thus romanticism originates in the deepest primordial subsoil of human nature. Historically speaking, however, the so-called Romantic Movement represents the turning-point of a Titanic assertion of human self-sufficiency which had begun to manifest itself as a dominant movement of mind in the sixteenth century. The romantic poets show us the crest of the wave just as it shatters itself against the cliffs of reality.[4]

Again we read: "Puritanism sloughs down into Unitarianism, Unitarianism sloughs down into a romantic transcendentalism" —this with regard to Emerson.

Now the rights and wrongs of such a view (which also carries with it a corresponding judgment with regard to the Victorian poets and by anticipation of contemporary poetry in what concerns the sources of their outlook) are to be judged, we believe, in the light of our foregoing historical review. The matter is not simple. There is much truth in the view that the story of the modern world is that of a great adventure in self-sufficiency which has brought its nemesis, meanwhile offering us a varied display of heretical and watered-down Christianity along the way. But this can be read in another way. Instead of seeing the self-sufficiency as a Titanism rebellious against due authority, it can be seen as the story of western man emerging from an epoch of law and entering into an epoch of responsible freedom with all the risks and dangers involved. When, in the Divine Comedy, Vergil had conducted Dante through the Inferno and led him to the Earthly Paradise, he says to him, now

> I crown and mitre thee lord over thyself.[5]

The Renaissance may be understood as an expression of this new autonomous responsibility of man and the accompanying

---

[4] *Op. cit.*, Vol. III, p. 511.

[5] "per ch' io te sopra te corono e mitrio," *Purgatorio,* Canto XXVII, line 142.

emancipation of his powers. In the Reformation the inevitable corollary of this moment in the religious sphere appears. In primary Protestantism the Christian heritage was restated with a depth and altitude corresponding to the greatness of the new task and its dangers. If any invitation to self-sufficiency or pride resides in Puritanism it is no more than the inseparable risk that attends the gospel just where it is most effective in establishing that freedom with which Christ hath made us free. The most fully personalized forms of Christianity are those which most richly release the energies of men—or most adequately set the creature free as an instrument of the divine working.

We would not then assign the antecedents of modern idolatries to Puritanism which after all rests on the anti-idolatrous principles of the sovereignty of God and justification by faith. Moreover, as a reviewer in the *Times Literary Supplement* (London) noted, Professor Fairchild has "underestimated the Augustinianism in the Puritan tradition," and therefore its critical resistance to Pelagian influences which made inroads on Protestantism and Catholicism alike. The fact is, moreover, that those vitalities which come to expression in romantic and post-romantic literature and whose expressions may not be couched in recognizable Christian forms, are not *ipso facto* to be defined as un-Christian or idolatrous. They may well be defensible expressions, versions, corollaries of what is inherent in the Christian faith and life; latent in orthodoxy or inadequately recognized there.

Professor Fairchild rightly demurs at that type of teaching of religious literature which is mainly concerned to "bring inspiring thoughts to the attention of the student" and to treat the material in a bracing and optimistic spirit "without encouraging habits of spiritual discrimination." "Unfortunately the facts as I see them compel me to regard the history of the literary expression of religious thought mainly as a study in spiritual pathology." [6] But what puzzles us in his whole treat-

[6] *Religious Perspectives in English Literature*, pp. 26, 27.

ment is his very conception of Christianity and of the way in which it relates itself to culture. He appears to think of Christianity in terms of a sharply definable doctrine and not to recognize that it is a living movement which is constantly involved in cultural penetration and therefore in risks, explorations and temptations. As Professor Trilling has said in his review of the third volume of the work:

> Professor Fairchild is at great pains to deny the integral and even symbiotic relationship which has always existed between romanticism and modern Christianity, including orthodoxy . . . [he] seems everywhere to imply that what is called Christianity is not really Christian at all. For him there is but a single Christian tradition . . . which is Catholicism in either its Anglican or its Roman form.

And Dr. Trilling speaks pungently of the way in which the author "goes in for close bargaining" with the romantic poets, begrudging all concessions.[7]

The matter is extremely important for our whole thesis in this book because our positive appreciation of many of the modern poets and the modern movement in literature and the arts, beginning with certain of the romantic school, rests on the view that they represent pioneering impulses occasioned by the limitations of "orthodoxy," so contributing to a new Christian formulation and pattern. In our brief discussion of Wordsworth, Emerson, etc., above it will be noted that we insist on a powerful latent Christian tradition in their work, assign a more positive religious value to it than does Mr. Fairchild, and are more ready to indulge any heresy that may be assigned to them since we are more dubious as to the definition of orthodoxy and more sympathetic with rebellion against the orthodox forms that obtained. We do, indeed, believe that the Christian faith and life find their center in the gospel of the revelation of God in the life, death and resurrection of

[7] *New York Times Book Review* (September 4, 1919), pp. 5, 13.

Christ. The ways, however, in which this faith and life are acknowledged and transmitted especially in art, and especially in particular historical circumstances where old patterns have become rigid if not fossilized and where new creative cultural movements are in process of assimilation by the faith, such ways are various and subtle. It is just here that the process of "testing the spirits" comes into play, and it is just here that any close bargaining with the unpredictable work of what may be the Holy Spirit will lead us astray.

All those concerned with the spiritual or theological assessment of modern literature will, however, be in immense debt to Professor Fairchild for his exhaustive study and for the clear thesis which gives order to his particular judgments. Those working from a different perspective can take over his conclusions in many respects if with some shift in the implications. We shall have occasion at many points to show the departure of modern culture and its expressions from a Christian norm as he has. And tribute must, moreover, be paid to his paper, *Religious Perspectives in English Literature*, referred to above, which so judiciously and searchingly states the responsibilities of a teacher of literature in the classroom today. The time was certainly ripe for an unevasive facing of what can only be called the theological responsibilities of the teacher in dealing with this subject matter.

III

CULTURAL CRISIS AND THE CONFUSION OF TONGUES

OUR analysis of the historical background and of the relation of poetry, Christianity and cultural change has prepared us for a diagnosis of our present situation in its cultural aspects. Here we find the real conditioning factors of contemporary poetry. What we are immediately concerned with is not the sociological forms of culture but rather all that underlies and animates them: the values and assumptions and dogmas that prevail. More than that it is the hurts and costs, the gropings and tensions, all those more subtle and intimate conditions of life today where our culture comes home to persons in their deeper experience. We are concerned with the spirit of our culture. We have to describe, as it were, the weather, the spiritual weather, in which men today are born, live, wrestle and die. It is of this that any Christian understanding and enterprise must take account as well as of the more external factors.

It is true that when we say culture we tend to think first of all of those strata of society that are somewhat privileged or sophisticated. We think of those minorities that we associate with literature and the arts, with the colleges and universities, with the interchange of ideas and the sponsorship of philosophies and cults. But though movements of culture may advertise themselves most visibly in such circles, they are pervasive in the whole of society. They rise from general conditions, and all men in a given time live in this same all-enveloping weather, and breathe the same air and suffer from the same pervasive toxins and infections.

St. Paul had his way of distinguishing between the visible and the invisible aspects of that world against which he conducted his great campaign. There were, indeed, the immense structures of social and political institutions that stood immediately before him, blocking his path, the age-old citadels of paganism. In the trade guilds and the municipalities—whether the *colonia* or the free cities—in the sacred college of priests of Diana of the Ephesians or the civic pieties of Athens, in the massive power of Rome itself, he was confronted by the incarnate forms of ancient evil and his collision with these concrete institutions left him with many scars. But when he said that despite the open door there were "many adversaries," or when he said that at Ephesus he had fought, as it were, with wild beasts, he was thinking of the deeper foes, those spiritual forces that animated these visible institutions. He expressed it most clearly when he said that "our wrestling is not against flesh and blood, but against the principalities, against the powers, against the world rulers of this darkness, against the spiritual hosts of wickedness in the heavenly places." And he speaks again of these deeper fortresses and fastnesses of wrong and of the proper means of their overthrow:

> For though we walk in the flesh, we do not war according to the flesh (for the weapons of our warfare are not of the flesh, but mighty before God to the casting down of strongholds); casting down imaginations, and every high thing that is exalted against the knowledge of God, and bringing every thought into captivity to the obedience of Christ.

That is, Paul recognized essential foes in the spirit of Greco-Roman culture, in its dogmas and loyalties, its "imaginations" and its "thoughts" (*noema:* "valuation"). To overthrow the outer citadels of blatant power he had to penetrate to the inmost keep where the evil was enthroned and where the visible tyrannies took their rise or received their sanction.

1. DISINTEGRATION: RECENT BACKGROUND

We have reviewed briefly in the preceding chapter the historical genesis of our present situation. The story of what happened to the modern world's faiths and assumptions, its traditions and loyalties, its order and its institutions since the medieval period is not as disturbing as it may at first sight appear. It bears upon the forms rather than upon the substance of Western society. The sum total of evil has probably not changed greatly, for the Middle Ages had their own way of brutalizing men and sabotaging the weal of successive generations, of condemning men and women before birth to attenuated and warped lives. And the very forces that have dissolved the older patterns of faith and social structure have brought real liberations. Nevertheless, the modern story is in large part a story of pride and of power, of new tyrannies for old, new tyrannies of the spirit as well as of the market place and the state. The particular constellations of evil today in our greater theatre require for their understanding some brief review of our more immediate past.

It has often been pointed out that our modern outlook dates rather from the Enlightenment and the eighteenth century than from the Renaissance and Reformation. A truly pervasive rationalism appears not with the first clear formulations of scientific method and empiricism in the sixteenth century, but two centuries later. Yet the secularization of Western society proceeded apace from the time of Bacon and Descartes. The new vitalities of the emerging nations of northern Europe burst the bonds of authority. A new self-consciousness of the individual emerged, at once more assertive and more complex. Wider and wider diffusion of the new curiosities collaborated with the rising rationalism to break up the hold of the classical and biblical world pictures. Men were coming out of the older securities and their nerves were exposed to experience in a way that made for fuller personal fulfillment but also for risks and anguish. Thus John Donne in his early sensitiveness to the new modes of consciousness, in his complexity and restlessness, was prophetic of our own modern outlook, and it is for this reason in part that he is so much cultivated by contemporary critics and writers.

In this different connection we note again that the romantic movement contributed to modern secularization and conditioned the modern consciousness. As a creative upsurge from the deeper energies of the northern European peoples it entered into various subtle combinations with the attenuated Christian heritage of the time and brought forth a host of literary and artistic creations. It animated a culture characterized by emotional exuberance, idealistic philosophies and revolutionary iconoclasm. The middle classes of today still live in a world blessed, and often misled, by the sentiments and valuations that were the legacy of that period. The religious ethos of middle-class Protestant life today bears the stamp of that experience. One of the pressing tasks of the church of today is to come to terms critically with the spell cast upon it by romanticism. A similar reaction is overdue on the part of many liberal religious bodies among us to the heritage of eighteenth-century rationalism. Granted that the larger part of our evangelical Protestantism needs more rather than less rationalism, nevertheless its chilling, impoverishing influence on some religious groups and on wider cultural circles is still evident.

But other and more recent influences have affected our contemporary picture. Here it is not science as a world view but the outcomes of science in technology and in the industrial revolution that demand attention. Randal Jarrell in "The Emancipators" addresses the older pioneers of science and confronts them with the sorry picture of today, asking them if they foresaw what "Trade" would do with their equations and inventions:

> You guessed this? The earth's face altering with iron,
> The smoke ranged like a wall against the day?
> The equations metamorphose into use: the free
> Drag their slight bones from tenements to vote
> To die with their children in your factories.
>
> Man is born in chains, yet everywhere we see him dead.
> On your earth they sell nothing but our lives.
> You knew that what you died for was our deaths?
> You learned, those years, that all men wish is Trade?
> It was you who understood, it is we who change.[1]

Setting aside the strictly social consequences of technology, no one can exaggerate its effects upon the spirit of modern culture. Empires of economic power have developed which have affected not only the economic but also the spiritual experience of men. Inherited faiths have been dissolved by the new social patterns even more effectively than by the march of scientism. If scientism has slain its thousands, a mercantile society and an industrial society following it have slain their ten thousands! And out of the changing economic scene sprang a new extension of science, the Marxian analysis of society with its convincing exposure of the self-deception that characterizes many of the ideals of men, the mask that veils the vast amoral or immoral forces of social organization. This disclosure of the realities of the common life furthered the discomfiture whether of religious faith or of the liberal tradition and constitutes one of the chief factors in contemporary negation. Insufficient awareness of all these matters constitutes one of the chief liabilities of the middle-class churches today.

A corresponding breach in the vestiges of our inherited securities was opened by the work of Freud and others. This too

[1] *Little Friend, Little Friend* by Randal Jarrell (New York: The Dial Press, 1945), p. 14.

was an extension of the field of science, only comparable in its significance with the work of Darwin and Marx. Here too a mask was torn off the realities of life, in this case the life of the soul. Men were made aware of the irrational factors in human conduct. The powerful cables, carriers of the high voltage of our profounder impulses and drives, were disclosed at work in all their potencies over our conscious behavior, values and rationality. Thus science on its various fronts seemed not only to have discredited the scriptural and traditional basis of religion and the validity of its ideals, but also to have identified realities in human behavior that are beyond the control of either reason or faith. Add to this the effects of war as we have known it since 1914 and the social costs of the great depression, and the wide prevalence of negation in the modern mood is understandable.

We may return to the figure of Nietzsche to find one who lived in the crosscurrents of our latter-day culture, and who illustrates points we have made and others we have had to pass over. He was also prophetic of what has since come to pass. He came from the petty *bourgeoisie* of a somewhat developed period of industrialism and philistinism, and protested against these. At the same time he was the product of a second wave of the romantic movement, one which attached its creative enthusiasm particularly to the idea of a German culture. Of this too Nietzsche became critical. He is in one chief aspect the representative iconoclast and the father of modern secular protestants, come-outers and Bohemians. But his protests are significant: against all prosaic naturalism and the philistinism consequent on industrialization; against the mechanization and depersonalization of modern life; against barbarism and mediocrity, and this carried with it a rejection of "democracy," socialism and Christianity, conceived as mass concepts intolerant of excellence and distinction; against all barren scholarship, historicism and metaphysics; and against the rising German nationalism. Nietzsche's appeal was to intuitional and instinctive authority. He opposed the hero to the saint. The solitude that he represented and confessed was not only that of the prophet but that of the self of our time whose roots are broken. He is the prototype of all the modern prophets who have fled the "bourgeois plain" because its atmosphere was too stifling and who have sought one or the other cult of salvation in irrationalism or mysticism to replace the God who was dead.

2. DISINTEGRATION: THE CONTEMPORARY PICTURE

The above retrospect has already suggested the chief features of our present disorder, but we have now to chart them more particularly and in their recent development as of today. The various resurgences toward new or renewed orders and faiths we defer to a third section.

We note first the loss of absolutes in our world. The situation is variously described as one characterized by eclecticism, by a loss of criteria, as "a crises in valuations." As Thomas Mann's Joseph found out in Egypt: "the world has many centers." This relativity extends, of course, to morals. Our historical review has shown the part of science in relativizing men's outlook. But it is not as though science itself spoke with a single voice. Says Max Planck: "We are living in a moment of crisis. In every branch of our spiritual and material civilization we seem to have arrived at a critical turning point . . . there is scarcely a scientific axiom that is not now-a-days denied by somebody." [1]

Healthy societies require a certain degree of agreement if not in general ideas at least in basic assumptions. John Oldham in *The Christian News-Letter* (No. 174) goes so far as to urge "the need of fundamental conformity." He is not countenancing official dogma or coercion from above, but he is warning that an anarchy of ideas and values will bring with it ruinous

---

[1] Quoted by Harry Slochauer, *No Voice Is Wholly Lost* (New York: Creative Age Press, 1945), p. vii.

social anarchy. History shows that creative communities and cultures have, each of them, possessed to a considerable extent a common outlook and common symbols. A particularly telling formulation of this truth comes from Karl Mannheim. Just as an individual knows himself and feels his identity most clearly in certain memorable and crucial experiences of his past which become therefore normative for him, so a society knows itself and orders itself in the light of decisive experiences in its past which illuminate existence. These common memories supply a people with what he calls its "primordial images" and "archetypes." They function as the rallying centers for group loyalties and cohesion. They take on symbolic and mythological development and thus more adequately objectify the faith by which the nation or the age lives. But for our time the archetypes are dimmed or dethroned. The great images of our cultural memory have been devaluated, and in their place has arisen a multiplicity of competing values. "God is dead," and the new gods that succeed Him clash at once in sanguinary conflict.

To describe our modern loss of absolutes in philosophy would take us too far afield. The same is true of ethics. What may be appropriately mentioned here is the sway of relativity in education. The presidential address at a recent meeting of the American Association of University Professors argued the advisability of a pluralism of viewpoints and values in the university. It was specifically stated that "anarchy" was the proper intellectual situation for such institutions. Thus the speaker set up his defenses against any and all academic conformism and safeguarded the utmost freedom of scientific investigation. But at the same time he was in effect excluding any proper guidance of society by the university in a time when that society is falling apart and when the personal costs are incalculable.

Another aspect of our situation, closely related to the loss of absolutes, is often referred to as the "loss of ritual." By this we mean much more than neglect of ecclesiastical rites and liturgies. We mean the loss of that communal ceremony and celebration, those feasts and fasts, pomps and jubilees, pilgrimages and holy days, which played so large a part in the older world. These focuses of sanctity in time and place constantly asserted and communicated the deeper sanctions for existence, and kept alive in men a sense of its mysterious and transcendent ground. At the same time they offered themselves as channels of discharge of all that nonrational reservoir of the unconscious in society and the individual which must have expression if it is not to find outlet in alienation and destruction.

The exposure of error in the religious and cultural traditions by science, the skepticism and relativity so long at work in the West, together with the influences of technology making for mechanization, these account in large part for the loss of ritual. "The ceremony of innocence is drowned," as Yeats wrote. "We have the press for wafer: suffrage for circumcision," as Pound put it; a situation which he and others wrongly ascribed to democracy rather than to more fundamental causes. That is, the creative and transfiguring central rites of church and synagogue have given place in our flat and sordid world to the "kitsch" and ugliness of the yellow journal and the pulp literature, life has been despiritualized, and a crass mediocrity has banished all sense of wonder and miracle from existence. In Henry Adams' terms we have the dynamo for the Virgin (or for Aphrodite before the Virgin) as the symbols of power for two different epochs.

The resulting sterility in the inner life of men, the mediocre taste of the Babbitt and the materialism of bourgeois ideals, have their correlatives in the visible face of our civilization, not only in the slums and the mining town and the "country slums," but in the ugliness of suburb and town, manners and crafts, amusements and recreation. This is particularly true of Anglo-Saxon countries. Industrialized France and Italy have their wastelands but there is a saving grace of artistic instinct in the Latin peoples, as in Japan and China and India, that defies materialism. In Milton's *Paradise Lost* it is only Mammon, "the least erect of spirits" who is perfectly content to accept hell as a permanent abiding place for the fallen angels. He could live there and not be conscious that there was anything better.

Evidently the loss of ritual, externally at least, is most clearly connected with the mechanization and standardization of life that go with our power civilization. Mass production and technical efficiency treat the sacred pieties of older cultures ruthlessly. Before it all ceremonies and sacred calendars go down —whether the Sunday of the Christian, the Sabbath and high holy days of the Jew, or the Ramadan of the Moslem. And there is little offered in its place. R. H. MacIver has well stated the matter: "No ceremonies salute the time-clock and the steam whistle, no hierophants unveil the mysteries of the counting house, no myths attend the tractor and the reaper-binder, no dragons breathe in the open-hearth furnace. For multitudes the art of living is detached from the business of living and must find what refuge it can in the now lengthened interval between today's work and tomorrow's." [2]

What T. S. Eliot has from his earliest writing so powerfully stated, he repeats in his more recent work:

> Here is a place of disaffection
> Time before and time after
> In a dim light . . .
>   Only a flicker
> Over the strained time-ridden faces
> Distracted from distraction by distraction
> Filled with fancies and empty of meaning
> Tumid apathy with no concentration
> Men and bits of paper, whirled by the cold wind
> That blows before and after time,
> Wind in and out of unwholesome lungs.[3]

---

[2] *Authority and The Individual* (Harvard Tercentenary Publications), p. 144.
[3] "Burnt Norton," from *Four Quartets* (New York: Harcourt, Brace, 1943), p. 6.

And Stanley Kunitz in "Reflections by a Mailbox" sees his fellows called to war as:

> . . . the powerful get of a dying age, corrupt
> And passion-smeared, with fluid on their lips,
> As if a soul had been given to petroleum.[4]

The contemporary picture of disintegration, again, can be studied in its aspect of the loss of roots. We can relate this to what has already been said. The loss of absolutes and the loss of ritual involved, as we saw, the devaluation of tradition. Men lost their peculiar fatherlands of the soul and became modern cosmopolites without a history. The deracinated Jew is like the deracinated Negro is like the deracinated European is like the deracinated American, as Gertrude Stein might put it. Our homes have no shrines, the Bible is not on our tables, we do not look toward Mecca or Jerusalem or the setting sun. We live in and for today. Our roots in older times are cut.

But the loss of roots has other aspects. For one thing multitudes of men have lost their connection with earth and mother nature. They are born and die in the city, they spend their days in the factory, the mine or the office. They have no living contact with the soil or the processes of nature. Between them and the living earth is the cement and the asphalt; between them and the stars are the skyscrapers and the apartment houses. They have only an indirect awareness of the procession of the seasons. It is no wonder that the ancient seasonal rituals have lost their hold, the feasts of solstice and equinox and the agricultural feasts of sowing and harvest. These multitudes are troglodytes in the artificial caverns of the machine age and the megalopolis. Something primordial is lost here. Even "natural religion" is precluded in such conditions, and natural religion is the basis of higher religion.

But more important is the loss of roots in community. Such

[4] From *Passport to the War* (New York: Henry Holt, 1944), p. 3.

conditions strike at community bonds even more effectively than at natural pieties and sentiments. Man is a social animal and his health depends on the psychological securities of the neighborhood and the tribe. We do not need to repeat what so many sociologists have said about the loss of community in modern life. The family itself, the basic molecule of society, is dissociated. The organic bonds that guarantee man status are broken, and we have an atomistic culture. The emancipation from feudal or patriarchal or rural patterns exacts its price in the depersonalization of man.

With this term, the "depersonalization" of man, we have reached the most significant and comprehensive datum of our analysis. This is the end result of our cultural disintegration, and it is at this point that efforts at reintegration take their rise and can be understood. But first note just what it means and what its costs are. It means that men are out of organic relations, isolated, both in the social and the spiritual sense, and that though they are integers in various power hierarchies, yet their field of responsible choice and their freedom of personal action have rapidly diminished. Current discussion has many terms for this "little man." It speaks of his "anonymity"; he has lost his name like the heroes of Kafka's novels. He is a "cowed (intimidated) cypher." In the economic context he is a robot, in the military, an expendable conscript. He has a sense of impotence over against the impersonal forces that underlie the business cycle or the outbreak of war. Or he is only too conscious of the personal authority of the dictator, the business czar or the boss. For the *Führer* in war has his counterpart in peace. Dylan Thomas dramatizes the fact of controlling power in a few hands or a single hand:

> The hand that signed the paper felled a city;
> Five sovereign fingers taxed the breath,
> Doubled the globe of dead and halved a country;
> These five kings did a king to death.[5]

[5] *The World I Breathe* (Norfolk, Conn.: New Directions Press, 1939), p. 47.

Psychologically and subjectively this modern man is the man without a face, who struggles for the sense of his identity and for status. The experience of isolation passes into that of alienation and neurosis. Not having organic personal relations by which to secure himself, not having a field of personal action, he becomes passive. He loses his power of resistance and consistency. Aldous Huxley in *Point Counter Point* describes such a state: "His mind was amoeboid, 'like a sea of spiritual protoplasm,' capable of flowing in all directions . . . At different times in his life and even at the same moment he had filled the most various molds . . . where was the self to which he could be loyal?" [6]

Much of modern literature reflects or studies these aspects of modern man. Two themes recur and can be illustrated by Franz Kafka's two best-known novels. One of them is that of the search for status, for belonging, for community. In *The Castle*, Kafka pictures an outsider, an alien, who tries to establish himself in a humble position in a village. The symbolic narration has a nightmare quality suggestive of the anxiety and anguish with which the hero seeks to escape from his insecurity and solitude. In the allegory of the story he stands not only for the insecure white collar employee of modern bureaucratic society seeking to secure himself economically, but more especially for modern man generally in his spiritual lostness under powers that veil themselves. The "castle" in this case, in or through which he must acquire his status, denies access to itself yet tantalizes with promises and concessions soon countermanded. This craving for place and recognition in the common life recurs in most of the major writers of today in the prominence given to the theme of the exile, the alien, the wanderer. We need only instance the significant place taken in contemporary works of Ulysses (Joyce), Joseph in Egypt

[6] *Point Counter Point* (New York: Harpers, 1928). Cited in Slochauer, *op. cit.*, p. 34.

(Thomas Mann), Ahasuerus—The Wandering Jew (Joyce again), Oedipus (Camus, and T. S. Eliot's *Family Reunion*).

Kafka's *The Trial* brings out another aspect of depersonalization, that of impotence in the face of the social and spiritual hierarchies of our day. It is true that we have spoken of the freedom of the modern man. But emancipation from medieval authority and other traditions nevertheless in the long run left him confronted by the insoluble problems of existence and those immitigable necessities which make no concessions to his desires. And these very emancipations smoothed the way for new political and economic tyrannies. The theme of *The Trial* is well known. The hero, "Joseph K.," an innocent employee, wakes up one morning to find himself under arrest and he is never able to clear himself or shake off the jurisdiction over his case of the mysterious but almighty authorities that indict him. His ambiguous situation and his endless expedients in the effort to justify and free himself constitute an allegory of original sin. Yet on another level we have a portrayal of the dependence and bondage of middle-class man over against the power centers of modern society. Kafka uses this latter theme, however, chiefly as a vehicle of the generalized sense of guilt and of disquietude that grips men. An expression of this on a less esoteric level is found in a poem of Kenneth Fearing's, "Confession Overheard in a Subway," in which every man gives voice to what is universally repressed:

> You will ask how I came to be eavesdropping, in the first place.
> The answer is, I was not.
> The man who confessed to these several crimes (call him John Doe) spoke into my right ear on a crowded subway train, while the man whom he addressed (call him Richard Roe) stood at my left.
> Thus, I stood between them, and they talked, or sometimes shouted, quite literally straight through me.

How could I help but overhear?
Perhaps I might have gone away to some other strap. But the aisles were full.
Besides, I felt, for some reason, curious.

"I do not deny my guilt," said John Doe. "My own, first, and after that my guilty knowledge of still further guilt.
I have counterfeited often, and successfully.
I have been guilty of ignorance, and talking with conviction. Of intolerable wisdom and keeping silent.
Through carelessness, or cowardice, I have shortened the lives of better men. And the name for that is murder.
All my life I have been a receiver of stolen goods."

"Personally, I always mind my own business," said Richard Roe. "Sensible people don't get into those scrapes.". . .

"Guilt," said John, "is always and everywhere nothing less than guilt.
I have always, at all times, been a willing accomplice of the crass and the crude.
I have overheard, daily, the smallest details of conspiracies against the human race, vast in their ultimate scope, and conspired, daily, to launch my own.
You have heard of innocent men who died in the chair. It was my greed that threw the switch.
I helped, and I do not deny it, to nail that guy to the cross, and shall continue to help.
Look into my eyes, you can see the guilt.
Look at my face, my hair, my very clothing, you will see guilt written plainly everywhere.
Guilt of the flesh. Of the soul. Of laughing, when others do not. Of breathing and eating and sleeping.
I am guilty of what? Of guilt. Guilty of guilt, that is all, and enough." [7]

The loss of absolutes, the loss of ritual, the loss of roots (in nature and community) suggest then the character of present-day culture and we have noted some of the costs involved.

[7] From *Afternoon of a Pawn-Broker and Other Poems* (New York: Harcourt, Brace, 1943), pp. 19-21.

This situation evidently sets special tasks for the church. And we must not forget that the church itself suffers the inroads of these conditions. We would, however, recur to a caution we have hitherto expressed. It is too simple to see the factors and the conditions as all negative. Much disintegration of old patterns and authorities is to be desired. There will be no gain, however, if the new patterns that replace them are unbaptized and inhumane, whatever the names (democracy! the Four Freedoms!) with which they may cover themselves. Much of the disintegration is desirable. But the *state* of disintegration is not desirable. Yet we should also note that human nature has a marvelous faculty of redeeming its worst liabilities and conditions. This mechanization, this rootlessness, this neuroticism of today do not, even so, starve out all affection, all natural impulse, all colorfulness and sanity by any means. The heart vibrates and the soul breathes even in a world where so much of its oxygen is removed. Indeed, as we move about in our age our temptation is to suppose that our fellows are in the large majority healthy, and that this world is not a sick world. After all, we say, this ruling middle class has its code of decency, its civic ideals and its humane responses to a neighbor's needs. The standard of living is the best in the world's history. Parents love their children and every large city has its symphony orchestra! Union members wear flowers in their buttonholes at their dances! But the surface of life should not deceive us. And the moving power of human nature to affirm itself against all blights and plagues should not blind us to the whole picture. We live in a tragic time.

3. REINTEGRATION: NEW ORDERS AND NEW CULTS

The picture of our culture includes not only the end results of disintegration but also many efforts at reintegration, some of them well advanced. Nature abhors a vacuum here also, and when old gods go, new gods arrive. In one aspect we may say that a period of analysis and criticism has brought forth its inevitable reaction in varied impulses toward synthesis. As Fichte already recognized: "We began to philosophize out of exuberance and therefore deprived ourselves of innocence. We noted our nakedness, and since then we philosophize out of our need for redemption." We see the same picture whether we look at philosophy, traditions, cults or communities. New faiths replace old; moribund traditions are revived; the multitudes, famished for significant symbols, flock to new rituals; and new or revived herd movements attract the individual terrified by his isolation. The appeal of the new loyalties is broadcast and amplified by the novel techniques of propaganda. Moreover, the power of resistance to false guides and irrational solutions has already been broken down by despair and enervation.

But we do not need to explain the emergence of such new forms and faiths. The depths of human nature are perennially explosive. Man is in a condition of perennial gestation. He brings forth dynamic creations which are as often destructive as otherwise. Tradition and ritual, religion and art, are the world-old dykes, or channels of these volcanic forces, and where they are suicidely removed the way is open to devastation. Those who rest upon the pleasant assurance that man has a divine spark in him that allies him to God sometimes confuse the divine spark with the blazing faggot that also burns in him. Let rationalism, idealism or romanticism take notice. Fortunately, some of the new impulses toward order and community today are disabused of such illusions and are constructive.

The flight from disintegration manifests itself particularly in the impulse toward community. Even though often blind and exploited this feature of our time is to be valued. It is one aspect of the "flight from freedom," i.e., from excess of freedom. The uprooted and lonely and dehumanized masses awaken to the danger of their situation, and troop toward any standard. Yet the banners that are lifted are no chance emblems. They represent profound hungers and coercive if partial aspirations.

For the proletariat: communism. For the middle class: fascism. And these two merge easily with racism or nationalism. Thus we get emotional ideologies that have the explosive force of religion, and they impregnate in various ways our whole culture. Literature and art are the first to register and to react to these intoxicating fumes and vapors which course through the world. But the point here is that these movements emerge as communities, destroying old community bonds and creating new ones around conceptions and loyalties incommensurate with the old. The minds of their devotees are impervious to our reasonings or appeals. And what we forget is that we ourselves, all unawares, are infected, so that even our best ideals are subtly corrupted. "Democracy" itself is misconceived and becomes a blind and a pretext for undemocratic attitudes. It can be made into an idol as we read into it a guarantee of whatever *status quo* or privilege our own interests dictate.

One redeeming aspect of this new collectivization is found in the numerous sporadic experiments in communal life—including cell-groups, cooperatives and work-camps—jealous to safeguard the true autonomy of the person, which have appeared both within and outside of the churches. Corresponding to these is the even more manifest summons to brotherhood and true personal "meeting" in contemporary literature. Mac-Leish defines love as the "pole star for this year." Miss Rukeyser ironically describes the weakness of love in a world of aliens: "We wound past armies of strangers, waving love's thin awkward plant among a crowd of salesmen." John Bunker sees a revolt of the masses animated paradoxically by a ruthless love:

> We must cleanse the earth
> With sorrow and hate . . .
> But mostly with love,
> Love pitiless, unrelenting, omnipotent,
> Love hungry with a great hunger—
> Love for mankind.[1]

[1] From *Revolt* (New York: Campion Press, 1940), p. 5.

And the term "love" recurs through the work of Auden:

> O every day in sleep and labor
> Our life and death are with our neighbor,
> And love illuminates again
> The city and the lion's den
> The world's great rage, the travel of young men.[2]

The flight from disintegration appears again—and here also often in a suspect form—in new mysticisms and cults. We have in mind chiefly all those irrational expressions that have arisen as a protest to the mechanization and sterility of modern life. Our age has had its pseudo prophets who have voiced one or another form of primitivism or vitalism or private mysticism. Arthur Koestler has spoken of "the Yogi and the commissar." Let the commissar stand as the representative of the totalitarian community described above. The Yogi stands for what we have here in view. Sometimes, indeed, direct if falsified importations of Hindu or Buddhist influence are present. Fundamentally, however, we have to do with neopagan impulses derived from the unbaptized vitalities of the West. These can be serviceable, but too often by excess of reaction they take the form of pride and irresponsibility. Nietzsche, on one side of his Protean nature, is a fountainhead of this phenomenon. D. H. Lawrence, though widely traduced, exemplifies it. There are about us countless inarticulate men and women who in their intimate values belong to the following of the Swamis. Their resistance to Christianity is not merely indifference or the love of pleasure as we tend to think. They follow false gods. In another age they would have been with the followers of Isis and Cybele, with the gnostics or the astrologers. Indeed, some of them are today. Likewise beneath the bohemianism and aestheticism of many sophisticated groups one discovers similar cults and pieties. Yet even here the baffling character of modern culture appears in the strange intermixture of valuable elements with the spurious. So many healthful influences

[2] W. H. Auden, "New Year Letter," *op. cit.*, p. 316.

NEW ORDERS AND NEW CULTS 63

continue in our time from the past that even the errorists are partly blessed by them. And a resort to the primitive in impulse and outlook is often a necessary if dangerous way of renewal of desiccated arts or a drought-stricken culture.

Lawrence was led to burst the strait jacket of middle-class non-conformist mores and conceptions where they had become most unlovely and constricting—namely, in such an industrialized area as his native Nottinghamshire. But his testimony ultimately took on the character of a generalized criticism of civilization. In Mexico and New Mexico, in Italy and Sardinia he found culture patterns that restored to him a true sense of life's mystery and power. Gauguin initiated the quest of the painters for a more immediate contact with unspoiled nature. It was not only that he sought the cultural primitivism of Samoa but that like his followers among various schools of modern artists and writers he declared for the sensibility of the child and even the infant. The freshness of such naive experience would more than compensate for the loss of sophistication where the latter had become cerebral or corrupt. Thus he wrote: "Barbarism means to me a return to youth. I went way back, farther back than the horses of the Parthenon . . . as far back as the *dada* of my infancy, and my toy wooden horse."[3] In a somewhat similar mood Robinson Jeffers turns from the corruption of man to the unstained and inhuman chastities of the Sierras and the western ocean, and to the purity of the rock and the wild creatures.

But primitivism and pseudoprimitivism have taken on many forms, some of them highly sophisticated. In Jeffers, in a variety of forms which it is unwise to attempt to reduce to a philosophy—since it is a poet and not a philosopher who speaks— there results a Titanism which from an immense height surveys, arraigns and prophecies evil ("Cassandra") for our civilization and our nation. In Aldous Huxley and in Gerald Heard an attempt is made in various ways to renew the mystical tradi-

[3] Cited in Slochauer, *op. cit.*, p. 132.

tion in Christianity or to fertilize it with themes and practices from the Orient. There is good in all these attempts to cure our ills, and Christianity at its best has known how to encourage and sanctify both man's natural religion and his pagan traditions. But it has also known how to judge them and to be severe in selection and rejection, "bringing every thought (valuation) into captivity to the obedience of Christ," submitting *eros* to *agape*, and refusing all intoxications and heady gnosticisms which in the name of freedom open the door to irresponsibility. It is forewarned out of long experience that the irrationalism of the private cult easily passes into the irrationalism of soil or blood or state. Man's nature is so extravagant and prodigal that even the primary and healthy currents toward fullness of life and creation that arise in the soul too easily run in the channels of sensuality, self-aggrandizement or power.

The Negro in the conditions of city life today offers a good example of the clash between native impulse and the factors that smother and repress these, an example all the more revealing in view of his greater gifts of spontaneity. Gwendolyn Brooks tellingly evokes the instinct for the dramatic and the colorful of this people so harshly inhibited by the character of our culture, and in "The Sundays of Satin-Legs Smith"[4] she is really generalizing about multitudes today whether black or white. Satin-Legs' starved aspiration toward richness and splendor finds its inadequate compensation in his

> wonder suits in yellow and in wine,
> Sarcastic greens and zebra-striped cobalt . . .

And,

> Here are hats
> Like bright umbrellas; and hysterical ties
> Like narrow banners for some gathering war.

[4] *A Street in Bronzeville* (New York: Harpers, 1945), p. 26.

NEW ORDERS AND NEW CULTS

But the immitigable limitations on all such hungers are only too clear and too cruel, limitations, that is, in such an order or disorder as ours. The "gold impulse" is thwarted:

> Below the tinkling trade of little coins
> The gold impulse not possible to show
> Or spend. Promise piled over and betrayed.

Is it any wonder that the betrayed impulse turns to some sidetracked or destructive expression in private fad, group orgy or mad ideology, and finally violence? Such a culture confronts Christianity with needs at various points. When the chain of evil reaches outward expression in violence and conflict, Christianity has to formulate its views of the maintenance of public order and the relative rights of competing power groups. At the more fundamental level of the underlying conditions Christianity has a twofold task. It must criticize the society and the culture that thus stifle the growth of youth toward adequate emotional and spiritual expression and offer it the ritual and drama and depth that belong to it. And it must know meanwhile how to "save" the individual and the family even where the damning general conditions continue.

The same situation which prompts the esthetic and religious cults of which we have been speaking also goes far to explain many more generalized features of our culture. Special mention should be made here of the character of amusements and recreation in our society. What is called the "jazz age" has passed through several successive phases, but the febrile satisfactions bestowed continue to illuminate the background of a mechanized and rationalized existence. The special forms taken by the drama, the moving picture, the novel and periodical or ephemeral publication tell their story. They speak eloquently of the omnipresent demands, whether for excitement, escape, distraction or partisanship. The accent in many of our social expressions, as witness sports, and performances and exhibitions of many kinds, is on heightened forms of the dramatic, on the shock valve; and alcohol, sensuality and gambling, one or more, are associated with most of our recreation. The depersonalized psyche, the numbed and enervated worker, requires high-tension stimuli to recover a transient awareness of his own identity.

The flight from disintegration and rootlessness, finally, takes a third form in a return to tradition. Here we have a return to absolutes that are defined by history. Thus we have neo-orthodoxies of various schools. Among these, neo-humanism has the greatest difficulty in lifting its voice in these days but we still hear appeals to the sanity of Socrates, Erasmus and Goethe. Educators fight a defensive battle for Greek and Latin, and now hope to take advantage of the panic induced by these catastrophic times to restore the humane arts and letters to their former place. But this kind of traditionalism is doubly weak today. It starts with the handicap of little direct knowledge from the inside of the new forces of today, and it lacks an adequate philosophy. Either it represents only an aesthetic eclecticism or if it appeals to the *philosophia perennis* it too evidently stops short of the authoritative appeal of either Aquinas or Calvin.

Neo-Thomism and the various forms of return to the Reformation are, indeed, live options today. The former also has its various shadings. On one side it merges imperceptibly with an academic humanism such as we have just mentioned. The term Neo-Thomism is loosely and mistakenly assigned to any who appeal to the great distinction of natural and supernatural revelation or who invoke reason, virtue and the soul in intellectual or political discussion. Neo-Thomism proper, however, requires a grave intellectual decision or series of decisions, in essential agreement with Aristotle and Aquinas, which set aside perhaps much of the error of the modern world but therewith also much of its experience. This is only the most articulate and influential form of appeal of non-Protestant Christian philosophy. There are Catholics who appeal rather to Duns Scotus, and others, in this case Anglicans, who appeal to a Platonistic theology. The great question with all of these is whether they are simply and solely reaction or whether they represent a serious coming-to-terms with modern experience and thought.

Protestant neo-orthodoxy whether on its Calvinist or Lutheran wings raises the same question. For our diagnosis of contemporary culture we are not concerned first of all with the theological issues. The significance for us of Barthianism in its various senses is whether it constitutes a repudiation of modern experience or an attempt to digest and incorporate it. We should not at any time deprecate the repossession of tradition. But tradition should be repossessed in the light of the present. The past becomes a safe guide only where, by a spiritual effort, it is comprehended as part of a larger present. We make ourselves contemporaries of those that have gone before so that their experiences and decisions become our responsibility along with the experiences and decisions of today.

But too much of the neo-orthodoxy as of the Neo-Thomism of today is in the bad sense reactionary. The past remains the past and men imitate it or accept its authority by way of a bondage rather than responsible renewal. This kind of grasping for absolutes in a day of relativity, while it offers a specious refuge, is no real solution of the problems of depersonalization and deracination. Here again, as with capitulation to the Commissar or the Yogi, men only find status by acceptance of new overlords whether political or spiritual.

What should be added here, however, is that the great faiths in their legitimate forms, do have the character of absolutes. But these absolutes derive their authority from the immediate apprehension of God and the living consent of the soul and not from any more concrete or objectified authority such as institution, creed or book. The latter are, indeed, essential carriers or vehicles of the faith but the faith itself must remain personal. More adequate symbols and rites of the Christian faith, suggestive both of its depth and of its ancient continuity, are a paramount claim upon religious reform today. But where these take the place of personal faith and responsibility, there Christianity today is confronted by false absolutisms even in the church itself.

We have sought to portray the disorder of our time and to trace its origin in intellectual and cultural influences of past and present. We should not, however, assign too great a significance to the role of ideas and movements, or let ourselves be beguiled into a deterministic view of these evils. The moral factor is primary.

> Accurate scholarship can
> Unearth the whole offense
> From Luther until now
> That has driven a culture mad,
> Find what occurred at Linz,
> What huge imago made
> A psychopathic god:
> I and the public know
> What all school children learn,
> Those to whom evil is done
> Do evil in return.[5]

The hurts and costs of contemporary life are deeply conditioned by prevailing faiths and unfaiths. Multitudes of men grow and live under the sway of false dogmas and under the tyranny of circumstances that limit their responsibility, induce spiritual maladies, and provoke them to fraud or violence. But each human being possesses an area of freedom and action which constitutes liberty. To this, Christianity must address its message and its demand at the same time that it passes judgment on the pagan structures and valuations which limit that freedom.

[5] W. H. Auden, "September 1, 1939," *op. cit.*, p. 57.

IV

RE-ASSESSING "TRADITIONAL" POETRY

WITH this picture of contemporary culture before us it would be natural to pass immediately to an examination of the new poetry which so directly reflects it. But it will be worthwhile for a number of reasons to pause and recognize the stubborn persistence on a wide scale of poetry in the Victorian and idealistic tradition, both at the end of the nineteenth century and since. Whatever diverse views may be held as to its quality, it is still widely popular in many quarters—so far as poetry is popular at all. Moreover, it includes a good many examples of what can be called specifically Christian poetry and invites our special interest for this reason, and, indeed, our genuine appreciation. But what makes its consideration especially relevant to this book is the fact that we can use it by way of comparison and contrast to exhibit both the cleavages in contemporary culture and the distinctiveness of the strictly "modern" temper and "modern" poetry.

Just as our children in school today still read "The Vision of Sir Launfall," "The Idylls of the King" and "The Village Blacksmith" so they read more recent poems of Edwin Markham, Vachel Lindsay and Francis Thompson, and still more recent work of Robert Frost, Carl Sandburg and Steven Vincent Benêt. A list of names will suggest the variety and wide appeal of contemporary poets commonly identified as traditional. There are Georgian and post-Georgian poets of the countryside like W. H. Davies, W. W. Gibson, Miss V. Sackville-West and Edmund Blunden in England. There are poets like Robert

P. Tristram Coffin, David Morton and Wilson MacDonald in America and Canada, much of whose work similarly is concerned with nature and rural life. Poets of this type are often called regional, but as in the case of Frost and E. A. Robinson they are usually something more. There are poets in whom the personal lyric gift predominates, as different as Alfred Noyes, Edna St. Vincent Millay, Robert Nathan, Walter de la Mare and Laurence Binyon. There are the Irish poets of the type of Padraic Colum and James Stephens, Catholic poets of the kind that appear in the journal and anthologies of the Catholic Poetry Society of America, and other types, mystical, socially-minded, and devotional. Nor should we forget the various types of less ambitious verse, homespun and dialect poetry in the tradition of Paul Lawrence Dunbar and the work of Ogden Nash and the humorists. Such a review reminds us of the universality of the poetic art and the way in which poetry emerges from and celebrates the whole dense texture of human experience. Such a reminder also forewarns us against cliquish or coterie attitudes or esthetic snobbishness. All such writers of traditional poetry today not only represent a many-sided tradition of craft and theme but have their own considerable audience, and a wide variety of poetry magazines characterized by this kind of content.

The word "traditional" as applied to such poets is hazardous, since the new poets also can and do lay claim to it. All depends on which tradition is involved. But we shall use the term in its more limited sense to refer to poets today who remain apart from the new movements in the art.

We propose to defend poets of this kind against the excessive intolerance often exhibited against them. But we must make distinctions, and above all we must measure all poets by an austere standard over against which few poets of any time, of whatever tradition, can be assigned notable excellence. Moreover, we must indicate the shrinking cultural tradition to which such post-Victorian artists belong and the fateful limitations of

A CULTURAL SURVIVAL

which they are prisoners. The new poets have corresponding handicaps constituted by the transitional character of our immediate period.

Those concerned with religious poetry in any strict sense cannot but be peculiarly interested in the present question since many of them will be hesitant as yet to relinquish "The Hound of Heaven," "The Congo," "The Everlasting Mercy," or "The Testament of Beauty" in favor of the recent work of T. S. Eliot or Robert Lowell. Yet distinctions and valuations must be made. There is no reason why both schools and all schools may not be appreciated, always under condition that we understand the works in question and test them discerningly.

1. "TRADITIONAL" POETRY AS A CULTURAL SURVIVAL

The sharp and even rancorous controversies of our time with regard to poetry would not take place except for the fact that divergent ways of life are at issue. Polemic like that to which the articles by Professor Robert Hillyer in June 1949 gave rise,[1] involve not only poetic craft but cultural philosophies and life experience. What is significant here is that Christian poets and critics can be found on both sides. In the arts today there are Christian traditionalists (in the narrow sense) and Christian modernists. What divides men here is not their faith but their sensibility, their experience of our time. The traditionalist finds the modern Roman Catholic poet just as alien as he does the modern nihilist. The nihilist poet and Mr. Auden have it in common that they have broken with the traditionalists' outlook and way of life. Where such fundamental divergence is involved there are naturally radically different views of poetry and styles of poetry. There results also an incapacity for mutual appreciation.

[1] "Poetry's New Priesthood," from the *Saturday Review of Literature* (June 18, 1949); "Treason's Strange Fruit" (June 11, 1949). Cf. "The Case Against the *Saturday Review of Literature*" from *Poetry, A Magazine of Verse* (Chicago: October, 1949).

We have here only one example of the confusion of tongues in contemporary society of which we have spoken in the preceding chapter. The same situation holds in the other arts. To do justice to post-Victorian and Georgian poetry today on the part of "moderns" is very difficult, and a strictly esthetic judgment is almost inevitably slanted by partisan factors. This has appeared most clearly in the extreme depreciation some years back of even the most gifted nineteenth-century writers. What is required is that we make the same effort of appreciation across contemporary cultural lines that we make in our exercise of historical imagination in the appreciation of ancient writers or of non-Christian religious classics. We should "suspend" our particular disbeliefs even in dealing with contemporary writers and artists who belong to a different color in the mosaic of contemporary culture.

The historical background of our situation which we have presented in the second and third chapters above, and the resulting picture of contemporary man, prepare us to understand the pluralism of our cultural ideals and expressions today. The matter can be recognized most clearly in connection with our religious institutions and faiths. We have here stubborn communities, social groups and strata which have resisted the acids of modernity and which, like islands, perpetuate ways of life and culture patterns with little change from the past. This is true not only of those religious bodies that are strongly traditional, with defenses of polity, dogma and liturgy, which defend them from solvent forces; it is also true to a considerable extent of those left-wing Protestant bodies which have encouraged interchange with the forces of the age. All such religious groups are like islands of social as well as religious tradition. It is inevitable and understandable that the new generations shaped by these inherited patterns, should find meaningful not only the religious cult but also the artistic idiom of the past. Thus it is only with the greatest effort that those concerned to revitalize the sacred arts of the Catholic church today have been able to achieve any results, even though the reform of church music and graphic arts is presented in terms of an older Catholic tradition.[2] Similarly the characteristic Catholic poetry of today still resembles that of Francis Thompson rather than that of Hopkins or Robert Lowell.

The same thing holds with poetry which is at all close to Protestant church life. We take our observations here from the hymn or didactic poem, and what we find is in the tradition of Browning, Vachel Lindsay or Edwin Markham unless it wanders off in a mystical vein that suggests Tagore or Gibran. The conventional patterns of the verse here correspond to that of the Catholic poet. In either case there are occasional striking accomplishments, but the predominant feature is the persistence of familiar idioms in church circles. The special cultures and strata—Catholic, Lutheran, Anglican, Reformed, Hebrew, etc.—sustain older artistic and poetic patterns.

What is true of churches is true in a less demonstrable way of socio-economic strata, and, of course, the two overlap. There are cultural islands in the rapidly changing landscape of modern society fortified by various types of stabilizing factors, in which a nineteenth-century way of life continues under changing external aspects. Those who belong by upbringing and circumstances to these islands approve what is called "traditional poetry" and "traditional art." It is these groups which support the poetry magazines which print the work of "traditional" poets and confer prizes for this kind of writing. These strata of our population have not lost their roots as much of the modern world has. They therefore find *meaningful* the work of the past several generations out of which have come their religious, moral and social patterns and values. The contemporary arts, tastes, manners, symbols that are meaningful to them, that speak to them, will be continuous with those of the nineteenth century.

The poetry of this tradition can lay claim to qualities of

[2] See Ch. VI below.

order, pattern and coherence because of the relative coherence and continuity of the culture out of which it comes. The writer in this medium works in the framework of a language, an artistic convention, a range of responses and in a gamut of sentiment and imagination long familiar and long defined. In all such respects he has an advantage, and the reader comes to his work knowing in a sense what he will find, not merely in what concerns allusions and themes, but more importantly in what concerns the range of attitude and sensibility. From this perspective, evidently, the kind of order found in the new arts will seem disorder, and the kind of meanings, meaningless, and the kind of experience itself, inapprehensible or unimportant.

In this connection a justification of the apparent disorder of modern poetry is found in parable fashion in some lines of one of our most notable American poets, Wallace Stevens, in a poem that has the significant title, "The Poems of our Climate." Stevens declares that we today cannot be satisfied with simplicity and a familiar pattern of harmony, symbolized in the poem by a flower decoration of pink and white carnations in a brilliant bowl of clear water. *Our* paradise is the imperfect as a mark of escape from the too familiar, and our delight "lies in flawed words and stubborn sounds."

> Still one would want more, one would need more,
> More than a world of white and snowy scents.
>
> There would still remain the never-resting mind,
> So that one would want to escape, come back
> To what had been so long composed.
> The imperfect is our paradise.
> Note that, in this bitterness, delight,
> Since the imperfect is so hot in us,
> Lies in flawed words and stubborn sounds.[3]

[3] Reprinted from *Parts of a World* by Wallace Stevens by permission of Alfred A. Knopf, Inc., copyright 1942 by Wallace Stevens.

A CULTURAL SURVIVAL

We have spoken of these relatively stable groups or strata in contemporary society as "islands." They were once part of a continent of traditional culture which has been increasingly submerged. In the preceding chapter we described the forces which have undermined the patterns, loyalties and community bonds of the past and which have led to the shaping of new ones in their stead. Such a transition is inevitably a period of confusion and of aroused conflict. This, of course, is true in the field of social and political ideals. It is similarly true in esthetics just as it is in religion. One can say that an old world is dying and that a new world is being born. Such a judgment is to weight the scales heavily against the "traditionalist" in the sense we have been using the term. It would mean that his way of life and scale of values is on its way out. Or one can say that our traditions are reshaping themselves and that for the time being it is not clear which of the old will be rejected and which confirmed. At least one may assert that the familiar "traditional" poetry must be radically reinvigorated or it will not be relevant to the new experience which is rapidly coming to characterize the whole of society. On the other hand, we could also forecast that that new poetry which merely reflects the passing episodes and paroxysms of our cultural struggle can only become a curiosity in a short time.

The pluralism of which we have spoken is then defined first of all in connection with the main cleavage between the sea of new forces and the islands of surviving order. But the new forces themselves take on their differing patterns and ideologies, and gifted individuals represent them in various ways or themselves stand apart. When the bonds of an old culture are dissolved the insecurities and anguish of rootlessness and estrangement, as we have seen, lead men to various forms of new order and new faith. In such a moment the most significant poetry will arise out of the depths of the disarray rather than out of the compromised citadels of tradition or out of the tentative new homes of the spirit.

The crucial judgment to make with regard to our situation is that as to the vitality and survival-value of the older middle-class ideals and values. The conclusion we reach here will determine our view as to the prospect for traditional art and poetry. We may believe that the loss of absolutes, of ritual and of community of which we have spoken, is only a marginal and temporary phenomenon. In that case we would insist that the culture and arts we call traditonal would continue essentially unchanged and be typical for the future. On the other hand, we may well conclude on a deeper view that these islands of security are rapidly shrinking and that a general transformation is rapidly taking place in our whole culture and way of life. In that case all our social forms and even the character of our religious institutions are subject to the change, and it would follow inevitably that the prevailing types of artistic expression would change with them, or, as a matter of fact, before them.

The latter appears to us to be the truer view. The forces and trends described in the preceding chapter are effecting a revolution at all levels of our life and the results of it cannot but penetrate into even the most protected citadels. Expressions of the new phases of culture have therefore a special importance. This does not mean that we should not discriminate among them. Nor does it mean that we must henceforth refuse homage to those choice or priceless aspects of the traditional culture just because it approaches its term. We still have with us a pluralistic culture in this special sense, and we should not be blind to the artistic expressions of any part of the mosaic.

2. HANDICAPS OF THE "TRADITIONAL" POET

The strength and weakness of post-Victorian, Georgian and traditionalist poetry today reflect the strength and weakness of our culture at the turn of the century. We are concerned here with that surviving middle-class culture related especially to

Protestant church life which had not and has not still in certain quarters been unsettled by the factors described in the preceding chapter. Out of this kind of milieu came and still comes a stream of idealistic or post-romantic literature, suggested by such names as Houseman, Vachel Lindsay, Millay. Even the incorporation of more realistic elements as in Masefield, Edgar Lee Masters and Sandburg could take place without essentially modifying the picture.

Now the "tradition" in such literature as in this milieu is multiple. We have first the more immediate late nineteenth-century background which represents the greatest liability in certain aspects. For despite the vitality of this period and the real greatness of many of its writers the society of this period took on a quasi-Philistine character which had corollaries in the arts. A curious bifurcation seemed to be the rule between an extravagant materialism and an accompanying thin idealism. The spiritual expressions of culture, whether religious or artistic, were isolated or depreciated and became other-worldly or escapist. The poet could not manage the common material of life—the lump was too sodden. His very language became special and there was always the temptation to resort to archaism to assure himself of eloquence. The result too often was rhetoric in the bad sense. If a poet sought despite all to speak for the power and glory of the materialistic age as in one sense Kipling and Henley did, it necessarily involved him in a moralistic dilemma.

The burden of worldliness was compounded with limitations of taste and sensitiveness. The legacy of the frontier played its part here in the American scene. The story of the frontier was a story of heroism but the struggle with a new territory and the subsequent decades of western small town development handicapped the developments of the arts and of those wider curiosities that make for a rich culture, despite the planting of academies and colleges.

The religious heritage might have been expected to redeem

this situation but in many respects it connived with it. Protestant non-conformity was, indeed, still an ultimate dyke against sheer Mammonism, and the seed-bed of individuals who gave educational and spiritual leadership to the times. But, as we have seen, this heritage had gone underground and acted only indirectly on culture. Its institutional aspects too often had taken on a rigid character alienating the vital forces of the time, or in their liberal forms had surrendered to the spirit of the age. Thus the religious arts in this period have evidenced the lack of cultural soil.[1]

The English critic, Herbert Read, in a chapter entitled, "Why We English Have No Taste" admits to the influence of capitalism and of Puritanism. But he places the main emphasis upon the "social psychology" of English life: the exaltation of the "normal," the allergy to the "odd." Such conformism he notes is really a form of neurosis, a retreat from the reality of life, a nervous mask.[2] This has its parallel in American life. Taste and fertility of artistic invention cannot thrive in a competitive insecurity.

Behind the influences of this post-Civil War period lie those of the romantic movement. Our middle-class culture in the United States bears the marks of this phase both for good and for ill. The release of spontaneity, the deepening of the intuitive life, the exhilaration of experience especially with nature, represented a kind of deferred secular Great Awakening. Its force and scope are evident in the transcendentalist movement and in those writers whose work is characterized by Matthiessen as the "American Renaissance": Emerson, Thoreau, Hawthorne, Melville and Whitman. This experience conferred upon our people an endowment so powerful that all subsequent generations have tended to recur to it as the inevitable form of esthetic experience. Conscious or unconscious loyalty to it

---

[1] See Ch. IV: "The Problem of Religious Poetry in America" in A. N. Wilder, *Spiritual Aspects of the New Poetry*.

[2] *Poetry and Anarchism* (New York: Macmillan, 1939), Ch. III.

often occasions the vehement resistance that obtains to the new mood in the arts. Thus the traditionalist poet of today appeals back to both Victorian and romantic habits, to a background of emotional and moral idealism peculiarly determined by conditions of a century and a half ago. In this background, influences of the age of sentiment and the age of reason combine with romantic factors without obvious conflict to compose a common middle-class sensibility. For in the new world there was no sharp conflict of neo-classicism with what preceded it, or of romanticism with neo-classicism. American intellectual life does not bear the marks of a fateful cleavage of tradition like that which has harassed the French since the French Revolution, and which has its parallels in other European cultures.

Here it is significant and ironical that the new poetry can call itself "traditional" with good reason, precisely because it appeals back of the romantic movement to the seventeenth century and earlier. The heritage of the "traditional" poets is too partial and too recent. The tradition actually lived by in our Middletown culture similarly is too partial and recent. And the same could be said of our Protestant bodies until recently. For though some may appeal back to the Reformation and its dogma, and others to the liberalism of the eighteenth century, their real ethos is that of the last century, idealistic, activist, moralistic. This has been and still is animated by that Holy Spirit which is never wholly absent from the church and often characterized by utmost devotion and redemptive power. But the general picture of Protestant church life shares the features and handicaps of middle-class culture.

With regard to the religious factor in the cultural type of which we have been speaking, it is sometimes suggested that an ascetic trait in Puritanism lies behind the esthetic limitations. Professor Kenneth B. Murdock in his volume, *Literature and Theology in Colonial New England*,[3] has touched on this question. He specifically disproves the notion that the New

[3] Cambridge: Harvard University Press, 1949.

England Puritans were hostile to art or its embellishments in their writing. It is shown, however, that their theology led them deliberately to set aside the richer sensuous treatment of religious themes found in the best "divine poems" and "holy prose" of the age. The Puritan recognized that spiritual things must be represented in sensuous terms but he drew the line at much that the Catholic freely used. He appreciated the Anglican middle way in style but sought deliberately a rhetoric more fitting to his idea of holy living, Scripture and his audience.

So much can be agreed with. Judgment, however, still remains open here as to whether this constitutes an impoverishment. The conceits, preciousness and daring sensuous imagery of Crashaw and Herbert, even to those who are not indisposed to them theologically, need not be viewed as essential and preferable for adequate Christian symbolism. What is more damaging is the thesis that "the tendency to write only out of the moral, respectable, rational part of the poet's nature came chiefly after the Reformation 'when the whole realm of sense became increasingly suspect; Protestantism . . . represented a split in the integrity of human experience.'"[4] After citing views which suggest that the Protestant made a bifurcation between the "spiritual" and the "material" Professor Murdock cautiously concludes: "Most critics agree that strict English Protestantism—especially in its severer varieties—tends to distrust the senses and so to offer scantier materials for art than the tradition of Rome."[5]

This is too large a subject to pursue fully here. The relations of Christianity to culture in different periods vary for excellent reasons. Numerous phases of Christianity have been iconoclastic, also for excellent reasons. Likewise Christianity in all its vigorous periods has inspired directly or indirectly great cultural expression. The prevailing situation in taste, skills and

[4] *Op. cit.*, p. 16. Professor Murdock cites here an unsigned review from the *Times* (London) *Literary Supplement.*

[5] *Op. cit.*, p. 17.

temper is often decisive. That Protestantism has often inspired the work of supreme artists is evident in such cases as Milton, Bach, Rembrandt and Melville.[6] The relation of the Christian life to the natural order is always one of tension even where the decisive principle of incarnation is fully recognized. Tendencies to a false spirituality are perhaps less characteristic of Protestantism than of Catholicism.

What is more to the point here is that the split in the integrity of human experience above referred to did occur sometime in the seventeenth century and has constituted a liability for all subsequent English and American poetry. In Victorian and post-Victorian work the results are most clear. The familiar thesis rightly recognizes that the poet came to write only out of *part* of his nature. The whole human being is not in the work. Sometimes indeed it is the sensuous element and physical image that are missing. The experience of the poet is not unreservedly and naively married to the sense experience as it is in Job and Dante.

Brother George Every has well put the matter in connection with the insipidity of a great deal of our traditional religious art.

> Modern Christian art is compelled to make a detour to avoid the Christmas-card associations of painting and poetry about religion. . . . It is the physical imagery that is important. . . . Religious feeling has to be translated into terms of physical sensation if it is to be made real again to those who are finding their way from a belief that only the physical is real to a renewed belief in the reality of the metaphysical. In their eyes the Christmas card stands for an old story, a kind of fiction, but El Greco gives a sense of interior experience, of something that tore at the very vitals of man.[7]

---

[6] Cf. Joseph Crouch, *Puritanism and Art* (London: 1910).
[7] *Christian Discrimination* (London: 1940), pp. 58, 59.

Even more characteristically for the poetry with which we are concerned, though intelligence (or "wit") may have a place in it, it is there in insufficient degree or, more serious, it is there as an "alien body." It is not absorbed and metamorphosed into the vision, sensibility and discourse that constitute the poem. Thus the work is either sentimental, lacking a sufficient intelligence and realism, or it is didactic if the element of intelligence is extrinsic and prosaic. The poet must feel with his intellect and know with his five senses.

These things are always said more concisely by the poets themselves than by others. Thus Miss Marianne Moore in an oft quoted poem pleads for a reconciliation of realism and idealism, of matter and spirit in an art that represents genuine incarnation. She begins by agreeing with the man in the street in his distrust of conventional poetry:

> I, too, dislike it: there are things more important beyond
>   all this fiddle . . .
> nor till the poets among us can be 'literalists of the
>   imagination'—above insolence and triviality and can
>   present
> for inspection, imaginary gardens with real toads in them,
>   shall we have it . . . [8]

Another piquant note is similarly revealing. In a satirical observation addressed to some traditional poets and entitled "Roses Only," she writes:

> You do not seem to realize that beauty is a liability rather
>   than an asset . . .
> . . . you must have brains . . .
> your thorns are the best part of you.[9]

The point we are making will be clearer to many if we think of it in connection with the Protestant hymn book. There are

---

[8] "Poetry," in *Observations* (New York: The Dial Press, 1925), p. 31.
[9] *Op. cit.*, p. 41.

many Protestants who will admit to dissatisfaction with even the better hymns of the nineteenth and twentieth centuries. We have in mind here the words alone. Such hymns, we say, lack "objectivity." They center about our own moods rather than massive realities. "Modern liturgies are generally strong in aspiration, but ancient, medieval, and Reformed liturgies are stronger still in adoration. Where we wish, they announce; where we inquire, they affirm; where we wonder, they exult and praise."[10] If we examine modern hymns and liturgical material we find that they lack wholeness of experience: conviction is not wed to feeling. Message and ethic are not fused with vision. It is not so with the Psalmist, with St. Francis or with Luther.[11]

We can see the reason for the ineffectiveness of "traditional" poetry today if we illustrate at a dead-end level in connection with prevailing popular misconceptions and popular verse.

There is first the sentimental-escapist type which may be illustrated at its worst by such a saccharine hymn as "Beautiful Island of Somewhere," often sung at funeral services at the request of the family. The words are turgid and meaningless, the bath of emotion enervating. But this kind of traditional poetry (and music in hymns and cowboy songs and blues) has a wide gamut, much of it of a greater pretension to merit. It is not, we believe, out of an impulse of snobbishness that we make this judgment or out of a failure to acknowledge the relative justification of popular verse of many kinds. Much popular verse charged with sentiment has quality, including many spirituals, folk songs and college anthems. It is rather a question of emotional truth, energy, reality. The imputation of our charge here bears upon much popular escapist lyrical poetry of our time which invokes "Beauty," dreams, visions and ideals without relating them to things as they are. What

---

[10] Roger Hazelton, "Ecumenicity in Worship," *Andover Newton Bulletin* (February, 1950), p. 16.

[11] Cf. George Every, "Hymns Ancient and Modern," Ch. V in *Christian Discrimination* (London: Macmillan, 1940).

appeal they have grows out of the fact that they are at least pale echoes of great transcriptions of beauty in the past, or touch chords of feeling in connection with nature, love, motherhood, fraternity, patriotism or piety without an integral and related vision that suggests what is involved for the person. The sentiment is irresponsible. As we have said in another connection: "These poems are full of dreams and visions and splendors. In sum they recall the sentiment of college fraternity sings or lodge love-feasts where every eye is wet but no one believes a word of it."

The formula to use with regard to this kind of poetry is that it represents a shallow resolution of conflict. It takes on the character of a spell to exorcize reality and is therefore escapist in the bad sense. The better traditional poetry of our time is not chargeable to this degree, but we have chosen the inferior kinds to exhibit the dangers it incurs. There is such a thing as a justifiable "escapism," of course, whether in the experience of beauty, of mysticism or of piety. For beauty, thus, we can set the merit of Yeats' "Byzantium" over against poems of Alfred Noyes or Rupert Brooke; for mysticism we can set that of Tagore over against that of Kahlil Gibran; for piety we can set that of G. M. Hopkins or the "spirituals" over against that of Oxenham and the modern hymn. The whole matter has its background in the ambiguities of the romantic movement and the age of sentimentalism that preceded it. Here on the one hand are precedents for unreality in experience and on the other for artificiality and partiality of poetic discourse. But this does not involve a drastic depreciation of romantic poetry as such nor denial of the greatly enhanced grasp of reality which as Whitehead has shown was the peculiar contribution of the movement.

In the second place there is the moralistic type of traditional poetry today which may be suggested, again by way of extreme, in Kingsley's, "Be good, sweet maid, and let who will be clever," or the familiar lines:

> So many paths, so many creeds,
> So many ways that wind and wind
> When just the art of being kind
> Is all this sad world needs.

This type of verse, again, has a wide gamut of quality, much of it of a greater pretension to merit, and genuinely admirable. At its worst it becomes clear that it uses the prestige and associations of poetic form to make palatable a didactic theme. Art (such as it is) and instruction are really divorced, but thereupon forced upon each other. As has been made clear in our first chapter we are not of those who exclude a didactic poetry. There are too many great examples of it beginning with the Old Testament prophets and coming down through Vergil, Dante and Milton. There is, indeed, a legitimate place for didactic verse of a popular and unambitious kind. The point is that it should not be confused with significant poetry; and we should not be left confused as to real possibilities of didactic poetry.

Scrutiny of the weakest types of moralistic poetry as above shows us that the chief error lies in the false relation set up between will and imagination. If the essence of poetry is "Schauen," "seeing" in its richest sense, an act of sensitive and integrating imagination, this will inevitably involve the attitude, the "moral" attitude also, of the poet and his reader. There will be no need to dot the "i's" and cross the "t's" of the moral implications or to appeal to the will explicitly. Or, if the action of the will is involved, as in the Hebrew prophets or in passages in Milton's "Lycidas" and *Samson Agonistes,* or in Wordsworth's sonnets on Milton and Toussaint l'Ouverture, the appeal will rise out of the imaginative vision and have its roots in the incipient vision itself. Traditional poetry is handicapped here again by the split in the modern consciousness which identifies poetry not with the whole man in a total experience and with a conception of "existence" in which will and mind and emotion are one, but with special areas of his experience.

Traditional-minded readers of the new poetry have their difficulties just because they are inclined to accept the limitations of which we have spoken as axiomatic and in the nature of things. Their approach is in terms of the mentality and temper of the older culture we have described and affects likewise their understanding of religion, education and all else. The impulse of the "modern" poet and artist is to recover the wholeness of experience and the corresponding wholeness of words and language which have been compromised. What is strange about it to the traditional reader arises in large part because this reader himself has become inured to a cleavage in his own mental habit and experience, and because the cultural situation today generally makes a more total communication peculiarly difficult. In the two following chapters we shall compare the treatments of important areas of experience in traditional and modern poetry and seek to do justice to both.

V

NATURE IN TRADITIONAL AND MODERN POETRY

WE PROPOSE in this chapter and the one following to single out noteworthy examples of comparatively recent "traditional" poetry and set beside them examples drawn either from the new poetry or from writers considered to be precursors of it. This will give us occasion to observe more particularly certain areas of difference between "old" and "new" as well as to remind ourselves of the variety of excellence of both. We shall thus also have before us a body of work whose religious as well as cultural implications may invite attention and comparison. For our purpose we choose two chief areas, both of which have engaged the attention of poets through the centuries: nature, and religious devotion.

One prior observation may be made with regard to the attitude of "moderns" toward traditionalist poetry. The "modern" reader, captivated by the new arts, is very often specially conditioned in his reactions by his own personal complexity of experience, if not by his own psychological and spiritual insecurity, factors which similarly inspire the new arts in question. The reasons for this we have suggested in our third chapter. He has a mind and heart conditioned by the contemporary crisis. Indeed, his actual economic and social situation may well be highly insecure, whether his actual livelihood or those more subtle social relations which make for rapport and confidence. At both levels this situation makes for complexity, anxiety, estrangement—but also for openness, exposure and hospitality to new possibilities. "Blessed are the poor in spirit" has its relevance here, in that these exiles are detached from accepted satisfactions and receptive to new endowments and new meanings.

Thus the "modern" is not at home with the cultural legacy still precious to many. His state of mind indisposes him to a familiar "simpler" type of poetry or painting or music, however excellent. He is in some respects like a sick man for whom a customary diet is tasteless. A soldier emerging from the Battle of the Bulge is in no mood to read "The Charge of the Light Brigade" or the *Barrack Room Ballads* or even Rupert Brooke. It is to the point here to recall that it was the war poetry of Wilfred Owen and not that of Wilfred Grenfell or Rupert Brooke which met the mood of the post-war poets.

Certainly in one respect our present cultural situation is a crisis and in that sense temporary. Those conditioned by the crisis evidently cannot do justice to much that belongs to a more stable life. In the *Hamlet of Archibald MacLeish* the modern Hamlet exclaims in self-defense:

> thou wouldst not think
> How ill all's here about my heart.

This does not mean that the contemporary mood is simply and solely a tragic one. It is also characterized by special richness and sensitivity that goes with the tension. But much that is otherwise meaningful and simple tends to take on the character of the insipid for such readers. Even when the crisis phase of our time has passed traditional art will have to meet the demands of a new awareness.

These considerations bear upon our attitude to nature and upon the treatment of nature in poetry as well as more directly human concerns, and to this we now turn. We are accustomed to say that there are "enduring permanences" in man's experience which are largely unaffected by cultural transitions. Nature is one of these. Yet man's vision of nature and of his place in it has changed in every period.

The theme plays into the hand of our larger interests in this study in another way. In our relation to nature we have the ground of something universal in man which is, moreover, an unmistakable element of the religious consciousness. This element may often be starved in the conditions of modern life. For that very reason and because the religious tradition has lost its hold on many, the modern secular artist may turn to nature as a surrogate for other forfeited sources of meaning. Correspondingly, much traditional poetry deals with nature in a romantic or mystical fashion. We are thus confronted with difficult problems in distinguishing between a legitimate celebration of the creation in terms of what might be called "natural revelation" as over against shallow or intoxicated forms of pantheism incompatible with the Christian outlook. We are not of those who would scent out heresy in the great romantic poets and their followers, believing as we do that the Christian faith fulfils itself in many ways, and often by the incorporation of the great waves of impulse and vitality that pour into the new experience of the generations. But the risks and excesses of such hours of emancipation and intoxication must be assessed.

1. THE LAND, BY V. SACKVILLE-WEST[1]

The poem which we choose as representing a traditional treatment of nature to serve as a point of reference in the present chapter is not, however, of the romantic type. It may stand, rather, as representative of that kind of rural or regional poetry which holds the affections of men through the centuries, celebrating the pieties of the soil and the seasons, and the life and toil of the husbandman. It is a work that should be better known, and its length gives it here an advantage over shorter

[1] London: William Heinemann, 1926. Also, *Collected Poems*, Vol. I (London: Hogarth Press, 1933).

poems that might have served equally well from the writings of poets like Frost, Masefield, Edmund Blunden and Edward Thomas.

The Land is a book-length poem in four parts divided according to the seasons. It can best be described as a modern *georgic*. The bulk of the work is devoted to the sober detail of husbandry and all its arts and skills. It has the kind of objective sobriety and traditional movement which can seem placid if not insipid to the modern mood. But it is free from two things that specially alienate readers of this kind. There is no false idealization of the life of the soil, and there is no useless decoration or rhetoric. Further, what philosophy of life may be construed is not on the surface. The poem in every way keeps close to experience, to life itself. At the very beginning this ascetic design is asserted:

> I sing the cycle of my country's year,
> I sing the tillage, and the reaping sing,
> Classic monotony, that modes and wars
> Leave undisturbed, unbettered, for their best
> Was born immediate, of expediency.
> The sickle sought no art; the axe, the share
> Draped no superfluous beauty round their steel;
> The scythe desired no music for her stroke,
> Her stroke sufficed in music, as her blade
> Laid low the swathes . . .

And the poet asks with regard to her own task:

> Why then in little meadows hedge about
> A poet's pasture? shed a poet's cloak
> For fustian? cede a birthright, thus to map
> So small a corner of so great a world?

The answer comes: because

> The country habit has me by the heart,
>   . . . only here
> Lies peace after uneasy truancy;

> Here meet and marry many harmonies,
> —All harmonies being ultimately one,—
> Small mirroring majestic; for as earth
> Rolls on her journey, so her little fields
> Ripen or sleep, and the necessities
> Of seasons match the planetary law.
> So truly stride between the earth and heaven
> Sowers of grain: so truly in the spring
> Earth's orbit swings both blood and sap to rhythm,
> And infinite and humble are at one;
> So the brown hedger, through the evening lanes
> Homeward returning, sees above the ricks,
> Sickle in hand, the sickle in the sky.

It is recognized that the farmer's life is that of the wrestler. The poet also knows with regard to her own craft,

> that no miracle shall come to pass
> Informing man, no whisper from Demeter,—
> Miraculous strength, initiated lore.
> Nothing but toil shall serve him . . .

This ascetic mood gives its key to the work. When joy comes to the tiller and harvester it grows out of such realism. Those colors of sunset which have the most incredible luminosity and modulation arise out of a canopy of dull obscurity or womb of gray, just as the rainbow requires a base of cloud or mist. The diurnal course of the husbandman is presented in no romantic fashion, yet without bitterness.

> And since to live men labour, only knowing
> Life's little lantern between dark and dark,
> The fieldsman in his grave humility
> Goes about his centennial concerns,
> Bread for his race and fodder for his kine,
> Mating and breeding, since he only knows
> The life he sees, how it may best endure,
> (But on his Sabbath pacifies his God,
> Blindly, though storm may wreck his urgent crops,)
> And sees no beauty in his horny life,

With closer wisdom than soft poets use.
But I, like him, who strive
Closely with earth, and know her grudging mind,
Will sing no songs of bounty, for I see
Only the battle between man and earth,
The sweat, the weariness, the care, the balk;
See earth the slave and tyrant, mutinous,
Turning upon her tyrant and her slave,
Yielding reluctantly her fruits, to none
But most peremptory wooers.
Wherever waste eludes man's vigilance,
There spring the weeds and darnels; where he treads
Through woods a tangle nets and trips his steps;
His hands alone force fruitfulness and tilth;
Strange lovers, man and earth! their love and hate
Braided in mutual need; and of their strife
A tired contentment born.

The justification of this spare poetry rests on its closeness to fact. And here is the hope of its survival—just as the main tools of husbandry, their shape determined by changeless conditions, have remained the same.

Homer and Hesiod and Virgil knew
The ploughshare in its reasonable shape,
Classical from the moment it was new,
Sprung ready-armed, ordained without escape,
And never bettered though man's cunning grew,
And barbarous countries joined the classic reach:
Coulter and swingletree and share and haft
Frugal of ornament as peasants' speech,
Strong to their use and simple as their craft,
Whether to turn the ridge or cleave the rean.

Not only is this strictness the hope of continuance, but we may note also that it is a safeguard against hazardous idolizations and philosophies of nature. The exact fact, the artistic rectitude in observation, may suggest wider truth, but this poet largely leaves it to the reader to make his own. In these observations we are constantly reminded of Robert Frost who also observes an axe-helve or a scythe in action with loving attention. It has been said of him that his "minute particulars run out into great universals." It is because he is so scrupulous with the thing seen and so honest in its reporting that the greater implications arise. He is "a child of fact," (an epithet applied to the Nazarene, the force of whose parables rests largely upon the precision of the observation).[2] Rufus Jones, the New England Quaker, who knew well the life reported by Frost, accounted for the stature of Frost's work as against that of other poets also occupied with country life in the following terms. Frost never misses a shade or a detail, an inflection or a texture of what he observes. If a farmer in one part of New England says "stone-boat," Frost uses that word and not "drag" or "sledge." This earthy and humble reality is the foundation of all else.

So Miss Sackville-West in a striking passage on Craftsmen says:

> Control is theirs. They have ignored the subtle
> Release of spirit from the jail of shape.
> They have been concerned with prison, not escape;
> Pinioned the fact, and let the rest go free,
> And out of need made inadvertent art.
> All things designed to play a faithful part
> Build up their plain particular poetry.[3]

Miss Sackville-West's section on Spring runs through the multifarious activities of the farmer, and is interspersed with an occasional song. The author writes as one who knows not only of gardening and wild flowers, not only of the figures of the peddler, the reddleman, the tinker and the boggart (scarecrow) but also of the sowing, hops, livestock, and bees. Out of such experiences as the coming of the spring, despite all

---

[2] Compare "The Observer." *The Poet of Galilee* by William Ellery Leonard (New York: 1928), pp. 19-32.

[3] Cf. Robert Frost: "The fact is the sweetest dream that labor knows." ("Mowing.")

dissonance of our "great necessary Babel," there arise partial coherences suggesting an ultimate whole:

> Such truths as we have snared
> Into the spread conspiracy of our nets,
> Come to us fragmentary from a whole,
> As meteorites from space . . .
> There's some relation we may not adjust,
> Some concord of creation that the mind
> Only in perilous balance apprehends,
> Loth, fugitive, obscure.
> . . . But still endure
> Nature's renewal and man's fortitude,
> A common thing, a permanent common thing,
> So coarse, so stated, usual, and so rude,
> So quiet in performance, and so slow
> That hurrying wit outruns it. Yet with spring
> Life leaps; her fountains flow;
> And nimble foolish wit must humbled go.

In the conclusion of the last section on Autumn and of the poem there comes a climactic appeal to the Vergil of the *Georgics*. The poet brings together the vintage of Roman days with the harvest of England and utters her deepest word with regard to man and nature.

> Then all my deep acquaintance with that land,
> Crying for words, welled up; as man who knows
> That Nature, tender enemy, harsh friend,
> Takes from him soon the little that she gave,
> Yet for his span will labour to defend
> His courage, that his soul be not a slave,
> Whether on waxen tablet or on loam,
> Whether with stylus or with share and heft
> The record of his passage he engrave,
> And still, in toil, takes heart to love the rose.
>
> Then thought I, Virgil! how from Mantua reft,
> Shy as a peasant in the courts of Rome,
> Thou took'st the waxen tablets in thy hand,
> And out of anger cut calm tales of home.

We return to our preliminary questions. From "traditional" poetry of today or yesterday concerned with nature we could have selected a hundred other examples, and much of it of this quality. We might have chosen parts of Robert Bridges' *Testament of Beauty,* or single poems of W. S. Davies, Wilfred Gibson, John Drinkwater, Rupert Brooke, Mark Van Doren, Robert P. Tristram Coffin, David Morton, etc. What is the issue here as between the old and the new poets?

We first note that a strict test would eliminate a great deal of even the anthologized nature poetry. Too often Beauty or Nature or God are invoked by name, capitals and exclamation points rather than being realized through the alchemy and felicity of the art. So, for instance, with the frequently quoted "Vestigia" of Bliss Carmen whose first verse suggests the whole:

> I took a day to search for God,
> And found Him not. But as I trod
> By rocky ledge, through woods untamed,
> Just where one scarlet lily flamed,
> I saw His footprint on the sod.

Another frequent failing is to seek to enhance the power of nature by presenting it in Gothic and liturgical symbols. Thus Bliss Carmen again, in his sonnet "Winter," in which the world becomes a sanctuary; concluding with the lines:

> While down the soft blue-shadowed aisles of snow
> Night, like a sacristan with silent step,
> Passes to light the tapers of the stars.

To be sure, sanctuaries, shrines, temples, altars, screens, candles, have some association of awe, but these associations are by way of being "properties" here rather than acutely felt and potent symbols. When Francis Thompson uses such imagery in his "Ode to the Setting Sun" it is more convincing though not wholly so.

Miss Sackville-West's poem is free of such defects and of

others more obvious. It is traditional as Frost and Hardy are traditional, though a certain rigor in all of them exempts them from the weaknesses of much Georgian poetry. The complex and restless mood of the "modern" does not, however, encourage him to linger with the simple sobriety of such art as this. Moreover, the "modern" is uprooted from the soil to such an extent that he does not even have that nostalgia for it that many relatively stable urbanites have. Furthermore, those initiated into our crisis ask for something more of art. *The Land* is profound but not revelatory. It has been said of Blake—one of the poets who mean most today—that "we can see farther by one flash of his lightning than in the steady sunlight of some other poets."

Some would raise the interesting question, moreover, whether even *rural* life is not changing so radically today as a result of technology—both with respect to the relation of man to the land and with respect to his own cultural context and inner life—that poetry of the pastoral or Georgic kind loses that main relevance to culture that it has always had in some form down to the twentieth century. The axe and the ploughshare today have a very much reduced place in the world and even in agriculture. Thus the basic symbols of the poem are compromised. The farm becomes increasingly a factory and the fields a laboratory. The rural sections are urbanized and the ancient deities of hearth and boundary, fountain and grove, sowing and reaping, are banished like the redman or forgotten like Johnny Appleseed and Pocahontas. Yet man will always be a creature dependent on the fruits of the earth and the cycles of the seasons, aware that his very bloodstream relates him to the ebb and flow of the sea. This bond remains, though the way it is felt can change greatly.

In Miss Sackville-West's poem there is no overt celebration of the Christian heritage. It gives us rather a sense of the deep and enduring kinship between man and nature, a kind of natural religion underlying all faiths. This is by no means as negative as might be supposed. There is, indeed, no Dionysiac intoxication nor Christian transfiguration of nature as in some poets both traditional and modern. But there are songs of great sweetness and peace and here and there a climax of resolved beatitude. It is in short a sound and fragrant poetry testifying to one of the incomparable older traditions of the West, that of English rural life. This kind of poem must not be disparaged even if we are increasingly estranged from the patterns and securities it assumes.

2. NATURE IN APOCALYPSE: NORMAN NICHOLSON

If the question be raised as to how poetry today envisages nature, the parallel case of painting could be cited and the mind turns immediately to Van Gogh. Here, indeed, we can see further by a flash of his lightning than by the steady sunlight of some other painters. Modern schools of painting aim at conveying a revelatory sense of the meeting of man and natural object. Nature is even presented in hallucinatory guise to effect this. The turn to exotic and primitive lands and times furthers the rediscovery of the real quality and mystery of natural forms and scenes, as in the case of Gauguin. By such a standard the poem we have been considering and other work like it recedes in interest. We have to go back to Wordsworth to find a treatment of man's place in nature that at all satisfies this new hunger. And even here with a difference.

What we have said in the preceding chapter with regard to the split in the modern consciousness since the seventeenth century and its effects on poetry has a bearing here. The author, indeed, stays close to the fact and avoids rhetoric and a facile idealization. Her art, however, like that of Frost, buys its excellence at a cost. Her diction lacks in that boldness and shock which we associate with both older and more recent poets. And there is not that integral immediacy of experience which, as in modern painting, often distorts but transfigures older ways of seeing. In poetry, especially, such experience issues in more or less conscious presentation of potent mythical elements and a constant rich surprise in the wedding of otherwise incongruous or alien materials. The two kinds of poetry have their own values. With this last kind we feel that we are close to the gates of life, the act of creation. With poetry like that of *The Land* and much traditional poetry, on the other hand, we feel that we grasp in their most subtle and precious nuances and pieties the values of an incomparable human heritage.

For a suggestion of the new ways in which nature is felt and treated we turn first to a poet of Cumberland and the English Lake District who can pay his homage to his predecessor, Wordsworth, but writes in a strange modern style. We refer to Norman Nicholson.[1] Nicholson's nature is a nature in its own way like that of Van Gogh; a nature of the Bible—of creation, flood and judgment; a nature inhabited by angels, good and bad; a nature such that Hellvellyn, megalithic Gable, and Wetherham, mountains of his region, take their place with "Everest, Sinai and the seven-fold hill of Rome" as six peaks that burn and are consumed away to the glory of God on the Last Day.

A suggestion of the difference in spirit of such poetry may be conveyed by the opening lines of the apocalyptic poem, "The Holy Mountain," just alluded to. Nature here is not the ancient dependable setting of man but rather a dynamic and explosive panorama of the soul and yet real:

> Dawn flares like a bonfire behind the eastern fell,
> Rockets up to the sky and burns out the stars,
> Licks up the mists as an oven licks up steam,
> Pours down the rocks and the screens like molten slag,

[1] The special reference to Wordsworth will be found in the poem "To the River Duddon," in *Five Rivers* (London: Faber and Faber, 1944), p. 17. This author's critical volume, *Man and Literature* (London: SCM Press, 1943), is a theological study of recent literature in which the final chapter only is devoted to poetry.

Gushes down the water-courses, down forces and ghylls,
Spreads like oil on the tarns, like burning bracken on the tops,
Till the peaks blaze like braziers.
And lower on the slopes the larches catch the flame,
Bristling with fire they crackle beneath the brass rocks,
In the metallic forest, by the steel rods of birches,
And the fire burns white as a furnace.
The dale split out of the base of the fell,
Is brimful of light and open to the day,
And the river roots among the shingle and stirs the silt
Yellow as gold-dust in the cracks of the rocks.[2]

In this setting in the Lake District, Mr. Nicholson goes on to locate the Garden of Eden, tells the story of the marriage of the angels with the daughters of men and the origin of evil, and concludes with the transfiguration of the world by fire. That this modern sense for nature is not confined to the apocalyptic poems is evident when we note a poem addressed to the author of the "Elegy Written in a Country Churchyard" which comes pat to our purpose. For Nicholson is here making clear the difference between the traditional and the modern way of dealing with nature.

In brief the traditional poet looks on nature as an observer while the new poet is "Part of a landscape that [he] cannot view." The poem is entitled:

Thomas Gray in Patterdale [3]

I hold Helvellyn in my fingers, here
Ringed in the glass.[4] The clouds are still as paint,
And ghylls like tucks along the four-inch fells
Slant into neat diagonals. The lake
Is bright as sixpence; and if the wind
Bend back the bracken, it is but as hands
Rub shadows into plush against the pile.

---

[2] *Five Rivers* by Norman Nicholson (New York: E. P. Dutton & Co., Inc., 1945), p. 72.

[3] *Rock Face* (London: Faber and Faber, 1948), p. 31.

[4] The author here gives this note: "i.e., a Claude-glass—a small convex mirror in which it was possible to see the landscape whole and in perspective."

There's not a breath of word or air or water
To blur the picture at the mirror's mouth.
But outside the glass
The breeze moves like a man; October trees
Scatter charred manuscripts; the sun
Includes me in its practice—I become
Part of a landscape that I cannot view,
And under the numbers of the wind I hear
Melodramatic crags and frantic thorns
Whispering simple names I almost know.
What if I listen? What if I learn?
What if I break the glass and turn
And face the objective lake and see
The wide-eyed stranger sky-line look at *me?*

3. MAN AND NATURE IN DYLAN THOMAS

The turn towards the surrealistic treatment of nature evident in Nicholson's work has its best contemporary expression in the poetry of the Welsh writer, Dylan Thomas.[1] Born in 1914, he is one of a group of poets writing in English who made their mark in the late thirties in reaction to the socially-minded and polemic verse of the early Auden and his friends. The emphasis on social criticism and satire gave place to a sensuous poetry marked by fantasy, but fourth dimensional in its concern with death and resurrection, evil and redemption. In this context nature, again, includes man and the vision of nature is shot through with the illuminations of the inner revelation.

The symbolism of Nicholson, who belongs to this school, is dominantly biblical, though not Catholic. In the case of Thomas the biblical allusion and apocalyptic play a less overt part and are combined with other imaginative resources. The influence of William Blake, Hopkins and Joyce is observable. The work of this poet is, however, most significant as an index of that break through to a deeper level of awareness consequent on the cultural pressures of our time. There is here a continual

[1] See *Dylan Thomas: Selected Writings* (*New Directions*, 1946); also a study, *Dylan Thomas*, by Henry Treece (London: Lindsay Drummond, 1949).

DYLAN THOMAS

exploration of man at an existential level which as in the work of all the most significant writers of our time can only be called theological in its implications. In his later work, notably in the volume, *Death and Entrances*,[2] this poet turns "from the womb and the grave to the world of light; from the contemplation of the flesh and its declension to a metaphysical vision of resurrection" (J. L. Sweeney).

Thomas' central concern is with man but nature offers him the terms for the statement and has its own life. Thus when the October wind blows upon him with its intimations of winter and death, his heart bleeds its own speech and this speech is also heard in all he sees, in the "vowelled beeches," the oaks, even the roots and the waters.

> Especially when the October wind
> With frosty fingers punishes my hair,
> Caught by the crabbing sun I walk on fire
> And cast a shadow crab upon the land,
> By the sea's side, hearing the noise of birds,
> Hearing the raven cough in winter sticks,
> My busy heart who shudders as she talks
> Sheds the syllabic blood and drains her words.[3]

The poet then offers the words of nature which concur with those of his heart:

> Some let me make you of the vowelled beeches,
> Some of the oaken voices, from the roots
> Of many a thorny shire tell you notes,
> Some let me make you of the water's speeches.

The last stanza resumes the double theme:

> Especially when the October wind
> (Some let me make you of autumnal spells,

---

[2] London: Dent, 1946. The title goes back to John Donne's sermon, "Death's Duell."

[3] The sun goes backward to night: therefore "crabbing." The speaker's shadow is a "crab": it too goes backward to darkness.

102 NATURE IN TRADITIONAL AND MODERN POETRY

> The spider-tongued, and the loud hill of Wales)
> The fist of turnips punishes the land,
> Some let me make you of the heartless words.
> The heart is drained that, spelling in the scurry
> Of chemic blood, warned of the coming fury.
> By the sea's side hear the dark vowelled birds.[4]

This transcription of the voices of death in nature has its counterpart in poems like the familiar and magnificent "And Death Shall Have No Dominion"[5] and in "Holy Spring" in which the Christian theme is explicit. This is an Easter poem which invokes Christ in the symbolism of the Sun as alone able to salvage the soul out of its husk and its "toppling house" of mortality. After a first stanza which fearfully meditates the dereliction of our ruin the poet reacts: "No," he says,

> Praise that the spring time is all
> Gabriel and radiant shrubbery as the morning grows joyful
>   Out of the woebegone pyre
> And the multitude's sultry tear turns cool on the weeping wall,
>   My arising prodigal
> Sun the father his quiver full of the infants of pure fire,
>   But blessed be hail and upheaval
> That uncalm still it is sure alone to stand and sing
>   Alone in the husk of man's home
> And the mother and toppling house of the holy spring
>   If only for a last time.[6]

---

[4] Poem number 5, "Especially when the October Wind," *Selected Writings*, pp. 10, 11.

[5] *Ibid.*, p. 50.

[6] *Ibid.*, p. 69. Brief paraphrase: the spring time is all annunciation as the morning of resurrection rises from the fires of purification and tears are solaced. The Sun (Father and Christ), prodigal in grace, brings a host of radiant sons (Psalm 127:3-5). Though we dwell still in storm and convulsion, yet he is sure to abide and prevail, if only after death, beyond the body-husk and the "toppling house" of nature that mothered us.

4. NATURE AND THE IMMACULATE WORD IN ST.-JOHN PERSE

We have mentioned the name of the French poet, St.-John Perse. We may in his case again illustrate the possibilities in the treatment of nature by a modernist poet which, as with Van Gogh in painting, contrast sharply with older methods. This is a different vision of nature. Neither is it the kind of special vision we associate with the nature-mystic, so powerfully exemplified, for example, in Ralph Hodgson's fine rhapsody, "The Song of Honor." The mystical vision of nature takes on many expressions. Some arise in Indian soil (Tagore), some in western romantic (Wordsworth) or Celtic (A.E.). Reflection will point to the fact that almost all such poetry betrays itself in this way: what ultimately emerges is an interest in the observer rather than in the observed, in the "soul" rather than in nature. This soul may be the "Over-Soul" but in one form or other, nature itself comes off a poor second. The poet is interested in himself not in the creation. Such poetry often goes the limit of "solipsism." This feature, apart from its extremes, is not in itself to be condemned. Though nature serves the role of a mirror rather than an object, the self as subject-matter is legitimate. But distinctions need to be made. The superiority of Wordsworth lies in two features. Though he is finally concerned with the mysterious greatness of the soul as it is brought home to him in its commerce with nature so that "we feel that we are greater than we know," yet the objectivity and enduring permanences of nature are never surrendered. In the second place the self so revealed guards its moral character and is never dissipated into an ineffable blur.

The most vacuous kind of nature mysticism is suggested by inferior strains of pseudo-oriental or Celtic rhapsodies which suggest Ralph Waldo Trine's theme of being "in tune with the infinite." In such work there is no saving realism either as regards nature or man. A certain limited "band" of psychic gratification is tuned in entirely removed from personal relevance, as with some kinds of enervating popular music.

The nature-mysticism of D. H. Lawrence was in part a reaction against this kind of mood and poetry. It had the merit of insisting on a deeper organic bond in which not only the senses but the dark powers of the blood were involved rather than the "spirit" understood in some isolated way. Traditional poetry in this area as in others represented a bifurcation of experience which carried with it the increasing isolation of esthetics, giving it an ivory-tower role and justifying the view of the plain man that art was an optional matter and the business of queer people. Even the correctives of poets like Lawrence could not overcome this prejudice among the masses, unfortunately, since even the more integral artist is still an exile in our culture. But the way has been prepared for the healing of the breach in increasing circles of modern society.

The treatment of nature in the poetry of St.-John Perse is not mystical in the sense described above: in fact, nature appears in his work in a way subordinate to other concerns, and we do him an injustice in singling out this aspect. But the sea, the shore, the rain, snow and winds as they appear in his writing suggest how powerfully modern poetry can deal with this subject matter. This poet is, moreover, a highly "difficult" one and access to his meaning is facilitated if we approach him at this point.

St.-John Perse is the literary name of the French writer, Alexis Léger. He was born in the Antilles in 1889. His education in France led to a diplomatic career especially in the Far East, and as Permanent Secretary of the Foreign Office. His chief work in poetry has been marked by a kind of racial or planetary character, in keeping with his experience of East and West and his feeling for the most ancient memories and legacies of man. In 1924 he published the long poem *Anabase*, translated into English by T. S. Eliot in 1930, which immediately took a leading place among the influential works of modern literature. The theme of the poem may be said to be that of exploration, the world-old caravan of man. We have here, as has often been noted, a recurrent theme in contemporary literature, the theme of the voyager, of Ulysses, of MacLeish's *Conquistador,* of the Wandering Jew. Modern man, transcending his national pieties and literary heirlooms, is led to dwell on the racial story. At the same time he gathers up, as Ezra Pound does in his *Cantos,* the archives, libraries, museums, relics, and saga of all the millenia of racial memory. Since the emphasis falls on the origin of man's economics and arts and the building of cities, nature comes into the picture as the space in which man moves and settles, the quarry of his building stones, and the forces that delimit and impinge upon his social adventure.

During the last war Perse was an exile in the Americas and wrote the poems included in *Exile and Other Poems,* now available in the English translation of Denis Devlin.[1] This series is especially pertinent to our present interest, three of the four poems relating themselves especially to aspects of nature. "Exile" (1941) is written from the point of view of a cabin on a beach in New Jersey and takes its rise from the desolation of the sea and the sands. "Rains" (1943) is dated from Savannah, and "Snows" (1944) from New York. The poems are written in a kind of Dionysiac free verse, difficult because of its shifting levels of meaning and its rare terms, often resistant to translation. They have, however, extraordinary visionary power which both retains realistic objectivity and opens up the creative levels of the spiritual life.

Mr. MacLeish says of him: "There is no poetry, he maintains, no active creation, without complete reliance upon the subconscious. But by the same sign the subconscious must be treated rigorously, must be mastered by reason. For the farther

[1] The Bollingen Series XV, Pantheon Books (New York: 1949).

a poet lets himself go into the world of the mysterious . . . the greater becomes his need of memory and of will." [2]

For our present purposes it must suffice to quote from the third section of "Exile" in which the poet confronts the endless surge of the surf and reads all manner of news in it of origins and destinies:

> ". . . There has always been this clamour, there has always been this splendour,
> And like a great feat of arms on the march across the world, like a census of peoples in exodus, like a foundation of empires in praetorian tumult, ah! like an animation of lips over the birth of great Books,
> This huge muffled thing loose in the world, and suddenly growing huger like drunkenness . . .
>
> ". . . There has always been this clamour, there has always been this grandeur,
> This thing wandering about the world, this high trance about the world, and on all the shores of the world, by the same breath uttered, the same wave uttering
> One long phrase without pause forever unintelligible . . .
>
> ". . . There has always been this clamour, there has always been this furor,
> And this tall surf at the pitch of passion always, at the peak of desire, the same gull on the wing, the same gull under way, rallying with spread wings the stanzas of exile, and on all the shores of the world, by the same breath uttered, the same measureless lamentation
> Pursuing across the sands my Numidian soul . . ."
>
> I know you, monster-head! Once more face to face. We take up the long debate where we left off.
> And you may urge your arguments like snouts low over the water: I will let you no rest and no respite.

[2] *Op. cit.*, pp. 144, 145.

On too many frequented shores have my footsteps been washed away before the day, on too many deserted beds has my soul been delivered up to the cancer of silence.

What more do you want of me, O breath of origin? And You, what more would you drag from my live mouth,
O power wandering about my threshold, O Beggar-woman on our roads and on the trail of the Prodigal?
The wind tells us its age, the wind tells us its youth . . . Honour thine exile, O Prince!
And all at once all is power and presence for me, here where the theme of nothingness rises still in smoke.

". . . Higher, night by night, this silent clamour upon my sill, higher, night by night, this rising of the ages in their bristling scales,
And on all the shores of the world a fiercer iambic verse to be fed from my being! . . .

And here a greater murmur is rising around the world, like an insurrection of the soul . . .
You shall not cease, O clamour, until, upon the sands, I shall have sloughed off every human allegiance. (Who knows his birthplace still?)" ("Exile," 3, pp. 80-82)

Whatever else there be in these lines there is at least a magnificent communication of the ceaseless procession and tumult of the breakers about the shores of the world. Similar passages are found in "Rains" and "Snows."

It snowed, and behold, we shall tell the wonder of it: how dawn silent in its feathers, like a great fabulous owl under the breath of the spirit, swelled out in its white dahlia body. And from all sides there came upon us marvel and festival . . . ("Snows," 1, p. 132)

> It is snowing away down there towards the West, on the silos and the ranches and the vast, unhistorical plains marched over by pylons: on the layout of unborn cities and on the dead ashes where the camps were; on the high unbroken soil, poisoned with acids, and on the hordes of black fir trees entangled with barbed eagles, like war trophies . . .   ("Snows," 2, p. 134)

But the description of nature is powerful just because it is more than nature as commonly seen, and more in a different sense than in poetry of the Georgic or the mystical kind. While its features can be exactly perceived yet in their impact on man they connote all manner of revelation and portent. One theme that seas, snows and rains alike suggest, especially the latter, is that of cleansing and obliteration. Here we are reminded of Keats' sonnet, "Bright star . . . ," with its reference to

> The moving waters at their priestlike task
> Of pure ablution round earth's human shores.

Thus in "Rains" there is a series of stanzas invoking not the purifying but the obliteration and erasure of the immense accumulation of the human past, both the false and the true, to make room for the immaculate Word that is yet to come, for the "Princes of exile," the artist, the poet and the scientist.

> "Wash, wash the peoples' history from the tall tables of memory; the great official annals, the great Chronicles of the Clergy, the bulletins of the Academies . . . Wash bulls and charters, and the Memorials of the Third Estate; Covenants, Pacts of Alliance and the great Acts of Federation; wash, wash, O Rains! all the vellums and parchments, colored like the walls of asylums and Lazarhouses, colored like fossil ivory and old mules' teeth . . . Wash, wash, O Rains! the tall tables of memory.

"O Rains! wash from the heart of man the most beautiful sentence, the most beautiful sequence; the well-turned phrase, the noble page. Wash, wash from the hearts of men their taste for roundelays and for elegies; their taste for villanelles and rondeaux; their great felicities of expression; wash Attic salt and euphuist honey, wash, wash the bedding of dream and the litter of knowledge: from the heart of the man who makes no refusals, from the heart of the man who has no disgusts, wash, wash, O Rains! the most beautiful gifts of man . . . from the hearts of men most gifted for the works of reason."
("Rains," 7, pp. 124, 125)

There is a suggestion in this last stanza of the motive of the new poets who would free themselves from the "literature" of the past: its "well turned phrase," its roundelays and elegies, its "felicities of expression," its Attic classicism or its euphuisms. The new poet makes no refusals and has no disgusts. Along with the refuse of the past must go "the poems born yesterday" in favor of "a language free of usage and pure," as the poet says in "Exile."

Ah! let them burn, let them burn on the sand-capes, all this refuse of feather, fingernail, dyed hair, impure linen,
And the poems born yesterday, ah! the poems born one evening in the lightning's fork, what is left of them is, like ash in women's milk, but the faintest trace . . .
And I, from all winged things for which you have no use, composing a language free of usage and pure,
Now I have once more the design for a great delible poem . . . ("Exile," 4, p. 85)

Behind the theme of obliteration is the deeper theme of the denudation of the poet. He too strips off the past and all possessions. His actual exile is a type of the experience of the soul. The clamour of the surf aids him to slough off "every human allegiance." He honors his exile. So the Stranger on the sands exclaims: "The whole world is new to me." Since the forces of nature teach him change and obliteration, he will found his new song in fragile and evanescent things, just as he chose the desolation of the shore to make his voice heard:

> I have built upon the abyss and the spindrift and the sand-smoke. I shall lie down in cistern and hollow vessel,
> In all stale, and empty places where lies the taste of greatness. ("Exile," 2, p. 79)

It is evident in all this that nature is a great reality and instructor to the poet. In one sense it leads him to an intense point of dehumanization as he sheds society, history and self to find the new immaculate word. In this moment there is a crest of ecstasy, and we might think of the nihilist lyricism of Robinson Jeffers who too is led away from civilization in contemplation of the grandeur and chastity of natural forms. But there is an immense difference. In Perse we do not have nature-mysticism, properly understood, least of all pantheism in any form. Nature instructs him and challenges him. His ecstasy and his word remains his own. This is also true to a degree of Jeffers and of D. H. Lawrence. But in Perse, as MacLeish says, "the subconscious must be treated rigorously, must be mastered by reason . . . the further a poet lets himself go into the world of the mysterious . . . the greater becomes his need of memory and of will." A second difference appears: Perse is magnanimous with that of which he divests himself or which is denied him as an exile. There is no scorn for history and for society. In fact there is a loving cherishing of its archives and works, whether of artist or artisan. Over against the impulse that seeks beyond the human there is always the contrary movement back. Here he resembles his great French contemporary, Paul Valéry, who at the climax of his greatest poem, "Le cimitière marin," when his revery has carried him far beyond the human preoccupation is brought back to this world's reality by the rising of the wind and takes up again the diurnal human task:

> Le vent se leve! il faut tenter de vivre! [3]

In adducing these examples of the work of Norman Nicholson, Dylan Thomas and St.-John Perse, we have sought to suggest in this one area, the treatment of nature, that the method and scope of the traditional poet is subject to special limitations. The modern crisis when felt in its depth transforms the vision of nature as well as man and the modern resources of prosody lend themselves to this new vision to make possible new ranges of utterance.

[3] The wind rises, one must essay to live.

VI

THE RENEWAL OF CATHOLIC DEVOTIONAL POETRY

A SECOND area in which it is rewarding to study the dilemma of "traditional" poetry, and one which is specially pertinent to our main concern, is that of Christian devotional poetry. The religious arts tend to conservatism—certainly it is true of the ecclesiastical arts, at least—so that it is of special interest to observe those occasions like the present when they undergo a marked change. The inquiry is all the more significant if we restrict it to Catholic—in this case, Roman Catholic—work. For sacred or devotional poetry tends to follow the older patterns in those faiths marked by a strong dogmatic and liturgical continuity. The changes in general culture penetrate to the arts of the church only with difficulty in such cases. Today, however, so acute and profound is our general crisis that even in the case of Catholic devotion we can observe the effects.

The resulting change may well be looked upon by Roman Catholics as promising for Catholic art and poetry. Protestants are not the only ones who are disturbed with regard to the level of taste in church music, church architecture and other ecclesiastical arts. Not only in the American continents but in Europe Catholic worshippers of discrimination lament the level of taste reflected in the statuary and objects of piety of the kind associated with the shops on the Place Saint Sulpice in Paris. It can be argued that there has been no really great Catholic art or architecture since the Renaissance. In poetry the situation is somewhat analogous, apart from a rare individual here or there. The fact that "there was no Catholic magazine which would accept any poem of Hopkins in his lifetime" is pertinent.

Nor is it only Protestant choir masters and organists who today are rebelling against an enervating tradition in church music and who are returning to older models or welcoming initiatives in a "modern" religious music. Of special interest here is the progressive restoration, under Papal directives, of the Gregorian chant and of singing by the laiety of the common parts of the high mass as was the custom in the early formative years of the church. It is only a parallel of recent degeneration when we note that this early practice had to be suspended after the eleventh century "because of the infiltration into the church's song of themes from theatrical or dance music, from popular songs . . . and noisy musical instruments."

In what concerns the graphic arts a forcible statement made by Mr. Julian Green is illuminating—and it is to be noted that he is led to this consideration in connection with a discussion of the promise for Catholic *poetry* in the work of Charles Péguy. In his introduction to *Charles Péguy; Men and Saints*,[1] Mr. Green calls attention to the disastrous influence of the painter Raphael on religious art from his time to ours.

> To this day it is impossible to go into a church and not find some trace of that awful spell cast over the religious sensibility by the great man whom our fathers called Sanzio. In an evil hour for Christianity, this magnificent genius stereotyped all the incidents of the life of Christ . . . But Raphael did much more, he infected and saturated the minds of millions with dull commonplaces about the gospels. From one end of Europe to the other he not only lowered the spiritual plane of art for generations, but made easy, and therefore suspicious, a certain

[1] New York: Pantheon Books, 1944.

approach to the realm of interior vision, he crowded the invisible with chromos . . . Raphael is probably one of the most dangerous heretics since the Church began; his heresy is a subtle one which begins with a yawn and ends in nausea.[2]

If a general harmful influence on religious sensibility and art thus goes back to the sixteenth century we may add to it the special tendencies to sentimentality in a more recent period. It is against this background that we shall make our present observations.

1. FRANCIS THOMPSON'S "FROM THE NIGHT OF FOREBEING"

We shall choose as our point of reference an important poem of Francis Thompson, "From the Night of Forebeing." We have here, as in the case of *The Land,* a poem of "traditional" type which again will offer us an occasion for study of the changing climate of culture and, in this case, of piety. In the sequel we shall have occasion to refer to two Catholic poets roughly contemporary with Francis Thompson, whose work has only come into its own in the last two decades—namely, Gerard Manley Hopkins and Charles Péguy. These two poets, however different, had this in common, that they found it possible to escape the limitations of the religious poetry of their environment and thus to forecast that liberation of it which is now taking place. Of this liberation we shall give some illustration in the persons of Robert Lowell and Thomas Merton.

It is widely forgotten today that Francis Thompson wrote at least two poems of some length which approach the quality of "The Hound of Heaven." Of these, "The Ode to the Setting Sun" is the better known. The other is the one with which we are here concerned. The work of this poet has suffered considerably in critical circles. Even among Catholic readers the

[2] *Ibid.*, pp. 17, 18.

comparatively recent discovery of Gerard Manley Hopkins has tended to eclipse him. Thompson offers us a notable example of late nineteenth-century Christian poetry. The divorce of poetry from much of experience is evident in him, but at the same time the sensuous resource of the Catholic tradition. Poignantly marked here is the exile of the artist from the world compounded with the exile of the believer. In his day the "world" had not been led, as it has more recently, to the point of questioning itself. Thus a poet of Thompson's type did not think ordinarily of addressing it or speaking with it or for it as a religious poet may with more confidence in our situation today. He then spoke from an ivory tower or oratory or lonely spot on hill or shore. Witness A. E.'s Celtic solitudes and Vachel Lindsay's relative banishment. Today if a Catholic poet like Thomas Merton does in fact cloister himself as a Trappist, he can nevertheless address a considerable audience of non-believers in whom an earlier secularity has been undermined if only to result in an inchoate religious curiosity. Such communication is all the more possible because Merton like some other Catholic poets today uses a distinctly modern idiom.

"From the Night of Forebeing" has the sub-title, "An Ode after Easter." The title is illuminated by two prescripts. First is cited a passage from Sir Thomas Browne: "In the chaos of preordination, and night of our forebeings." [1] This is followed by the words from the first chapter of the Gospel of John: *"Et lux in tenebris erat, et tenebrae eam non comprehenderunt."* The poem was written in his last truly productive period in the years following 1892 when Francis Thompson was staying with the Capuchin monks at Pantasaph in Wales and was quickened by companionship there with Coventry Patmore. It comes, therefore, several years after "The Hound of Heaven" and belongs to a group which Thompson called "this latest,

---

[1] From *Hydrotaphia, Urn Burial*, Ch. V, Par. 17. The context reads: "Pious spirits, who pass their days in raptures of futurity, made little more of this world than the world that was before it, while they lay obscure in *the chaos of preordination and night of our forebeings.*"

highest of my work" and in which he believes that he has "modified much the excessive loading both of diction and imagery which disfigured my former work."

The poem, as the citation from Sir Thomas Browne indicates, hails the ultimate emergence of order and the day: this is predestined. But it is written out of present chaos and night. The light, indeed, already makes itself felt. But "the darkness comprehendeth it not." The man who knows the night of fore-being is chiefly aware of the night. If he has intimations of the dawn, it is by way of obscure struggles and tension set up in him by its approach, rather than by any illumination. The present is a larva experience, a "long ensepulture cold," the "snow-cloistered penance of the seed." It is not a state of utter stagnation. Such would be

> The solstitial slumber of the spirit,
> The blear and blank negation of all life:
> But these sharp questionings mean strife, and strife
> Is the negation of negation.

The fact that the poem is called "An Ode after Easter" and that it opens with triumphant descriptions of the spring does not mean that joy and light prevail. They are set in contrast, rather, with the "night" or stricken emptiness of the poet. Yet this emptiness passes insensibly towards pain and this pain eventually towards bliss.

The Ode is primarily a Christian study of hope. More precisely it is a study of birth, of birth by death—as are the other two major poems we have mentioned.

> And so of all which form inheriteth
>   The fall doth pass the rise in worth;
> For birth hath in itself the germ of death,
>   But death has in itself the germ of birth . . .
>   For there is nothing lives but something dies,
> And there is nothing dies but something lives . . .
>   ("Ode to the Setting Sun")

The generality of the theme of birth enables the poet to play back and forth with different applications. The winter becomes spring; death becomes resurrection; the world's old age is consummated in renewal; the individual,—the writer himself and then the writer as poet—senses the transition from death to life. So, as he says in the poem, "A Fallen Yew":

> Along my soul a bruit there is
> Of echoing images,
> Reverberations of mortality.

Only here we have reverberations and images of not only mortality but of rebirth. Yet the poem is free from any too facile solution. The last theme is fortitude in expectation.

The opening pages of the poem celebrate the spring. There is little here of the archaic excess and forced apostrophe which mark many of the weaker Odes.

> Spring is come home with her world-wandering feet,
> And all things are made young with young desires.

Through the gaiety and song a "higher and a solemn voice" of promise reaches him:

> O prophecy
> Of things that are, and are not, and shall be!
> The great-vanned Angel March
> Hath trumpeted
> His clangorous 'Sleep no more' to all the dead—
> Beat his strong vans o'er earth, and air, and sea.
> And they have heard;
> Hark to the *Jubilate* of the bird
> For them that found the dying way to life!

The following sections apply the promise as a portent to the goal of cyclic Man and "Mortality's great years":

> O Earth, unchilded, widowed Earth, so long
> Lifting in patient pine and ivy-tree
> Mournful belief and steadfast prophecy,
> Behold how all things are made true!
> Behold your bridegroom cometh in to you . . .

Then the parable is turned upon his own life amid its wreckage and loss, and it points him

> Toward the far completion, wherewith crowned
> Love unconsumed shall chant in his own furnace-fire.
> How many trampled and deciduous joys
> Enrich thy soul for joys deciduous still,
> Before the distance shall fulfil
> Cyclic unrest with solemn equipoise!
> Happiness is the shadow of things past,
> Which fools still take for that which is to be!
> And not all foolishly:
> For all the past, read true, is prophecy,
> And all the firsts are hauntings of some Last,
> And all the springs are flash-lights of one Spring.
> Then leaf, and flower, and fall-less fruit
> Shall hang together on the unyellowing bough;
> And silence shall be Music mute
> For her surchargèd heart. Hush thou!
> These things are far too sure that thou should'st dream
> Thereof, lest they appear as things that seem.

There follows a striking passage describing the paroxysm of anguish of the poet from whom the power of poetry is withheld, and then the

> . . . prevenient winnowings
> Of coming songs, that lift my hair and stir it . . .

This rightly leads on to the higher levels with which the poem concludes and which we cite in full:

> Nature enough! Within thy glass
> Too many and too stern the shadows pass.
> In this delighted season, flaming
> For thy resurrection-feast,
> Ah, more I think the long ensepulture cold,
> Than stony winter rolled
> From the unsealed mouth of the holy East;
> The snowdrop's saintly stoles less heed
> Than the snow-cloistered penance of the seed.

'Tis the weak flesh reclaiming
Against the ordinance
Which yet for just the accepting spirit scans.
Earth waits, and patient heaven,
Self-bonded God doth wait
Thrice-promulgated bans
Of his fair nuptial-date.
And power is man's,
With that great word of 'Wait,'
To still the sea of tears,
And shake the iron heart of Fate.
In that one word is strong
An else, alas, much-mortal song;
With sight to pass the frontier of all spheres,
And voice which does my sight such wrong.

Not without fortitude I wait
The dark majestical ensuit
Of destiny, nor peevish rate
Calm-knowledged Fate.
I, that no part have in the time's bragged way,
And its loud bruit;
I, in this house so rifted, marred,
So ill to live in, hard to leave;
I, so star-weary, over-warred,
That have no joy in this your day—
Rather foul fume englutting, that of day
Confounds all ray—
But only stand aside and grieve;
I yet have sight beyond the smoke,
And kiss the gods' feet, though they wreak
Upon me stroke and again stroke;
And this my seeing is not weak.
The Woman I behold, whose vision seek
All eyes and know not; t'ward whom climb
The steps o' the world, and beats all wing of rhyme,
And knows not; 'twixt the sun and moon
Her inexpressible front enstarred
Tempers the wrangling spheres to tune;
Their divergent harmonies
Concluded in the concord of her eyes,

And vestal dances of her glad regard.
I see, which fretteth with surmise
Much heads grown unsagacious-grey,
The slow aim of wise-hearted Time,
Which folded cycles within cycles cloak:
We pass, we pass, we pass; this does not pass away,
But holds the furrowing earth still harnessed to its yoke.
The stars still write their golden purposes
On heaven's high palimpsest, and no man sees,
Nor any therein Daniel; I do hear
From the revolving year
A voice which cries:
'All dies;
Low, how all dies! O seer,
And all things too arise:
All dies, and all is born;
But each resurgent morn, behold, more near the Perfect Morn.'

Firm is the man, and set beyond the cast
Of Fortune's game, and the iniquitous hour,
Whose falcon soul sits fast,
And not intends her high sagacious tour
Or ere the quarry sighted; who looks past
To slow much sweet from little instant sour,
And in the first does always see the last.

    What does this poem of Francis Thompson have to suggest to us, interested as we are in the changes in poetry and especially in religious poetry since his time? We must insist first that this is a notable work. Contemporary cross-currents of criticism should not obscure this fact. It is not surprising that the last seven lines of the poem spoke relevantly to the needs of the hour when they were quoted in the House of Commons in one of the crises on the brink of the last war.
    What we shall have to say with regard to this poet can be somewhat generalized in its bearing to cover a wide manifestation of the symbolist movement throughout Europe, which indicated "if not a definite return of the tide of spiritual faith,

at least a pause in that ebb—which Matthew Arnold had heard in the fifties by Dover Beach." "Symbolism," continues Professor C. H. Herford of the University of Manchester,

> is one of the symptoms of a far-reaching idealistic reaction traceable throughout Europe in the eighties and nineties. Here in England, such symptoms are the so-called Celtic poetry of Yeats and A. E., the discovery of Blake and Shelley, the Catholic mysticism of Francis Thompson; in Belgium the earlier drama of Maeterlinck, in Norway the later symbolistic plays of Ibsen, in Germany the Parsifal phase of Wagner, and the early poetry of Richard Dehmel, finally, in Russia, the creative prose of Tolstoy, Dostoyevski and Andreyev. The kinship of these voices of many tones cannot be disputed; what makes them kin is a temper which continually approaches religion.[2]

Having acknowledged the continuing value of the poem before us and of the best work of Francis Thompson generally we can properly now seek to define its limitations and inquire into the decline of this poet and of others of his approximate type in critical esteem today. We are not now especially concerned with him as a Catholic poet, though we shall illustrate what we have to say from the work of other poets of the same faith.

It is often helpful in seeking to define the limitations even of a great poet to look at his weakest work. In this his inherent limitations stand out most sharply. This procedure is often followed, for example, in the case of Wordsworth. The case of Shelley is germane to our present task since he was a poet peculiarly prized by Francis Thompson and the two are similar in important respects. The tenuous unreality of Shelley's inferior poems gives tell-tale evidence of the precarious and lim-

[2] "Some Approaches to Religion Through Poetry During the Past Two Generations." Reprint, *Bulletin of the John Rylands Library*, Vol. VII, No. 1 (July, 1922), p. 7.

ited grasp on concrete experience characteristic even of his best work. Shelley undoubtedly did sustain some genuine rapport with life as it is, but in a highly selective way. Only by such genuine rootage is a seer or visionary nourished. With the greatest of them, however, such rootage out of which their marked ideality and subjectivity springs, is widely ramified and related. If not, as in the cases of Shelley and Thompson, they are at the mercy of sporadic intensities of experience; they depend altogether upon "inspiration," and when that fails them they suffer with dumbness or essay to force their utterance.

Now it has been the special limitation of many romantic and post-romantic poets—and here they were conditioned by the isolation of the artist and the ambiguity of the religious tradition in the period—that they restricted or were obliged to restrict their exploitable experience. When we speak of the "subjectivity" or "spirituality" of such poets we are recognizing this, although these terms are not in themselves necessarily a matter of disparagement. When we identify a post-romantic poet with a concern for Beauty or the Ideal we similarly are recognizing this limitation. For such poets commonly tend to locate beauty in a limited area of experience. Beauty *rightly understood* may still be accepted as an ultimate test of esthetic experience, but to identify it by and large, if we may for the moment exaggerate, with roses, lilies, nightingales and the moon, as is so typical of much traditional sentiment, is to dwarf the experience and its resources.

Moreover, there is a close relation here between the experience assumed and its expression. It is not justifiable to distinguish content and style, but the style is a just index of the poetic experience. Post-romantic style, as in Francis Thompson, has very marked special conventions. In the feebler work of Shelley and Thompson these are familiar to us in what we speak of as the artificial, the archaic, the rhetorical. It becomes clear that there is a sharp distinction for them between what is considered poetic and anti-poetic—not only in theme but in vocabulary, syntax and even grammatical forms, not to mention verse forms such as rhythm and rhyme. This observation does not mean that poetic conventions are not valuable but that the categories of these employed, especially in their limitation and tendency to stereotype, are tell-tale indications of the limitations of the scope of experience.

It is these kinds of considerations which explain the caustic remarks with regard to the work of Francis Thompson by the "new critics." Thus John Peale Bishop writes: "The impulse which the romantics of the early nineteenth century had given poetry had long been exhausted. By the turn of the century it had so definitely expired that when Francis Thompson came along, it was scarcely possible for him, a belated romantic, to create poetry. He could only make elaborate garlands for its corpse."[3]

The "modern" consciousness, even in the case of a Roman Catholic, can find Francis Thompson's poetry wanting in full relevance because that consciousness is more complex and its experience and needs more diversified. The subjective drama of the inner life is, of course, always important to human beings, and personal wrestling with the issues of faith and despair is always a part of the life of the Christian. But for us the locus of this inner drama has changed. The factors which define our issues have changed. The polarities and tensions demanding artistic resolution have become more varied. A poetry which does not answer to these must be set aside even for lesser work that is more at home in the experience.

To illustrate these remarks we point out elements in "From the Night of Forebeing" which can be accounted weaknesses and which suggest the dangers of the tradition in which Francis Thompson writes. At the close of the section which deals with the premonitions of songs to be granted to the poet comes a highly infelicitous section given to a bathetic image: the poet

[3] *The Collected Essays of John Peale Bishop* (New York: Scribners, 1948), p. 84.

in relation to his new-born Joy is compared to a woolly dam which recoils from the infant lip of the suckling lamb!

> O youngling Joy carest!
> That on my now first-mothered breast
> Pliest the strange wonder of thine infant lip,
> What this aghast surprise of keenest panging,
> Wherefrom I blench . . . ?

Again the grief section with a polemical reference dealing with freedom in the third stanza is likewise forced.[4] We need not object too strongly to words like "distinct," "meinie," "vidual," but there are recurrent effete expressions, such as spices "fit for Paradise"—and coinages and hyphenated terms which cannot but give a sense of the artificial. Some would further hold that the poem contains a shallow doctrine of progress vaguely related to the current evolutionism, but we cannot altogether agree with this. It is true that this poet can exhibit a conventional social philosophy as is evident in his later odes like those on the occasion of the diamond jubilee of Queen Victoria and his poem on the death of Cecil Rhodes. But the consummation and goal of life is envisaged commonly in truly religious rather than utopian terms as in the celebrated passage in the present poem already quoted, beginning:

> The Woman I behold, whose vision seek
> All eyes and know not . . .

Nevertheless one feels in Francis Thompson as in many of the Christian writers of the period that secular aspirations of the age often furnish the drive of the utterance, though it garbs

[4] We refer to the passage:
> Lo, the Earth eased of rule:
> Unsummered, granted to her own worst smart
> The dear wish of the fool—
> Disintegration, merely which man's heart
> For freedom understands
> Amid the frog-like errors from the damp
> And quaking swamp
> Of the low popular levels spawned in all the lands.

itself in Christian symbolism. Thus Professor Herford says with regard to him in the article already quoted:

> We may even say that Catholicism only supplied the less vital symbols of an imagination which heard the stars shout together and brought offerings to the Sun, 'To thee, O Sun—or is't perchance to Christ?' As Christ Himself appears, not in the half-faded guise of convention, but in imagery at once startlingly new and yet primeval, as of the youth of the world—the Hound of Heaven, akin somehow to Yeats' hunter God winding his lonely horn across whatever theological gulfs in the dewy twilight.[5]

Thus over against some of the weaknesses indicated above we may set a citation from the work of Hopkins. In him the older sensuousness and integrity of poetry which we associate with the seventeenth century reappears more perfectly. We shall present the life and work of this Jesuit poet of the nineteenth century in the next chapter. We quote here three stanzas of address to God.

1

Thou mastering me
God! giver of breath and bread;
World's strand, sway of the sea;
Lord of living and dead;
Thou hast bound bones and veins in me, fastened me flesh,
And after it almost unmade, what with dread,
Thy doing: and dost thou touch me afresh?
Over again I feel thy finger and find thee.

9

Be adored among men,
God, three-numbered form;
Wring thy rebel, dogged in den,
Man's malice, with wrecking and storm.

---

[5] "Some Approaches to Religion . . . ," p. 7.

Beyond saying sweet, past telling of tongue,
Thou art lightning and love, I found it, a
    winter and warm;
Father and fondler of heart thou hast wrung:
Hast thy dark descending and most art merciful then.

32

I admire thee, master of the tides,
Of the Yore-flood, of the year's fall;
The recurb and the recovery of the gulf's sides,
The girth of it and the wharf of it and the wall;
Stanching, quenching ocean of a motionable mind;
Ground of being, and granite of it: past all
Grasp God, throned behind
Death with a sovereignty that heeds but hides,
    bodes but abides;[6]

Further citations from Hopkins (see below) will make it still clearer that one aspect of his superiority to Thompson, the Rossettis and the Meynells is his more immediate realism and earthiness, as well as the intellectual power in his work.

2. THE DILEMMA OF CATHOLIC SYMBOLISM

A further observation that arises out of our consideration of the poetry of Francis Thompson is that of the increasingly isolated and alien character of the Catholic symbolism in our secularized culture. Granted the vitality of Roman and Anglican Catholicism in this century, yet the modern cultural trend has created a kind of man for whom this stream of Christian experience and piety takes on an archaic and even cabalistic character. In a situation where "Christendom" is no longer defined by the widespread continuing ritual and "myth" of the older faith, the Catholic tradition becomes increasingly a private if cherished heritage, a "family" habit and usage of certain

---

[6] "The Wreck of the Deutschland," stanzas 1, 9, 32. *Poems of Gerard Manley Hopkins,* 2nd edition (London: Oxford University Press, 1930), pp. 11, 14, 22.

limited strata and circles. We have in mind here the more intimate conventions of Catholic devotion, not the central themes of Christian faith shared with all Christians. The agnostic today may, as we have said, be more hospitable to religious impressions; but special versions of piety with their long consecrated idiosyncracy become increasingly alien to him. The situation of the King James Bible offers an analogy on the Protestant side. It still speaks eloquently to those brought up in it. But to increasing multitudes it does not so speak.

Judaism offers an even better analogy. It appears that the most significant creative work by Jewish writers in our period is not available to readers of English, French, German, etc. There is an incomparably precious body of Hebrew literature and poetry which is quite out of reach of most of us: first, because it is in Hebrew or Yiddish; second, because it has a character all but incommensurable with other traditions; but, thirdly, because its meaningfulness rests upon an ancient legacy of folkways, memories and associations that have belonged to the isolated and even clandestine life of Israel.

This same kind of privacy belongs to a less degree to Christian art and poetry there where it is at all closely related to the inmost cult or piety. Today the Christian Church (especially the Catholic Church) and Christendom are by no means the same thing or even closely related. Many of those who belong to Christendom today are not acquainted with the language of the religious community proper.

Therefore the poetry of Francis Thompson so far as it celebrates the liturgy and the dogmas will be restricted in its appeal. It is true that "The Hound of Heaven" has a universal appeal for all sects, but this poem is the exception that proves the rule: there is not a line in it of peculiar Catholic symbolism. But much of this author's poetry, especially the later work, does confine itself to the celebration of the mass and its inherent dogma in keeping with the expressed purpose of the poet.

One aspect of the private or esoteric character of Catholic poetry is that nature is so often interpreted in terms of the liturgy. We have shown how artificial the use of liturgical symbols can be in nature poetry but with Francis Thompson these are often impassioned and genuine. "In this new mystical poetry which Thompson made peculiarly his own, Nature and the Catholic Church are one in their ritual; the former, in her changes and pageantry, merely offers on a larger scale the same homage to God as the Church in her solemn offices."[1] As in the "Orient Ode" the rising and setting sun represents the host in the eucharist,[2] so in the "Ode to the Setting Sun" it represents Christ on the cross:

> Thou art of Him a type memorial.
> Like Him thou hang'st in dreadful pomp of blood
> Upon thy Western rood;
> And His stained brow did vail like thine
>   to night,
> Yet lift once more its light,
> And, risen, again departed from our ball,
> But when it set on earth arose in Heaven.
> Thus hath He unto death His beauty given . . .

The following objection can be made to our present thesis. It will be urged that the rich body of Catholic symbolism is at least one of the imaginative resources of the west and that poets can properly anticipate acquaintance with it on the part of their readers as they do of classical mythology and literature or of such material as the Golden Bough offers in abundance. Thus altogether "modern" writers avail themselves of

---

[1] "The Poetry of Francis Thompson" by E. G. Gardner: *The Month* (London: February, 1898).

[2] Thompson wrote to Patmore soon after "The Orient Ode" was completed: "As a matter of fact it was written soon after Easter, and was suggested by passages in the liturgies of Holy Saturday, some of which—at rather appalling length—I have quoted at the head of its two parts." *Poems of Francis Thompson,* Revised Edition, ed. T. L. Connolly, S. J. (New York and London: Appleton-Century, 1941), p. 450. There follow one and one-half pages of translation of the passages from the Vulgate closely followed by Thompson in the poem.

elements from medieval piety, mariolatry or St. John of the Cross without demur. They take over echoes from Dante and the Golden Legend, from Crashaw, Vaughan and John Donne of the most intimately Catholic kind. The point is, however, that they use it from a different center. It is when the special Catholic ethos is dominant that the work is a hard saying to modern ears, not only because of unbelief but because that special spiritual orientation has become only one among the numerous legacies of the Christian past. It may still be one of the most articulated and massive, in fact, it may be the only one that has that character. But in this very distinctiveness it has lost touch with the movement of the modern spirit. Art conceived in this tradition speaks primarily to those formed in the piety of this wing of the church.

These considerations are illuminating in connection with the work of Catholic poets today as will appear below. The predominate Catholic elements in poets like Hopkins, Péguy and the later Eliot—where they predominate, which is not a matter of consistency—operate as a real barrier between them and modern readers, even where these readers are not agnostic. The most remarkable feature in many such writers is the degree to which the main channel of Catholic piety is abandoned or obscured, in which the Catholic imagination is modified in the direction of secular experience and motifs, even to the point of what looks like heresy. This is particularly evident in the case of French Catholic novelists as we shall show.

The handicaps of a Catholic or Christian literature that arise from the use of a private language are overcome in two ways. A radical iconoclasm may discard what may appear to have become an esoteric and archaic pattern. Thus Protestantism in different phases sought to recover and retain the tradition but discarded precious liturgical and artistic usages which had served as vehicles for it. Similarly today there are poets conscious of writing in the Christian tradition who have more or less deliberately extricated themselves from the private utterance of Catholic mystical piety. On the other hand, without going so far, a Catholic poet today may commend his liturgical and doctrinal tradition of faith by accommodating his utterance to the new resources of poetic method. Certain Catholic poets of today, while as always orienting their work about the great themes of the faith and the liturgy, have freed themselves from the cherished idiom of the household of faith and have transformed it by a great contemporary freedom of imagery and resource.

3. *PÉGUY: POET OF CHRISTIAN FRANCE*
The problem of the renewal of the Catholic and, indeed, of all Christian art and imagination is highlighted in the work of a number of French Catholic writers of the immediate past and present. We have in mind especially Léon Bloy, Charles Péguy, Georges Rouault, Paul Claudel, and the novelists Mauriac and Bernanos. We shall here give special attention to Péguy.

One of the most extraordinary centers of Christian revival in the last two generations has certainly been that formed by the extraordinary figure of Léon Bloy and his friends and converts including a number of those mentioned above. We are fortunate today in having a group of volumes in English which describe the lives, conflicts and influence of these men and present their writings and art.[1] Bloy, who lived from 1846-1917, mainly in Paris, cannot here be described in detail. He was a

[1] Raissa Maritain's two volumes: *We have been Friends Together: Memoirs* (1942) and *Adventures in Grace* (1945), both published by Longmans, Green and Co., New York. Pantheon Press has provided English translations of the work of Bloy and Péguy: *Léon Bloy: Pilgrim of the Absolute* (1947); *Charles Péguy: Basic Verities* (1943); *Charles Péguy: Men and Saints* (1944); *Charles Péguy: God Speaks* (1945). To these add the volumes by Daniel Halévy and Wallace Fowlie mentioned below. The volume, Karl Pfleger, *Wrestlers with Christ* (New York: Sheed and Ward, 1936), has chapters on Bloy and Péguy which are informing but of limited value. See also a highly instructive, if unsympathetic, study of French Catholic literature: Rayner Heppenstall, *The Double Image: Mutations of Christian Mythology in the Work of Four French Catholic Writers of Today* (London: Secker and Warburg, 1947).

writer with a "ferociously Spanish imagination." He was an "angry and pitiful visionary" concerned with justice and the suffering of men. He was a devout Catholic who felt the obligation of poverty for the Christian and that of suffering. These two themes, poverty and suffering, took on a deep mystical character for him. He lived with his family in chronic destitution and anxiety, but found in that situation an occasion for humility and love. He was a man of God of a biblical stamp, a scandal to the world, as Maritain says, "a Job on the dung heap of modern culture." His writings have a breath of genius and his personality succeeded often in awakening agnostics to the dimensions of Christianity and so to conversion. Rouault the painter, the two Maritains, husband and wife, and Charles Péguy were among those touched by Bloy.

Rouault, who was born in 1871, is to be regarded as the chief pathfinder in the renewal of Catholic religious painting. To quote Mr. Wallace Fowlie:

> The nineteenth and twentieth centuries in France form one of the richest periods in the history of painting. It is markedly characterized by an absence of religious works in the production of its leading painters. With the exception of Rouault. It is even possible because of the magnitude of Rouault's work, that he is opening up a new era. Since the Renaissance there has been no art, particularly in the field of painting, which can properly be called Christian art.[2]

But Rouault is a thoroughly modern painter, for all that he is called also a "medievalist," having passed through the school

---

[2] *Jacob's Night: The Religious Renascence in France* (New York: Sheed and Ward, 1947), p. 28. See the whole chapter (Ch. II) devoted to Rouault. Mr. Fowlie in this same connection adds: "One of the most regrettable facts in Catholicism of the last two hundred years has been its strangely closed and even hostile attitude toward major artistic events. Recognition of the work of Rouault may help to change this. It is to be hoped that the Church, its clergy and its monastic orders will study and accept the life work of this ardent Catholic and painter. Rouault is much more than a mere painter of religious subjects. He is a religious painter." *Ibid.*, pp. 28, 29.

of the *fauves* and shared in the revolt against impressionism. Mr. Fowlie connects his work with that of the tragic visionary Bloy and with the T. S. Eliot of the *Waste Land*. The continued depiction of the Cross in Rouault's work evidences the Catholic theme treated, however, with the sensibility of a modern. Rouault is at one with the great contemporary novelists, says Fowlie, in his vision of humanity; with Joyce, Proust, Mauriac, and the dramatists, Cocteau and Sartre. Yet he "stands apart from these artists in giving to the one theme common to them all its deeply Christian aspect. This doctrine of the last things is called by the philosophical term 'eschatology.' Rouault is an eschatological artist. He paints the last things because of the new rise they predict, because of the hope which can come only after despair. The idea of salvation dominates his entire work." [3]

In the case of the French publicist and poet, Charles Péguy (1873-1914), we have another example of the renewal of conventional Catholic art. During the last decade of the nineteenth century and up to his death in 1914, Péguy carried on a stormy series of crusades in connection with politics, anti-Semitism and education, but a parallel secret calling as poet accompanied these. One by one his lengthy and puzzling poems, his "mysteries" and "tapestries" were published in his celebrated review, the *Cahiers de la Quinzaine,* along with the writings of Romain Rolland, Benda, and others, only to meet complete neglect. Today they are recognized as productions of extraordinary importance. Here the ancient heart of Catholic France beats. All those circles of French youth which have not been attracted to Marxism or skeptical liberalism, have found in them and in Péguy's heroic example a chief inspiration. His short life, marred by intransigence and broken friendships, had

[3] *Jacob's Night,* p. 45. Cf. the remarks of Jacques Maritain on Rouault in his *Art and Poetry* (New York: Philosophical Library, 1943), pp. 22-29. "There is in him . . . an intense religious feeling, the faith of a stubborn hermit, that led him to Huysmans and to Léon Bloy, and that made him discover the image of the divine Lamb in all the abandoned and rejected whom he commiserates . . .," p. 25.

nevertheless a strange mark of destiny and a mysterious blessing upon it, and he opened up springs of charity and faith which are contributing to the renewal of Christian France.

The writing of Péguy has been made available to English readers in this country recently in the volumes mentioned above in the excellent translation accomplished by Anne and Julian Green. Daniel Halévy's *Péguy and Les Cahiers de la Quinzaine* offers us an invaluable guide to the background of the poetry in the life and faith of the man.[4] Péguy came from humble peasant stock of the region of the Loire. In his early life as a fighting socialist he outwardly rejected the church. Later he identified himself with the faith but was withheld from the offices of the church by special scruples and the circumstances of his marriage. In any case he was an individualist always averse to clericalism.

> Within the Church itself, it is permissible to distinguish a specifically Roman tradition and a specifically Christian one. Péguy's adolescence was strongly impregnated with Christian influences, but the Roman strain as such was far less close.[5]

We have then some background for explaining the unique character of Péguy's Catholic poetry. It was not dominated by traditional patterns, whether devotional or sacramental, as in the case of many Catholic poets—with the result that their work partakes of the hermetic. The themes and even the rhythm of his work can, indeed, come from the missal.[6] But the strength of the work comes from his peasant realism and the related medieval realism, for it was to the age of Joan of Arc that he was drawn by all his patriotic, cultural and spiritual ardor. His poetry largely takes the form of free verse, a prose-like

---

[4] New York: Longmans, 1947. English edition; (London: Dennis Dobson, 1946). Our references shall be to the American edition.
[5] Halévy, *op. cit.*, pp. 152, 153.
[6] Julian Green, *Charles Péguy: Men and Saints.* Introduction, pp. 18-20.

verse, which moves slowly with a very large element of repetition. Totally unlike the work of Hopkins, it nevertheless resembles it in its fibre and toughness, in its basic realism, so that we have here again a reinvigoration of Christian devotional poetry coming from a contemporary of Francis Thompson. It must be stressed that Péguy is not related to the line of the post-romantics and symbolists in France to which we owe our major debt for the enrichment of poetry. Other present-day Catholic poets have owed a debt to Baudelaire, Rimbaud, Laforgue and others. Neither Péguy nor Hopkins were in this line or were exposed to the same climate. Nevertheless they both found their own way out of those temptations to tepidity and sentimentality which were so strong in their time.

The crux of the matter is the recovery of wholeness in sentiment and language, as we have repeatedly said. In Péguy the claims of tangible fact and actuality are evident in the extraordinary, even childlike, naivete of his work, and particularly in his presentation of "spiritual" matters. He has transcended the gulf. His Joan of Arc is a "child of Lorraine mourning over her plundered village and her ravaged countryside; she is, too, a Christian suffering for the incursion of evil in creation. She is both, serving both reigns, time and eternity; the twofold task is not one, but concerted."[7] It is in this connection that Halévy cites lines of Péguy which document this wholeness of his vision and poetry:

> Et l'arbre de la grace et l'arbre de nature
> Ont lié leur deux troncs de noeuds si solennels,
> Ils ont tant confondu leurs destins fraternels
> Que c'est la même essence et la même stature.[8]

[7] Halévy, op. cit., p. 35.
[8] The tree of grace and the tree of nature
Have linked their two trunks with such solemn bonds,
Have so interwoven their common fate,
That there is but one essence and one stature.
Ibid.

The one passage of some length which we wish to quote, however, is taken from Péguy's *Mystère des Saints-Innocents*, which appeared in the *Cahiers*, series VIII, number 12, in March, 1912. We cite it in the English translation by Anne and Julian Green where it can be found in more complete form. We call attention to the theme of hope, of the future and its frail beginnings, of Spring and its premonitions of new life, which we saw instanced in "From the Night of Forebeing."

I am, says God, Master of the Three Virtues.

Faith is a faithful wife.
Charity is an ardent mother.
But hope is a tiny girl.

I am, says God, the Master of Virtues . . .

Faith is a church, a cathedral rooted in the soil of France.
Charity is a hospital, an almshouse which gathers up all
    the miseries of the world.
But if it weren't for hope, all that would be nothing but
    a cemetery . . .

I am, says God, Lord of the Three Virtues.

Faith is a great tree, an oak rooted in the heart of France.
And under the wings of that tree, Charity, my daughter
    Charity shelters all the woes of the world.
And my little hope is nothing but that little earnest of a
    bud which shows itself at the beginning of April.

And when one sees the tree, when one looks at the oak,
That rough bark of the oak thirteen and fourteen hundred
    years old,
Which will be a centenarian and centuries old for
    centuries and centuries,
That hard, rough bark and those limbs which are like
    a confusion of huge arms,
(A confusion which is an order),
And those roots which thrust into the soil and lay hold
    of it like a confusion of huge legs,

(A confusion which is an order),
When one sees such strength and such roughness, the tender little bud no longer seems to be anything at all.
It is the bud that looks as if it were the tree's parasite . . .
And yet it is from that bud, on the contrary, that everything comes. Without a bud that once appeared, the tree would not exist. Without those thousands of buds that come out once at the beginning of April and sometimes in the last days of March, nothing would last, the tree would not last and would not keep its place as a tree (that place must be kept), without that sap which rises and weeps in the month of May, without those thousands of buds that begin to grow tenderly at the armpits of the hard limbs.
Every place must be kept. All life comes from tenderness. All life comes from that tender, delicate April bud and from that sap that weeps in May, and from the cotton-wool and the down of that delicate white bud that is clad, that is warmly, that is tenderly protected by the tuft of the fleece of a vegetable wool, the wool of a tree. In that cotton-like tuft lies the secret of all life. The rough bark looks like a cuirass in comparison with that tender bud. But the rough bark is nothing but a hardened bud, a bud grown old. And that is why the tender bud always pierces through, always springs up from under the rough bark . . .

Without that bud which does not look like anything, which seems as nothing, all that would be as dead wood.
And the dead wood will be cast into the fire.

Now I tell you, says God, that without that late April budding, without those thousands of buds, without that one little budding of hope, which obviously anyone can break off, without that tender, cotton-like bud, which the first man who comes along can snap off with his nail, the whole of my creation would be nothing but dead wood.
And the dead wood will be cast into the fire.[9]

[9] *Men and Saints*, pp. 233-241.

If other passages of Péguy could be quoted it would become clear why André Gide spoke of his poetry as follows:

> Péguy's style resembles the style of very old litanies. It is like Arabian songs, like monotonous moorland songs; it is comparable to the desert, sand desert, stone desert . . . Péguy's style is like the stones of the desert, one here, another there resembling it, each like the other, but just a little different; and the difference is underlined, insisted upon, repeated, seeming to be repeated, is emphasized, asserted ever more clearly, and so we progress . . ." [10]

If this style is like that of old litanies we may find an analogy for its tonic contribution to contemporary devotional poetry in the return today of church musicians to Gregorian chants.

4. CONTEMPORARY CATHOLIC POETRY

In a prolonged correspondence between Jean Cocteau and Jacques Maritain concerning the relations of art and Christianity, the latter at one point sketches his hopes for a new poetry. It is to be a poetry "freed from Rimbaud while remaining aware of what it owes to Rimbaud" (that is, a beneficiary of the explorations of the deeper life and of revolt which the young Rimbaud inaugurated). "I see a sure promise in the moving effort, pursued for ten or fifteen years, to throw away all the dead weight of carnal denseness, ostentation, complacency, false understanding, adulterated perfection, that literary perfection carries along." [1] So Maritain characterizes the struggle of the new poetry for integrity. Further, the contribution made to poetry by the surrealists in the wake of Lautréamont is not to be despised: the study of dreams and the mystic state can "renew the language's resources, the deeper life of verbal imagination, it can help to purify words of the soiling

---

[10] Cited in Halévy, op. cit., p. 129.

[1] Jacques Maritain, Art and Faith (New York: Philosophical Library, 1938), p. 106.

of common usage; [but] it will furnish after all only a technique." [2] What actual form this new poetry will take, Maritain does not venture further to define, but he commits the task to Cocteau and Max Jacob.

It is of interest, in this context, to turn to two Roman Catholic poets in this country who give evidence of their initiation at least indirectly into the modern influences of which Maritain speaks. We pass over Anglo-Catholic writers, including Eliot, though their work is to be borne in mind. We also pass over here that considerable range of poetry written by Catholic writers which finds its medium in the publications of the Catholic Poetry Society of America, in its review, *Spirit, A Magazine of Verse*, and in the anthologies made up from time to time from its pages.[3] The greater part of this is "traditional" in character and while exquisite work is found here our chief present interest is in figures in whom the renewal of the Catholic arts is evidenced. We must confine ourselves to brief illustration.

Mr. Robert Lowell's first book, *Land of Unlikeness*,[4] was published in 1944 with an introduction by Mr. Allen Tate. On the title page is found a legend from Saint Bernard:

> *Inde anima dissimilis deo*
> *Inde dissimilis est et sibi*
>
> As the soul becomes unlike God,
> So also it becomes unlike itself.

The strife in the soul so suggested finds its echoes in the poems, and also in the title of the author's second volume: *Lord Weary's Castle* [5] (the sketch on the title page in this case represents presumably the murder of Abel). With regard to this

---

[2] *Ibid.*, p. 107.
[3] *Drink from the Rock*, 1944. See also *Return to Poetry: Critical Essays from Spirit* (New York: the Declan X. McMullen Co., 1947).
[4] Massachusetts: Commington Press, 1944.
[5] New York: Harcourt, Brace, 1946.

title, Mr. Lowell says in a note: "My title comes from an old ballad:

> 'Its Lambkin was a mason good
> As ever built wi' stane:
> He built Lord Wearie's castle
> But payment got he nane . . .'"

We may well include here some biographical information about the poet included in a review of his second volume by Mr. Selden Rodman in 1946:

> At 29, Lowell's career already matches in stubborn heresy such of his forebears as "Rebel John," who grew orchids under glass in protest against Jefferson's plebeian politics, Imagist poet, Amy with her long Manila cigars, and that Robert Traill Spence Lowell, his namesake, who took a slum parish in Newark, and then, "wearying of the high pulpit," became headmaster of St. Mark's and author of the narrative poem, "The Relief of Lucknow." Young Lowell, who began to write at St. Mark's and Harvard . . . tried to enlist twice (in 1943) but when drafted refused to serve on the ground that the country was out of danger and that the bombing of civilians was unprincipled. He served six months in a federal prison, became a Catholic and, in 1944, published 250 copies of "Land of Unlikeness" . . .[6]

The poems embody an ironical and even savage commentary on the Babylon of this world rather than celebration of the faith. The satire is specially directed at that New England spiritual penury from which his own conversion will presumably have delivered him. The work of the poet is still at too early a phase to justify generalization. His complex resource of prosody, however, which has a soberly ornate character and that added interest which virtuosity and sophistication lend, suggest immediately one form that religious poetry can take

[6] "Poems from a Boston Jeremiah," *New York Times Book Review*, November 3, 1946.

today. In the following stanza from "A Prayer for My Grandfather to Our Lady" we note the tonic combination of many elements, classic and colloquial, audacious and traditional.

> Mother, for these three hundred years or more
> Neither our clippers nor our slavers reached
> The haven of your peace in this Bay State:
> Neither my father nor his father. Beached
> On these dry flats of fishy real estate,
> O Mother, I implore
> Your scorched, blue thunderbreasts of love to pour
> Buckets of blessings on my burning head
> Until I rise like Lazarus from the dead:
> Lavabis nos et super nivem dealbabor.[7]

In his introduction to the earlier book Mr. Tate says that the "symbolic language often has the effect of being *willed;* for it is an intellectual style compounded of brilliant puns and shifts of tone." Further, the satirical direction of the Christian symbolism "points to the disappearance of the Christian experience from the modern world, and stands, perhaps, for the poet's own effort to recover it."[8] In the best and most developed of the poems in the later volume, "The Quaker Graveyard in Nantucket," any such defensive use of the gospel is transcended. The bold imagery retains its effectiveness, and the powerful symbols of Moby Dick are employed to convey the enigma of evil in which grace operates. The sections are punctuated with intercession. Thus the attack on the white whale and the disaster to the Pequod are described and lead to an exclamation of prayer:

> . . . and gulls go round the stoven timbers
> Where the morning stars sing out together
> And thunder shakes the white surf and dismembers
> The red flag hammered in the mast-head. Hide,
> Our steel, Jonas Messias, in Thy side.[9]

[7] *Lord Weary's Castle,* p. 22.
[8] *Land of Unlikeness,* Introduction.
[9] *Op. cit.,* p. 12.

This is an intricate poetry which as yet fails to meet the possibilities for Catholic work that Maritain expresses. But it suggests some of the new elements that will be available.

The same holds for the work of Thomas Merton,[10] whose prose work written from a Trappist monastery has become so widely known. Merton, we feel, has genuinely cloistered himself. His poetry revolves continually about the devotional life and the liturgy. That nature which is here taken up into grace is largely rural. We hear little of the cities and glories of men except as under judgment. The arts and treasures of the centuries are not drawn on. On the other hand, Robert Lowell packs his lines with memories and allusions, and like Peter who through the centuries in one of his poems,

> Walks on the waters of a draining Rome
> To bank his catch in the Celestial City [11]

so he "banks his catch" of the world's wisdom and beauty in his heavily encrusted and formal stanzas. Yet while Merton devotes his poetry constantly to the intimate patterns of Catholic devotion he has appropriated many of the liberties of the new poetry which make for directness and wholeness of speech. This is not devotional poetry of the first rank. But it is of interest to see Christian verse freed from the esotericism that threatened it in its traditional forms. Merton has learned to use audacious figures from the classical Catholic poets, no doubt. Thus, we quote from "The Communion":

> O sweet escape! O smiling flight!
> O what white secret breaks our jails of flesh?
> For we are fled, among the shining vineyards,
> And ride in praises in the hills of wheat,
> To find our hero, in His tents of light!
> O sweet escape! O smiling flight!

[10] *A Man in the Divided Sea*, 1946; *Figures for an Apocalypse*, 1947; *The Tears of the Blind Lions*, 1949; all published by New Directions Press.
[11] *Lord Weary's Castle*, p. 49.

> O sweet escape! O smiling flight!
> The vineyards break our fetters with their laughter!
> Our souls walk home as quiet as skies.
> The snares that death, our subtle hunter, set,
> Are all undone by beams of light!
> O sweet escape! O smiling flight! . . .
>
> We'll rob your vines and raid your hills of wheat,
> Until you lock us, Jesus in Your jails of light!
> O sweet escape! O smiling flight! [12]

To appreciate the variety of this poet's work it would be necessary to quote such poems as the beautiful lines to his "To My Brother Reported Missing in Action" (p. 126 in the same volume), and the highly effective poem in memory of the Spanish poet, Lorca (*Ibid.*, pp. 138, 139). An even more original work is the sequence "Figures for an Apocalypse" which occupies fifteen pages at the beginning of the book of that name. Here we have a version of the end of the world including a section, "In the Ruins of New York" with its epitaph:

> This was a city
> That dressed herself in paper money:
> She lived four hundred years
> With nickles running in her veins
> She loved the waters of the seven purple seas,
> And burned on her own green harbor
> Higher and whiter than ever any Tyre.
> She was as callous as a taxi;
> Her high-heeled eyes were sometimes blue as gin,
> And she nailed them, all the days of her life
> Through the hearts of her six million poor.
> Now she has died in the terrors of a sudden contemplation
> —Drowned in the waters of her own, her poisoned well. [13]

In "The Captives—A Psalm" Merton writes a modern version of psalm 137 with its theme: "How shall I sing the Lord's song

---

[12] *A Man in the Divided Sea*, p. 131.
[13] P. 23.

in a strange land?" The "strange land" here is no state or nation but a city without vision and a Babylon of idols—so that the cruel words of the original Psalm can be taken up without blame.

> Blessed is the army that will one day crush you, city,
> Like a golden spider.
> Blest are they that hate you. Blest are they
> That dash your brats against the stones.
> The children of God have died, O Babylon,
> Of thy wild algebra.
>
> Days, days are the journey
> From wall to wall. And miles
> Miles of houses shelter terror.
> And we lie chained to their dry roots, O Israel! . . .
> May my bones burn and ravens eat my flesh
> If I forget thee, contemplation!
> May language perish from my tongue
> If I do not remember thee, O Sion, city of vision,
> Whose heights have windows finer than the firmament
> When night pours down her canticles
> And peace sings on thy watch-towers like the stars of Job.[14]

The examples we have chosen at least make it clear that devotional poetry, Catholic or not, can be freed from the limitations broadly characteristic of such poets as Francis Thompson, the Rossettis and Alfred Noyes, and of many Protestant evangelical writers in the tradition of Lanier and Vachel Lindsay. Such reinforcement comes on the one hand from a vigorously discriminating structure of faith which safeguards the writer in question from shallow and spurious moods, and keeps clear the distinction between Christian vision on the one hand and romantic intoxication on the other. We see such a structure of faith behind all the work of Hopkins, but we are not at all sure that we see it consistently behind the work of

[14] *The Tears of the Blind Lions* (Norfolk, Conn.: New Directions Press, 1949), pp. 20, 21.

Thompson. Such reinforcement comes, on the other hand, from the general movement of artistic renewal today. Lowell and Merton illustrate this aspect. The names of Eliot and Auden could be added except that we have purposely excluded here discussion of writers of Anglo-Catholic affiliation.

But even with these elements of strength Catholic symbolism has an esoteric character for vast groups of men in the world today. It takes on more and more the character of a survival along with the "mythology" and intimate idiom of any liturgical heritage. The adoption of a modernized expression for such art or poetry as by Rouault in painting or T. S. Eliot in poetry only alleviates the difficulty. What can serve the modern temper better is the revolutionary substitution of a quite new vehicle and language, responsive to the time, though without surrender of the perennial elements of the Christian revelation. What is needed could be described as a secularized Christian art which would, however, still be Christian. Some of it may have explicit Christian themes; in the case of devotional poetry it would. If one danger to be averted is neo-pagan forms of art and culture, another danger is that of an undue stereotyping of the patterns of orthodoxy, either in Catholicism or Protestantism. It is true that Protestants today are often glad to return to the hymns of Isaac Watts, Cowper or Luther as a refuge from the tepidity of the contemporary hymn. But this does not mean that good modern hymns must echo those of the writers named. It is possible to have the vigorous structure of faith of which we have spoken without necessarily also clinging to one or other precious but archaic heritage among those which different families in Christendom have cherished.

Indeed, a poet whose formation identifies him with a restricted dogmatic and liturgical heritage must pay the price in what concerns the scope of his art. If he lets his horizon be bounded in large part by his form of faith, his audience will be confined largely to his own sect except in the case of the exceptionally gifted like Hopkins. Furthermore, his allegiance tends to isolate him not only from secular experience but from that frontier of experience where the growing edges of religion are in fruitful interplay and conflict with the world. The nourishing soil of imaginative creation is thus circumscribed. We shall give attention to this matter in the case of Hopkins, the Jesuit poet, and recognize that there are special vocations in which restriction of experience has its compensations.

The most revealing phenomenon in this connection is the curiously ambiguous relation to their faith of the most notable Catholic writers of our age, especially the French novelists Mauriac and Bernanos and the poet Claudel. The latitude of the Catholic religious imagination as exemplified in these figures is truly extraordinary. An outsider can well wonder what the church makes of these strange sons in whom, to use Heppenstall's phrase, there has certainly been an astonishing "mutation of the Christian mythology." The same strange preoccupations appear in the English novelist, Graham Greene, especially in his work, *The Power and the Glory*. No one can read the novels of Bernanos—*The Sun of Satan, Joy, The Diary of a Country Priest*, or in French, *L'Imposteur*—without being struck not only by the manicheism, but the obsession with demonic powers and exorcism. Heppenstall goes farther and sees a veritable reversion to witchcraft and obsession with the scapegoat theme, all, indeed, put to the service of literary power.

> The work of Georges Bernanos is at bottom primitive, pre-Christian. At the same time, its appeal is also post-Christian and not at all uncongenial to an audience conditioned by the theories of Freud and his successors. As music plays directly upon the rhythms of the heart-beat and the bowels, Bernanos, though he uses Christian stage-properties and Christian prestige, plays upon the most deeply flowing mass—impulses of mankind. Bernanos (in his fiction) is a witch-doctor. He is also a psycho-analyst

for whom and for his patients, primitive magic is still operative and primitive *tabus* still valid . . . And always in the center of the stage stands the figure of the scapegoat priest, on whom we load all our sins and send him out into the wilderness and who is the point at which primitive belief assumes the Christian paraphernalia.[15]

Mr. Heppenstall is right as to the materials but we believe he is unjust in his implications. There is such a thing as Christian exorcism just as vicarious sacrifice is a perennial reality. The primitive scapegoat has its valid and direct relationship to the solidarities involved in redemption, however much our use of the symbol needs to be guarded. Bernanos has, however, incorporated large elements of secular awareness into his religion and writing. Thus we do not say that the novels of Bernanos are not works of profound Christian inspiration, but they represent a highly esoteric Christianity that reminds us of Ignatius of Antioch or of the tortured or dead Christs of Spanish or Latin-American art. Something of the same kind could be said with regard to Mauriac. We recall also that Péguy could never quite decide whether he was a Catholic or a socialist in his earlier years. His abstention from the mass throughout his life after his conversion because of family impediments is in any case a symbol of the independence of his pattern of faith. Our point is that these first-rank Catholic writers escape the handicaps of which we have spoken and enter the rich arena of imaginative resource just because they transgress the limits of traditional liturgical and theological patterns. The same principle holds for Protestant artists. The renewal of Christian devotion and devotional art hangs upon a greater initiation in the "world." One may say that a little heresy is a good thing in some phases of orthodoxy, in the same way that David Harum said that a few fleas are good for a dog, and that Arnold Toynbee has reminded us that a few

[15] *Op. cit.*, p. 36. Cf. Donat O'Donnell, "The Faust of Georges Bernanos," *The Kenyon Review*, XI, 3 (Summer, 1949), pp. 405-23.

large fish are good for the herring in the seine: it keeps them lively.

The general character of the work of the most sensitive and gifted Catholic writers of today, however, when seen in conjunction with that of the Joyces who have left the church, makes it clear that that Christian mold, apart from the armature of its polity, is in a state of advanced dissolution or transformation. The more adventurous sheep scatter to new pastures and the shepherd is hard beset to keep track of them. Since the arts anticipate the doctrine auguries of similar theological scandal would not be misplaced. In view of the pressure of the new times this branch of the church appears to be in a period like that which preceded the Reformation.

VII

GERARD MANLEY HOPKINS: THE PRIEST AS POET

1. *AMA NESCIRI*

IN 1918 a volume of poems was published in London by the good offices of Robert Bridges, the author of these poems having died almost thirty years earlier. No verse of his had ever been published before, except that Bridges had included a half a dozen short pieces in his anthology, *The Spirit of Man*, and a few others had found their place in other collections. There was little indication that the small volume of 1918 would ever win any considerable attention. Only four hundred copies were sold in two years and it was ten years before the edition of 750 copies was exhausted.

Yet in the later twenties and early thirties these poems found an excited audience and became a decisive influence on a new generation of rising poets. A writer who had done his work in the midst of the Victorian era, in the seventies and eighties, made a powerful impact upon the modernizing poets of the group whose leaders included W. H. Auden, Stephen Spender, C. Day Lewis. The American poet, Richard Eberhart, was a student at Cambridge University at this time, and he subsequently wrote: "It is difficult now to describe the excitement of that discovery. In a world at war one cannot imagine such a joy . . . The absolute sensuous immediacy of Hopkins, his power to overwhelm, to convince, to lift the spirit, to give joy, will shine through all the trials of commentators upon sometimes seemingly intractable material, and will overcome criticism." [1]

But our surprise is increased as we realize that the poet who attained to this influence on an emancipated school of modern and left-wing writers was a man with a religious vocation, a Catholic, a priest, a Jesuit, who, to use his own phrase, was "strung by duty" in the discipline of his order.

We have at least a two-fold reason for devoting a chapter to Hopkins in this book. He is one of the few first-rank religious poets of the last century and his work is apropos to the subject matter of the preceding chapter and offers many facets of interest to those concerned with the relations of poetry and the Christian faith. Furthermore, there are aspects of his work which are essential in any appreciation of the new poetry, aspects which distinguish him from his Victorian contemporaries and which explain his congeniality to the writers of our time.

The history of literature and of thought occasionally offers us these striking paradoxes and reversals. It is not so rare that a forgotten writer should re-emerge from obscurity after a generation or two or even after centuries, after the fashion of the stellar phenomena known as *nova,* and take on a sudden brilliance altogether disproportionate to that hitherto existing. But the present instance is even more of a mystery. It is like a resurrection from the dead. For Hopkins had not only been indifferent to publication but had very early in his work made it a matter of principle not to further its publication. He was by no means indifferent to his art. His letters to his poet friends, Patmore and Bridges, show how eloquently he could speak of the importance to a poet of readers, of an audience, of praise. Thus he wrote to Dixon in 1878:

> I knew what I should feel myself in your position if I had written and published works, the extreme beauty of

[1] *Poetry, A Magazine of Verse,* LXII, VI (Sept., 1943), p. 347.

which the author most keenly feels, and they had fallen out of sight at once and have been (you will not mind my saying it, as it is, I suppose, plainly true) almost wholly unknown.

And he continues that he therefore feels it

a sort of duty of charity to make up, so far as one voice can do, for the disappointment you must, at least at times, I think, have felt over your rich and exquisite work almost thrown away.[2]

Despite this awareness in the case of others, Hopkins adopted a point of view that is all but incredible to us. In effect he left his poems to shift for themselves. There is no doubt that he suffered acutely at times from a sense of frustration as regards the fate of his writing, and that he wrote very much less than he would have if he had permitted himself the usual approaches to publication. Yet he discouraged attempts by his friends to further publication. His motive, as we shall see, was religious. His vocation led him to avoid "the disquiet and the thoughts of vain-glory" and to reproach himself for "backward glances" toward the temptations of his earlier years. He wrote on another occasion to Dixon, with regard to the neglect of his friend's poems, pointing him to Christ as the final critic, the unfailing judge of the gifts which He, Christ, had bestowed. And there are other words of Hopkins' evidencing his willingness to leave the ultimate fate of his own work to the wisdom of God.[3] He finally consigned his manuscripts to his friend Robert Bridges before his death in 1889, but with little anticipation that the circumstances would favor publication, and without encouraging it.

No doubt there is some relation between this scruple and the purity of Hopkins' work. We may well raise some consid-

---

[2] Cited in E. E. Phare, *The Poetry of G. M. Hopkins* (Cambridge, Eng.: The University Press, 1942), pp. 90, 91.

[3] Eleanor Ruggles, *Gerard Manley Hopkins, A Life* (New York: W. W. Norton, 1944), p. 206.

erations here as to the spirit in which art and literature are pursued today. There is little of the reticence and anonymity which conditioned some of the greatest art of the past. The following quotation is from an article of the novelist, E. M. Forster.

> In the past neither writers nor readers attached the high importance to personality that we do today. It did not trouble Homer or the various people who were Homer. It did not trouble the writers in the Greek Anthology, who could write and rewrite the same poem in almost identical language, their notion being that the poem, not the poet, is the important thing . . . It did not trouble the medieval balladists, who like the cathedral builders, left their works unsigned. It troubled neither the composers nor the translators of the Bible.

We make a great deal of the personality and success of the artist. One can almost say that our modern audiences, concert-goers and readers of book-review sections, are more interested in the man than in the work. They want the success-story rather than the symphony. They want a picture of the poet with his dogs and his pipe rather than the poems.

Some years ago some private letters of Vachel Lindsay were published which showed by his own testimony that he loved adulation and was deeply injured by it.

> I am almost wrecked by good will. By September or October when the reviews of the *Collected Poems* come roaring in, I will be more demoralized than ever. Above all I need a Handy Guide to Privacy, to serenity, to meditation, to delicacy of fancy, to village quietness, to secret prayer . . . My manager, Armstrong, is determined to national-tour me again, Bryanize me if possible. My publishers back the idea, and I am sure of flattery and fried chicken in every town, while slowly disintegrating . . .[4]

[4] C. P. Lee, "Adulation and the Artist," *Saturday Review of Literature,* XXII, XV (August, 1940), p. 18.

It is commonly agreed that the artist must have some appreciation to produce. Hopkins himself could quote Milton's lines:

> Fame is the spur that the clear spirit doth raise
> To shun delights and live laborious days,

a spur, he goes on, "very hard to find a substitute for or to do without."

A striking parallel, however, to the unworldliness and scruple of the Jesuit Hopkins is offered in the attitude of the American sculptor, John B. Flanagan, who had no such special religious grounds for his retirement. "Man should not praise himself," he said, "but kneel in adoration before the vastness of the creation." He took pains on every occasion to avoid notice and attention. Walter Pach says of him that he had "the Assisi point of view." His life-long devotion to the sculpture of animals meant for him a deliberate and restorative repudiation of what he called our "narcissistic" obsession with the human and the human figure. His favorite counsel to other artists was the ancient motto of the saints: *Ama Nesciri*, love to be unknown. "He was medieval," says Pach, "in his disinterestedness and in his truly mystical passion for humility and anonymity." [5]

2. "STRUNG BY DUTY AND STRAINED TO BEAUTY"

Gerard Manley Hopkins was born in Essex County, England, in 1844 and died in 1889. He came of a cultivated Anglican family. He went to Oxford in 1863, where he was spoken of as "the star of Baliol" because of his scholarship and gifts. He was a pupil of Jowett and Walter Pater. It was at this time that he became the friend of Robert Bridges and of other men later distinguished in letters. He was sensitive to the religious and philosophical currents flowing strongly in the university at this time. The height of the controversy attendant on the

---

[5] Walter Pach, "John B. Flanagan, American Sculptor," *The Kenyon Review*, V, 3 (Summer, 1943), 384-93.

Oxford Movement had occurred just prior to his arrival and Newman's *Apologia* was published during his first year as a student. First a disciple of Pusey and Liddon, he then came under the influence of Newman who had left Oxford by this time. He was converted to the Roman Catholic faith in 1866 and after his graduation with the highest honors in classics in 1867, he began his novitiate in the Company of Jesus in the following year. This is the decisive event in his life and in his poetry. The remaining years include the long educational and spiritual training in his order and the various services he was called upon to render as teacher, parish priest, preacher, and finally teacher again. He was not notably effective in these functions. Ill health, excessive burdens, conscientiousness, fastidiousness of taste, seem to have been factors here. He cultivated music and painting and special intellectual interests. But the important thing is that he took his vocation with extreme seriousness, sought to attain the highest standards with unflinching rigor, and left an impression of near-saintliness as well as of exquisite tastes upon his associates. His last years were spent as professor of classics at University College, Dublin, and it was in this period that the testing of his vocation became most severe and that he wrote some of his greatest poems.

The year of his Jesuit vocation, 1868, is significant for any survey of his poetry. Previous to this his work was indeed highly talented but rich to the point of lushness. This work he destroyed, as far as he was able, lest it constitute an attachment to the world that might in whatever way qualify his entire commitment to his new life. Moreover, he refrained from writing poetry for a period of seven years. Then a superior in the order suggested that he write an elegy apropos of the tragic shipwreck of the *Deutschland* in which five nuns lost their lives. We have quoted three stanzas of this poem in Chapter VI. In "The Wreck of the Deutschland" many of the technical features appear which were to characterize his later work. After this time he wrote infrequently until his death twelve years later. His collected poems include fifty-one poems beside fragments and minor remains.

We shall be obliged here to refer readers to the collected poems of Hopkins, assuming some knowledge on their part of the poems at least as found in current anthologies. Our present citations will confine themselves largely to the later sonnets but we shall first offer two of the earlier poems to suggest the character of the prosody and the variety of the themes. This will prepare the immediately following discussion of the lineage and affiliation of the poet.

"The Starlight Night" is quoted rather than the more familiar "God's Grandeur" to illustrate Hopkins' treatment of nature. As against the way in which it is handled in Miss Sackville-West's poem, *The Land,* and in Francis Thompson, we may note the audacity, sensuousness and density of image, and at the same time the complexity of experience *enacted on the page* rather than merely meditated.

> Look at the stars! look, look up at the skies!
>   O look at all the fire-folk sitting in the air!
>   The bright boroughs, the circle-citadels there!
> Down in dim woods the diamond delves! the elves'-eyes!
> The grey lawns cold where gold, where quickgold lies!
>   Wind-beat whitebeam! airy abeles set on a flare!
>   Flake-doves sent floating forth at a farmyard scare!—
> Ah well! it is all a purchase, all is a prize.
>
> Buy then! bid then!—What?—Prayer, patience, alms, vows.
> Look, look: a May-mess, like on orchard boughs!
>   Look! March-bloom, like on mealed-with-yellow sallows!
> These are indeed the barn; withindoors house
> The shocks. This piece-bright paling shuts the spouse
>   Christ home, Christ and his mother and all his hallows.[1]

The other poem here quoted is chosen as representing Hopkins' poems dealing with individual human beings, children,

---

[1] *Poems of Gerard Manley Hopkins,* 2nd ed. (London: Oxford University Press, 1930), p. 26.

etc., and growing out of his pastoral activity. Here, in "Felix Randal" we see the last hours of a once powerful blacksmith and the ministration of the priest. The poem illustrates the "common speech rhythms" which replace in the work of this poet the familiar cadenced feet of our usual prosody and, equally important, the informal tone of one who speaks naturally within himself. What makes a poem like this so extraordinary is that with this naturalness of rhythm and tone there goes also such an acme of artistic fastidiousness even to the last detail.

> Felix Randal the farrier, O he is dead then? my duty all ended,
> Who have watched his mould of man, big-boned and hardy-handsome
> Pining, pining, till time when reason rambled in it and some
> Fatal four disorders, fleshed there, all contended?
>
> Sickness broke him. Impatient he cursed at first, but mended
> Being anointed and all; though a heavenlier heart began some
> Months earlier, since I had our sweet reprieve and ransom
> Tendered to him. Ah well, God rest him all road ever he offended!
>
> This seeing the sick endears them to us, us too it endears.
> My tongue had taught thee comfort, touch had quenched thy tears,
> Thy tears that touched my heart, child, Felix, poor Felix Randal;
>
> How far from then forethought of, all thy more boisterous years,
> When thou at the random grim forge, powerful amidst peers,
> Didst fettle for the great grey drayhorse his bright and battering sandal! [2]

[2] *Op. cit.*, p. 48.

3. LINEAGE AND MODERN RELEVANCE

What is the relation of Hopkins to the cultural chart or transformation which we have outlined in our second and third chapters? If he is counted as a precursor of the new poets, it is hardly because he was involved in the same kind of emerging cultural and spiritual crisis which conditioned the sensibility of his contemporaries, the French post-romantics, and later figures in England and America like Pound, Joyce and D. H. Lawrence. This new climate came late in England; at least the artist here was in some sense beguiled longer by the unique traditionalism of English society so that it was only with the first World War that writers like Aldous Huxley awoke to what was happening to the life of the West with any great clairvoyance. In France the writer and artist had for long a more detached situation and this, combined with their greater sensitivity for the cultural climate and the Latin vigilance against industrial dehumanization, accounts for the emergence of writers like Baudelaire, Rimbaud and Mallarmé a half a century and more before that of parallel figures in Anglo-Saxon countries.

Moreover, the commitment of Hopkins to the Catholic faith, especially since it was in terms of the vocation of an order, shielded him from the forces of the age for better and for worse. It carried with it what Leavis has called a "restriction in the nourishing interests behind his poetry," to be understood also in the sense of exemption from the wider theatre of complex tensions which qualify a poet to speak more representatively for his age. This "strange disease of modern life," as Leavis suggests, had no more real place in his life and poetry than it had in that of Matthew Arnold. One aspect of the concentration of Hopkins' attention, negatively illustrated, is the naivete of his treatment of patriotic matters and of buglers, sailors and schoolboys.[1] This isolation is even true of a lay

[1] F. R. Leavis, "Metaphysical Isolation" in *Gerard Manley Hopkins, by the Kenyon Critics* (New Directions, 1944), pp. 128-130.

Catholic poet like Péguy who, though he was a participant in the social battles of the period, was by his peasant background so profoundly medieval a French Catholic that he only partially appreciated the forces making for a new age, forces that came to expression supremely in the work of André Gide, the great empiricist and humanist. Hopkins' relevance to the modern poetry movement was not, therefore, in this realm. Nevertheless, he did in many respects transcend his Victorian setting.

Interesting attempts have been made to "place" this poet with reference to poetic lineage. C. Day Lewis spoke of him as a phenomenon "out of the blue." Hopkins' letters and note books register the same demurral against Victorian writers as is characteristic of the modernist poets. Of Dickens he says: "Like, I believe, Lang, I cannot stand Dickens' pathos; or rather I can stand it, keep a thoroughly dry eye and unwavering waistcoat," though he admits to an admiration for Dick Swiveller and Kit and Quelp. "The Brownings are fine, too, in their ghastly way," he remarks. He also has some discriminating remarks about Tennyson. He appears to agree with Bridges in his praise of Doughty as one "free from the taint of Victorian English," though he also asks whether Doughty is free from the taint of Elizabethan English, which he, Hopkins, holds had been a corpse now these three centuries. All such models, he says, even Shakespeare, move him to admire and then to go and do otherwise.

We have noted that Hopkins differs enormously from Francis Thompson, and from the Georgian poets generally. The religious element in his work suggests classification with poets like George Herbert, Vaughan and John Donne. C. C. Abbott in his edition of the letters to Bridges well points up the shared features with Donne: "Kinship in mental strife, restless curiosity, candour, complexity, and density of texture." One of the most curious classifications suggested and one supported by a word of Hopkins himself is with none other than Walt Whitman. "I always knew in my heart Walt Whitman's mind to be more like my own than any other man's living. As he is a very great scoundrel, this is not a pleasant confession." The attempt to find similarity between Hopkins and Milton by Bridges and Charles Williams is not very convincing. And Miss Phare's detailed comparison of Hopkins and Wordsworth is chiefly significant for the differences brought out in their treatment of nature and common people.

Poets of the post-war period were drawn to Hopkins for one thing, as we have said, because his poetry is based on the rhythms of common speech. This break with conventional poetic rhythm brought poetry closer home to honest feeling and spontaneous discourse. There is plenty of older precedent for it in English poetry. He was led to it not by any iconoclastic impulse, but by technical study of prosody and by a sense of the dramatic demands of the art, calling for greater flexibility in the utterance. Ordinarily he did not completely abandon the values of our familiar verse rhythms but he liberated them or compounded them with this more irregular movement.

> What the heart is! which, like carriers let fly—
> Doff darkness, homing nature knows the rest— [2]

One can simplify the explanation of Hopkins' famous "sprung rhythm" by saying that for him "stress"—that is, the fall of stressed and unstressed syllables—supersedes the fixed number of syllables to the foot as the basis of his prosody. The count of syllables and the regularity of accent are no longer the norm, and thereby, as Day Lewis says, this poetry rejoins common speech rhythms, though with the support of the familiar structure underneath. In the second quarter of this century this principle explains much of the work of contemporary poets.

But beyond this Hopkins did carry his innovations very far. And these studies in technique interested our new poets later.

[2] "The Handsome Heart," *op. cit.*, p. 47.

They were but a part, it is true, of the inevitable liberation of English poetic discourse which was to come with so wide a ramification throughout the English-speaking world as its culture moved away from its older moorings. In this sense the explorations and shapings of new vehicles of communication by such writers as Pound, Lawrence, Joyce, Stein and Eliot are only further responses to needs which our traditional poets have not encountered. Similar transformations have taken place in the other arts under similar compulsions. But language itself, the word, registers most instantaneously of all the arts an alternation in the consciousness of mankind or any significant body of it.

With the new play of rhythm at his service, Hopkins was able to make poetry a flexible instrument for all sorts of dramatic subject matter. And his innovations included also various lesser devices and licenses: inversions, word-coinages, alliterative and chiming sequences, many of which his imitators have more easily copied than they have his greater qualities.

Beyond these matters this poet is appreciated for other qualities. Hopkins was remarkable for his richness of culture, intellectual power, sensibility, nobility of taste, and for the gamut and contrasts of qualities which combined in him. Thus his verse represents an articulation of a vast area of complex experience: sensuous and intellectual, immediate and contemplative, introspective and social. Again, he is with all this the artist, the craftsman. One feels always in him the strictness, the rigor, the economy, the honesty. "He aimed at an unattainable perfection of language," said Bridges. Beside him a great deal of even distinguished poetry appears loose, imprecise, bought at too cheap a price, too slack an effort.

We sometimes come upon a poet who is interesting to us— apart from the question of his stature—because all his work carries the stamp of a very particular experience of the world and perspective upon it. He is all the more strange at first and has to be given opportunity to create in the reader the taste by which he is to be enjoyed. After we enter into his novel witness to things, it becomes increasingly exciting. It is our own world but seen at a special angle. This is precisely true of Hopkins and his often-stated conviction with regard to both life and art clarifies this point. For he had a special philosophy with regard to individuality which he assigned to the Franciscan Duns Scotus, who in this area as in others differed from the more widely held views of Aquinas. After two stanzas devoted to Oxford in his poem "Duns Scotus's Oxford," he pays tribute to the philosopher:

> Yet ah! this air I gather and I release
> He lived on; these weeds and waters, these walls are what
> He haunted who of all men most sways my spirits to peace;
>
> Of realty the rarest-veined unraveller . . .[3]

In the philosophy of Duns Scotus the particularity of the individual and the concrete particularity of the object took precedence over generalization. Thus Hopkins' theory and practice represented a constant effort to elicit the precious and unique design, or "inscape" (to use his own word) of things and people, to

> Deal out that being indoors each one dwells.

Each one of us lives "indoors" and has his own wealth, his own "chambers of imagery." In his incomparable note books and in his letters as well as in his poems, this writer dwells upon the taste and savor of oneself as something unique which converts and qualifies all experience. This largely accounts for the impression of naive candor which the poems convey. But it is when the Christian experience of the writer voices itself in these terms that the effects are truly extraordinary.

[3] *Op. cit.,* p. 40.

4. THE TERRIBLE CRYSTAL

For the purposes of the present volume we cannot do better than select the so-called "terrible sonnets" for special attention. Here we have not only examples of his greatest work and of his special style as it had been perfected in his last years, but also that part of his work which most interests the student of Christian devotional poetry. They are further relevant to us because they have a bearing upon the conflict in him of vocation and artist, a matter to which we shall return in our next and concluding section.

There are seven sonnets (listed in the *Collected Poems* as Nos. 40, 41, 44, 45, 46, 47, 50) which represent such astonishing spiritual throes and expostulation with God that they inevitably recall the outcries in the appalling "confessions" of Jeremiah. The term, "the terrible crystal," taken from Ezekiel 1:22, has been applied to the central moment of this experience, as it has been applied to the metaphysical anxiety of Kierkegaard and his followers, to suggest the inhuman and many-faceted revelation of the creature in confrontation with the unconditioned.[1] If such a relating of Hopkins to the existential school is somewhat excessive, nevertheless there is some truth in it, and we thus note a further point at which he anticipated the spiritual situation of the twentieth century. In the sonnet number "41" we find the lines:

> O the mind, mind has mountains; cliffs of fall
> Frightful, sheer, no-man-fathomed. Hold them cheap
> May who n'er hung there . . .

No comparable expression of the "sense of the abyss" or "metaphysical dread" is to be found in the nineteenth-century poets outside of the work of the French symbolists and possibly Edgar Allen Poe.

---

[1] M. Channing-Pearce, *The Terrible Crystal: Studies in Kierkegaard and Modern Christianity* (New York: Oxford Press, 1941).

We can best begin with the sonnet number "50" which has, as prescript, words of Jeremiah which provide the poem also with its opening lines.[2]

Justus quidem tu es, Domine, si disputem tecum; verumtamen justa loquar ad te: Quare via impiorum prosperatur? Etc.

Thou art indeed just, Lord, if I contend
With thee; but, sir, so what I plead is just.
Why do sinners' ways prosper? and why must
Disappointment all I endeavour end?

Wert thou my enemy, O thou my friend,
How wouldst thou worse, I wonder, than thou dost
Defeat, thwart me? Oh, the sots and thralls of lust
Do in spare hours more thrive than I that spend,
Sir, life upon thy cause. See, banks and brakes
Now, leavèd how thick! lacèd they are again
With fretty chervil, look, and fresh wind shakes
Them; birds build—but not I build; no, but strain,
Time's eunuch, and not breed one work that wakes.
Mine, O thou lord of life, send my roots rain.[3]

The sense of frustration here builds up to its climax in the expression, "time's eunuch." One should not too immediately conclude that the miscarried "work" refers to his art. But we have fortunately supporting evidence from a letter in which he writes: ". . . if I could but get on, if I could but *produce* work, I should not mind its being buried, silenced, and going no further; but it kills me to be time's eunuch and never to beget." To be included here are lines from the sonnet number "44":

[2] "Righteous art thou, O Lord, when I contend with thee; yet would I reason the cause with thee: wherefore doth the way of the wicked prosper?" Jer. 12:1.

[3] *Op. cit.*, pp. 68, 69.

> Only what word
> Wisest my heart breeds dark heaven's baffling ban
> Bars or hell's spell thwarts. This to hoard unheard,
> Heard unheeded, leaves me a lonely began.[4]

The same poem defines the term "lonely" further with reference to Hopkins' lot "to seem the stranger," separated from family both by distance and faith, and from England.

But the depth of the distress is only first felt when we turn to poem "45" when it becomes clear that it is a separation from God which is involved.

> I wake and feel the fell of dark, not day.
> What hours, O what black hours we have spent
> This night! what sights you, heart, saw; ways you went!
> And more must, in yet longer light's delay.
> With witness I speak this. But where I say
> Hours I mean years, mean life. And my lament
> Is cries countless, cries like dead letters sent
> To dearest him that lives alas! away.

Thus the octet, with its horrendous sense of life spent in fruitless invoking of God as by "dead letters" sent by a lover. There follows the sestet with its close written out of the Inferno but introduced by a play on the pathetic appeal of Job 10:8-13:

> Thy hands have framed me and fashioned me
> Together round about; yet thou dost destroy me.
> Remember, I beseech thee, that thou hast
>   fashioned me as clay;
> And wilt thou bring me unto dust again?
> Hast thou not poured me out as milk
> And curdled me like cheese?
> *Thou hast clothed me with skin and flesh,*
> *And knit me together with bones and sinews*
> Thou hast granted me life and loving kindness;
> And thy visitation hath preserved my spirit.
> Yet these things thou didst hide in thy heart.[5]

[4] *Ibid.*, p. 65.
[5] American Standard Revised Version.

The sestet is as follows:

> I am gall, I am heartburn. God's most deep decree
> Bitter would have me taste: my taste was me;
> Bones built in me, flesh filled, blood brimmed the curse.
>   Selfyeast of spirit a dull dough sours. I see
> The lost are like this, and their scourge to be
> As I am mine, their sweating selves; but worse.[6]

It will be recalled that in the first stanza of "The Wreck of the Deutschland" quoted earlier the same passage from Job is used:

> Thou hast bound bones and veins in me, fastened
>   me flesh,
> And after it almost unmade, what with dread
>   thy doing. . . .[7]

Sonnet number "41" is important for our examination. For after expostulation:

> No worst, there is none. Pitched past pitch of grief,
> More pangs will, schooled at forepangs, wilder wring.
> Comforter, where, where is your comforting?
> Mary, mother of us, where is your relief? . . .

it is evident that the pangs are not personal but a sharing of

> . . . a chief
> Woe, world-sorrow; on an age-old anvil wince and sing—[8]

This becomes clear in the positive sonnet number "40" as it does in the ninth and tenth stanzas of "The Wreck of the Deutschland" where the image of the anvil is also found and God is seen as forging his will in man. We can only mention the sonnets number "46" and "47" in which provisional ways

---

[6] *Op. cit.*, p. 65.
[7] *Ibid.*, p. 11.
[8] *Ibid.*, p. 62.

of supporting the awful ordeal are glanced at: in the former by the way of patience, and in the latter, in a poem of incomparable poignancy and virtuosity, by the way of invitation to an hour of amnesty:

> My own heart let me have more pity on . . .
> Soul, self; come, poor Jackself, I do advise
> You, jaded, let be; call off thoughts awhile
> Elsewhere; leave comfort root-room; . . .[9]

But poem number "40" ("Carrion Comfort") brings out the ultimate secret of the wrestling and shows that the adversary is God and at the same time insists that man must of his own will sustain the encounter to the uttermost.

> Not, I'll not, carrion comfort, Despair, not feast on thee;
> Not untwist—slack they may be—these last strands of man
> In me or, most weary, cry *I can no more.* I can;
> Can something, hope, wish day come, not choose not to be.
> But ah, but O thou terrible, why wouldst thou rude on me
> Thy wring-world right foot rock? lay a lionlimb against
>   me? scan
> With darksome devouring eyes my bruisèd bones? and fan,
> O in turns of tempest, me heaped there; me frantic to
>   avoid thee and flee?
>
>   Why? That my chaff might fly; my grain lie, sheer
>   and clear.
> Nay in all that toil, that coil, since (seems) I kissed the rod,
> Hand rather, my heart lo! lapped strength, stole joy,
>   would laugh, cheer.
> Cheer whom though? the hero whose heaven-handling
>   flung me, foot trod
> Me? or me that fought him? O which one? is it each
>   one? That night, that year
> Of now done darkness I wretch lay wrestling with (my
>   God!) my God.[10]

[9] *Ibid.*, p. 66.
[10] *Ibid.*, pp. 61, 62.

Especially in connection with this sonnet it is evident how partial a review is ours here in virtually passing up all mention of the detail. The reader is referred to the numerous reference works available. Our chief concern within the limits of our study, is to relate Hopkins to the chief themes of our book. In this connection it is highly significant that in these major poems, though the Christian theology remains basic, the poet has either risen above, or for some reason dispensed with, the usual quasi-esoteric idiom of Catholic devotional piety. (We have noted that this same is true of Francis Thompson's "The Hound of Heaven" for what this may be worth in the case of a lesser poem.) This is not because he is less truly Catholic but, we venture to say, because he is more so. Here he rejoins that which is common to the Christian consciousness and for that very reason speaks a language and evokes an inner drama which are familiar to the deeper secular mind of today.

The Christian heritage makes itself felt in modern devotional poetry, whether Catholic or Protestant, but where it is powerful it can only find adequate expression by liberating itself in two senses: first, in transcending the stereotypes of traditional religious sensibility and symbol; and, second, by breaking with the special "poetic" and rhetoric which has been the familiar medium of religious poetry. What is even more interesting here is that, on its side, "secular" poets under pressure from the spiritual crisis of our time and employing the new media of utterance find themselves within immediate range of the perennial subjects of religious poetry. Here a quotation from Jacques Maritain is revealing:

> I have often repeated that art is brought remarkably close to religious use by the most daring modern researches, requiring as they do much formal purification. It is not the newness of their means, but rather the spirit from which they seek inspiration that often keeps them apart from such usage.[11]

[11] *Art and Poetry*, p. 37.

Thus in our time a common experience outside and inside the church, and a common purified rhetoric are working together to reconcile the church and the world or remnants of the one and the other and to make possible both a truer Christianity and a greater Christian art.

5. ART AND RELIGIOUS VOCATION

In tracing the deepening levels of Hopkins' anguish we began with that factor constituted by the frustration of his art: the "time's eunuch" theme. This, we are convinced, was only a superficial level of what was involved in his "terrible pathos," but also the personal occasion of something that went deeper. The profounder tones of his ordeal make it clear that we have to do here with what religious psychology has agreed to call the experience of "the dark night of the soul." This is to be understood not merely as an alternating mood of depression in the religious life, least of all a pathology or abnormality in it, but as a necessary stage in the process of dying and rising of the self in its movement toward God. In Hopkins' case, however, it was in connection with his talent and, indeed, vocation *as artist* that the deeper trial arose. If he had not been a priest and Jesuit it would have arisen in another form for him, as a Christian. His vocation made the struggle more acute and imposed highly restrictive barriers upon the artistic activity ensuing, but at the same time thereby intensified it. Those secular critics who have been constitutionally incapable of appreciating the validity and demands of such a religious vocation have made the crass charge that it was this which was responsible for the suffering evident in Hopkins' later poems and for what they conceive to be the miscarriage of his poetic gift and the meagreness of his production. There is some truth in the charge. But every poet works under certain personal limitations and circumstances which serve both to confine and to stimulate his writing. A Protestant Christian will first pay homage to the consecration of life and talent evident in the case of Hopkins and connect his greatest achievement with it. He will at the same time regret that special Christian vocation should be construed in the rigid pattern of such orders, which perpetuate a once valid form of monastic protest and action without sufficient modification down into the cultural situation of our times.

The discussion of this matter by Catholic writers takes two directions. On the one hand, the sound view is upheld, for example, in the volume by Mr. John Pick [1] that it was just because the poet was "strung by duty" and by that exalted dedication involved in the discipline of his order, that he could have the sensitivity and the purity of vision to write his best work. On the other hand, a view disparaging to poetry is sometimes presented, as in the article by Chester A. Burns, S. J., in the symposium, *Immortal Diamond.*[2] Here it is, indeed, rightly held that poetry must sometimes be sacrificed to other demands. But the writer goes further and gives the impression that he thinks of poetry as only an estimable but essentially frivolous pursuit carried out for the solace of men or the adornment of life. In terms of a supernaturalist dialectic it is not hard to see how such a view arises. Hopkins himself tried to maintain it but not altogether successfully. He no doubt held that his poetry was far less significant than his vocation. But the question to be asked is whether there could be such a disjunction between the two. In what follows the issues here can be clarified by reference to Hopkins' correspondence.

The letters exchanged between the poet and Richard Watson Dixon with regard to the relation of poetry to a religious vocation are here of notable interest, raising, as they do, the deepest questions as to the ultimate importance of the arts and their service to mankind, and the ever ambiguous questions involved in asceticism. As a foil to the discussion, we might recall the

[1] *Gerard Manley Hopkins: Priest and Poet*, Oxford, 1942.
[2] "Gerard Manley Hopkins: Poet of Ascetic and Aesthetic Conflict," *op. cit.*, ed. by Normand Weyand, S. J. (New York: Sheed and Ward, 1949).

noble terms in which Milton saw his own vocation as a Christian poet and his feeling that no greater service could be rendered to a nation or the church than through the dedication of the poet's talents to their service.

Relevant also to the discussion is a correspondence that went on between the great Catholic theologian, the Baron von Hügel, and the poet, Yeats. The former in effect called on Yeats to accept the Christian faith and submit his imagination to the great heritage of the church. Yeats responds in a number of poems included in the group entitled, "Vacillation" [3] refusing, on grounds that are suggested in the following lines:

> Must we part, Von Hügel, though much alike, for we
> Accept the miracles of the saints and honour sanctity?
> I . . . though heart might find relief
> Did I become a Christian man and choose for my belief
> What seems most welcome in the tomb—play a
>   predestined part.
> Homer is my example and his unchristened heart.
> The honey and the honeycomb, what has Scripture
>   said?
> So get you gone, Von Hügel, though with blessings on
>   your head.[4]

The same reply appears in another section:

> The Soul: Isaiah's coal, what more can man desire?
> The Heart: Struck dumb in the simplicity of fire!
> The Soul: Look on that fire, salvation walks within.
> The Heart: What theme had Homer but original sin?[5]

Thus Yeats believes that the Christian faith would involve for him an asceticism which would rule out the larger part of the passion and drama of life where he had found his chief material. He does not envisage the possibility, we may add, that

[3] *The Collected Poems of William Butler Yeats* (New York: Macmillan, 1937), pp. 287-290.
[4] *Ibid.*, p. 290.
[5] *Ibid.*

this faith might amply compensate him with a different heritage of imagination and symbolic wealth, or even the same one in a different perspective.

But to return to Dixon and Hopkins, the former writes that he hopes Hopkins is going on with his poetry.

> I can understand that your present position, seclusion, and exercises would give to your writings a rare charm—they have done so in those that I have seen: something that I cannot describe, but know to myself by the inadequate word *terrible pathos*—something of what you call temper in poetry: a right temper which goes to the point of the terrible: the terrible crystal. (26 October, 1881.)

And with regard to Hopkins' scruples:

> I ought not in your present circumstances tease you with the regret that much of [your letter] gives me: to hear of your having destroyed poems, and feeling that you have a vocation in comparison of which poetry and the fame that might assuredly be yours is nothing. I could say much, for my heart bleeds: but I ought also to feel the same: and do not as I ought, though I thought myself very indifferent to fame. So I will say nothing but cling to the hope that you will find it consistent with all that you have undertaken to pursue poetry still, as occasion might serve: and that in so doing you may be sanctioned and encouraged by the great society to which you belong, which has given so many ornaments to literature. Surely one vocation cannot destroy another: and such a society as yours will not remain ignorant that you have such gifts as have seldom been given by God to man.
> (4 November, 1881.) [6]

---

[6] These letters are cited in G. F. Lahey, S. J., *Gerard Manley Hopkins* (London: Oxford University Press, 1930), pp. 81, 82, and will be found in C. C. Abbott, ed.: *The Correspondence of Gerard Manley Hopkins and Richard Watson Dixon* (London: Oxford University Press, 1935), pp. 80 and 89-90.

ART AND RELIGIOUS VOCATION 171

The position maintained by Hopkins is illuminated by the *Spiritual Exercises* of Loyola, a writing which lies at the foundation of the discipline of the Jesuits. Mr. Pick has discussed this in his study.[7] The piety that inspires the *Exercises* is not one that excludes or depreciates the creaturely goods of life or their proper enjoyment. The "Principle and Foundation" of the treatise, a sort of preface to the regimen of the Jesuits, states that all

> the other things on the face of the earth were created for man's sake, and in order to aid him in the prosecution of the end for which he was created. Whence it follows, that man ought to make use of them just so far as they help him to attain his end [that is, the praise and service of God] and ought to withdraw himself from them just so far as they hinder him. It is, therefore, necessary that we should make ourselves *indifferent* to all created things in all that is left to the liberty of our free will, and is not forbidden; in such sort that we do not for our own part wish for health rather than sickness, for wealth rather than poverty, for honor rather than dishonor . . .

It is further to be noted that supreme stress is laid on the counsel of perfection that man should aim at positive identification with Christ, should aspire to be an *alter Christus*. Now Hopkins accepted his vocation with the most resolute and uncompromising dedication. Everything indicates that he pursued it with the most costly and austere self-abandonment. We can therefore understand his attitude to nature, to his art, and to publication and fame. To quote one of the letters which gave rise to Dixon's pleas:

> This I say: my vocation puts before me a standard so high that a higher can be found nowhere else. The question then for me is not whether I am willing . . . to make a sacrifice of hopes of fame (let us suppose), but whether

[7] *Op. cit.*, Ch. 2; pp. 117, 118, etc.

> I am not to undergo a severe judgment of God for the lothness I have shewn in making it, for the reserves I may have in my heart made, for the backward glances I have given with my hand upon the plough, for the waste of time the very compositions you admire may have caused and their preoccupation of the mind which belonged to more sacred or more binding duties, for the disquiet and the thoughts of vain glory they have given rise to.

In the same letter Hopkins thus speaks of his further intentions with regard to his poetry.

> However, I shall, in my present mind, continue to compose, as occasion shall fairly allow, which I am afraid will be seldom and indeed for some years past has been scarcely ever, and let what I produce wait and take its chance; for a very spiritual man once told me that with things like composition the best sacrifice was not to destroy one's work but to leave it entirely to be disposed of by obedience. But I can scarcely fancy myself asking a superior to publish a volume of my verses and I own that humanly there is very little likelihood of that ever coming to pass. And to be sure if I chose to look at things on one side and not the other I could of course regret this bitterly. But there is more peace and it is holier to be unknown than to be known.[8]

As for nature: Hopkins was able to put a highly positive interpretation upon it. The instructions of Loyola himself justify a view of it as sacramental and as a pathway to God, and this was confirmed for our poet by his mentor, Duns Scotus, who "was very forceful in the statement of a sacramental view of the world, for he contended that God created the world to make it possible for man to look upon the visible beauties of the universe and experience them as a bridge between the finite and the infinite. Individual 'inscape,' forms splendidly

---

[8] C. C. Abbott, ed. *op. cit.*, pp. 88, 89.

ART AND RELIGIOUS VOCATION 173

shining on matter, are images, similitudes, representations, analogues of Divine Ideas." [9]

The issue was not then for Hopkins a matter of asceticism in the sense that either nature or art were of themselves suspect. Neither does it appear that Hopkins thought meanly of poetry. The infinite pains involved in his best work and the themes and concerns to which he devoted it would show that. On the one hand, however, it could usurp upon the attention more properly given to his professional and vocational duties— and here it would seem a wiser disposition might have been made by the due authorities. Thus a more liberal policy appears to be followed in the case of the Trappist poet, Thomas Merton, a member of an order in some ways even more rigorous in its discipline than is the Company of Jesus. In either case the Protestant will be forgiven for raising the question as to the advisability of admitting to such orders those whose spiritual gifts (*charismata*) are so marked in other directions. The poet is closely related to the prophet and his role cannot be identified with that of the soldier without deformation and loss. More generally we may say that the very special pattern of Christian discipleship to which Hopkins subjected himself —that of the Jesuits—no doubt bears its supernatural fruits, and did in his case; but this pattern might well be reconceived in the light of the modern experience of the church and its modern task without loss of its essential devotion. The subtly varying gifts and unique vocations of Christians, quite apart from those with extraordinary talents, should warn the church against any excessive stereotyping of the life of the "religious," especially as modern culture and "personality" diversify themselves, and as the church repeats the experience of Israel in passing from law to freedom.

More basic, however, than the question of the special regimen of the order in Hopkins' case is that of the nature of poetry. It was not only because his art conflicted with his

[9] Pick, *op. cit.*, p. 36.

professional duties as a priest and Jesuit that he minimized it. He was also tempted to think of it, in common with Thomist esthetics, as an activity that belonged to the natural order as over against the supernatural order of religious exercise. It would appear, however, that his preferences for Duns Scotus combined with his own feeling as to religious art to leave him unsatisfied as to this oversimple scholastic distinction. The fact is that a Christian poet often carries out the role of a Christian prophet and opens the wells of the "supernatural" life in ways impossible for the priest or the fixed channels of grace. Hopkins' dilemma and anguish arise here. It was not that he was not free to enjoy his gift, nor was it a desire for fame and honor. It was rather that he could not more freely carry out the prophetic function to which he was called.

The religious life is not as simple as these scholastic categories would make it, nor are the processes of revelation and redemption. We have noted an analogous distinction by Mr. Auden (see above, Ch. I) between art as "frivolous" and the moral life as serious, offered in a context distinguishing the layman from the priest. The truth that underlies these arbitrary distinctions is that grace is specially though irregularly potent in the visible church and its ministries. But the laiety, and the laiety in their quasi-secular functions, can often be the channels of grace. Dogmatic distinctions oversimplify the matter. Poetry has a religious character, for better or worse. This carries risks with it. It may take on a character of demonic magic or it may serve as a medium of revelation and of central Christian revelation. The poet is, therefore, all the more responsible. If he is a gifted Christian poet he may be called on as a bearer of the Word and he may mediate it sacramentally to circles quite outside the reach of the pulpit and the stated exercises of the church. Such a calling has its own costs and discipline and none can be said to be higher.

With whatever uncertainties and vacillations here, however, Hopkins acted conscientiously and heroically in the light given

ART AND RELIGIOUS VOCATION

him and the options open to him. His decisions for the priesthood and the order are understandable ones. The essential *ascesis* could have taken place in other ways, but in whatever way it conferred upon him finally a strength and a sobriety that compensate in part for the loss of other things. Again we cite his line: "Strung by duty and strained to beauty."

As for his attitude to publication, we find here what is surely a rare victory over what is generally conceded even to the best, the desire for fame, that last infirmity of noble minds. Such disinterestedness goes *pari passu* with the love of the object: love of man, love of beauty, or love of God. The version of this love held by Hopkins is well represented by the words of St. Ignatius at the climax of the *Spiritual Exercises:*

> Take, Lord, and receive all my liberty, my memory, my intellect and my will—all that I have and possess Thou gavest it to me: to thee, Lord, I return it! All is Thine, dispose of it according to all Thy will. Give me Thy love and grace, for this is enough for me.

How God did dispose of the works of His servant, Gerard, and justify again the trust that all His servants place in Him, is now in part a matter of history.

VIII

SECULAR INVOLVEMENT: POETRY OF PROTESTANT AND ANGLICAN BACKGROUND

THE most significant art of the twentieth century—Stravinski, Picasso, Joyce, Kafka, Pound, Eliot—is that which comes immediately out of the epochal convulsions of the time, out of full immersion in the condition of man today. Faithful transcription of this experience into art cannot take place if the artist is trammeled by formal patterns suitable to a less dynamic experience. Nor can it take place within the frame of a religious symbolism or dogma which inhibits the full experience. This does not mean that the modern awareness cannot be construed in Christian terms but any element of stereotype in such terms will distort the experience and inhibit the power. The Christian faith has its criteria but these need not exclude the Christian artist from full identification with the spiritual crisis of today as would a rigid dogmatic legacy. It is the spirit, as the Christian understands it, which searcheth all things and which underlies all the dynamic impulses of our crisis. Therefore the Christian is in the best position to understand them, to diagnose the age, and to "interpret the times." The command to "test the spirits," that is, to assess and distinguish among the spiritual and cultural impulses of a situation, this command rests on an appeal to the Holy Spirit in the church. This Spirit while it is related to the whole history of the church is not bound by any time-conditioned formulations of the church.

The conclusion is that the Christian faith understood in terms of Protestant freedom offers the artist today the best basis for full grasp and interpretation of the modern experience. But such an approach must evidently be distinguished from a Protestant dogmatism or a parochial Protestant evangelicalism. It must represent the height and depth of the gospel. Those non-Roman poets of today who have most powerfully dealt with the crisis in question in Christian terms, T. S. Eliot and W. H. Auden, have availed themselves of Anglo-Catholic tradition to safeguard the dimensions of the faith but combined this with an empiricism in experience which marks a Protestant freedom. Preceding and underlying the Catholic elements in their work there lie decades of secular involvement and immersion. In these decades, though tacit Christian orientation and assumptions operated, they were able without inhibiting frames of reference to identify themselves fully with the disintegration and estrangement, the Waste Land and anxiety of the time and its secular artistic expressions. It is our belief that their adoption of specifically Catholic doctrine and symbolism, so far as these are not simply the perennial foundations of Christianity itself, has tended to handicap their representativeness as voices of the modern situation and their most adequate Christian interpretation of it. This is less true of Mr. Auden. Even in the case of Mr. Eliot there is such a rich eclecticism in his religious symbolism that the narrowing and isolating consequences are less felt.

In the absence of first rank artists and poets whose orientation is consistently and recognizably Protestant, we can turn to those secular artists whose background at least is Protestant and in whom this background makes its appearance indirectly, or to writers whose background is Catholic but who have abandoned that faith. In such men we see a secular presentation of the modern experience and its spiritual and moral issues at a level that tends to pass into a Christian formulation. Such writers point to a new version of Christianity which is neither Catholic nor Protestant in the more limited senses of these terms. But the empiricism of their outlook and their radical secular involvement is only reconcilable to what Paul Tillich has defined as the Protestant principle—namely, the ever present disposition to judge and reject the successive embodiments and authorities set up by culture and church.

The problem and prospects of a Christian art today, as we are implying, is tied up with the willingness of the church to enter fully into the rich if ambiguous life of contemporary men. This is a perennial issue and involves much more than religious art.

1. THE CHRISTIAN ARTIST AND THE WORLD: THE THREE ALTERNATIVES

From the earliest days of the Christian church the greatest dilemmas it has faced have had to do with its inevitable but perilous entanglements with the "world." When it moved out into the pagan Hellenistic civilization it could not remain unchanged but neither could it safely accommodate itself to that culture. Here the new Israel, in the struggle for the survival of its essential faith, was only repeating the experience of the Hebrew tribes of the desert when they took up the new agricultural life of Canaan. Their desert deity had to come to terms with the Baals that gave the wine and the oil. The Christian church today faces just this sort of major adjustment.

In the first and second centuries, as always in such a situation, there were three possible solutions. One group of the early Christians wished to Judaize, to retain the existing Jewish-Christian patterns of belief and cult. Another group took the course of "acute Hellenization," that is, of taking over the forms of paganism to such a point that it surrendered the substance of the faith. Out from between these two extremes finally emerged the early Catholic church. Through a period of vacillation and conflict it had succeeded in transforming and at the same time enriching itself and its faith so as to survive and operate in the new theatre. This was only possible because it had freely undergone identification with the new milieu in its deepest levels and yet without betrayal. Herein it was only carrying out the example of the incarnation. It did, indeed, die to live.

It would incidentally be interesting to observe the character of the symbolic forms and literature produced by these three tendencies in the early church. The reactionary Judaizing sects, the Ebionites and their like, have left us only devitalized gospel fragments and polemic material. On the other wing, the gnostic Christians produced some respectable hymns but their group had surrendered one of the poles which generated power and the hymns tend toward the vacuous. The main stream of the church produced the later writings of the New Testament including the Fourth Gospel, the naive and radiant early liturgical elements and sober but resonant passages in the rhetoric of the early apologists. These latter elements were born out of the full engagement of the church with the pagan world.

In these three directions which invited the early church we find an analogy to the present dilemma of Christianity confronted with a new situation in western culture. It is only an analogy since for one thing our present culture is Christian in its backgrounds, so that we shall hasten to qualify it.

The Roman church we may say "Judaizes" in the sense that it withholds itself from full involvement in the forces that have made the modern situation. On the other wing, we have "acute Hellenization" in the sense today of "acute secularization." This includes all those especially Protestant elements which have allowed themselves to be taken over by modern movements and ideologies, rationalistic, romantic, neo-pagan, Marxist, or a combination of these. In between we have the central stream of Protestantism and Anglo-Catholicism. But this element is today in a peculiar condition of disarray. It can be said to include a vast number of men and women whose commitment is for the moment uncertain or withheld, who could not espouse either of the other solutions, and who are, in fact, waiting for this central way of life to clarify itself before they return to it. But their return to the faith as is already evident will necessarily be by a different way, through new country, unfamiliar fields and strange cities.

Each of these three directions has its corollaries in what concerns the arts. Roman Catholic art and its limitations we have described. On the other wing, instances are at hand of naturalistic, neo-pagan or Marxist art and literature which have divorced themselves from Christian connections. In between we have imaginative creations sometimes explicitly and sometimes only implicitly related to the Christian heritage, but in either case witnessing to full initiation into the encounter of our spiritual traditions with the present crisis.

When we speak of the involvement of the church in the world it is always, of course, a matter of degree and kind. This is because incarnation is of the essence of the gospel. The question cannot be one of embodiment or disembodiment, but of successive re-embodiments. The gospel must be free continually to re-embody itself and the church must continually die to live.

It is true that Catholicism makes more of the idea of incarnation in many respects than Protestantism. The place assigned in its worship to the arts, the senses, to action and drama, is one aspect of this. As we have seen, Catholic mystical and devotional poetry and prose employ sensuous and sexual symbol which Puritan writers denied themselves. Moreover, the relation of the Mass, the cult of Mary and other prominent features of piety to universal elements in fertility religion, etc., testify to a wide syncretistic hospitality. We believe, however, that at least in our period this church has largely foreclosed the possibilities of such continued "incarnation," commerce with and borrowings from the general life of men, except in lesser matters. Meanwhile the older embodiments take on an archaic character. Since Trent, the Roman church has made itself more rigid and failed to come to terms fully with the great movements that have conditioned the lot and outlook of men and societies. It is not enough to point to the evil in such movements. They must be bereaved of their pride and error and the values incorporated.

Of course, Christianity in all its forms is by its nature irrepressible and universal, and many deep interactions between the Roman church and the non-Roman world have continued. But when tradition is assigned the same sacrosanct authority as revelation there inevitably follows an uncompromising parochialism of standpoint and ethos which precludes the kind of transformations which took place in the creative period of the early church.

In such a situation the influences of the environing culture can often only introduce themselves in a clandestine and ambiguous way. One example here would be the infiltration of sub-Christian elements in Latin American popular Catholicism. The atavistic folk art and symbolism which reflect this, exhibit, indeed, a contact with the non-Christian milieu, but to the loss rather than the gain of the faith. The regenerative power of the church is checked by the fixed character of its forms. On a more sophisticated level our review of a number of the most gifted French Catholic writers revealed an extraordinary heterodoxy of inspiration, indicating, indeed, an involvement of Catholics in the secular wisdoms and forces of the modern world, but one whose enrichment and instruction of the church remains frustrated. The restiveness of the Catholic imagination here becomes apparent, in any case.

There are certainly strong impulses toward a beneficial secularization in Catholic life and art today as in Protestantism, but the nature of this church is such as to limit rather than encourage it. The renewal of the ecclesiastical arts and the musical tradition are now being furthered by Rome. But the massive character of the liturgy, discipline and doctrine are such as to isolate the believer and the orthodox artist from either the crisis or the constructive contributions of the age.

Where Protestantism adheres closely to the patterns of its past the same may be said. Communities and sects of a strongly traditional Calvinist or Lutheran type engage only diffidently in the arena of modern social and cultural conflict, and it is significant that they often seek to provide their own schools and colleges for their youth. They perpetuate relatively pure and redemptive channels of Reformed Christianity, but the figure that befits them, as churches, is hardly that of the leaven, and least of all that of the seed that dies. The same may be said of the neo-orthodoxy of the continent. Either type of Protestantism lacks the sensuous and artistic heritage of Catholicism yet like the Catholicism of our period is not disposed to the kind of fertilizing secularism which would nourish the religious artist.

Anglo-Catholicism is as always in a unique position in all these matters. With regard to those who are rigorously Catholic in their sacramental views much of what we have said about Roman Catholicism would apply. There remain, however, the special factors in the tradition of the English church which somewhat modify the picture. An analogous factor operates in the case of French Catholic writers and helps to account for the "mutations" of the Catholic imagination which we found there. Our best example of the receptivity of the Anglo-Catholic writer to secular involvement is Mr. W. H. Auden, and it may be significant in his case that much of his work was done before the marks of this orientation appeared upon his poetry and prose. Anglicans and Episcopalians who are not deeply formed in or committed to the Catholic view of the mass and priesthood resemble the great body of Protestants in their exposure to secular influences and to the modern situation with all its emancipations and confusions.

2. *ACUTE SECULARIZATION*

We have begun by speaking of those aspects of the church which, according to our analogy, "Judaize," which avoid giving hostages to the world or admitting Trojan horses into their midst. Their arts are characteristically in a pattern of the past, in special "traditions" which like all traditions change but which lag when a revolutionary period is upon them.

On the opposite wing in western culture is to be found those groups and individuals that have reacted violently against the whole Christian heritage and represent an "acute secularization." In our third chapter we have spoken of Nietzsche as the representative iconoclast and father of modern secular protestants, come-outers and bohemians, and the prototype of all modern prophets who have sought one or another cult of salvation in irrationalism or mysticism to replace the God who is dead. We have spoken also of D. H. Lawrence and of Robinson Jeffers, who in various ways, also illustrated by modern musicians and artists, have sought to return to a pre-Christian and even pre-classical level of experience to discover renewal and freedom. We have spoken also of those who would refresh the vitalities of a dehumanized order by way either of the Yogis with their cults, or the Commissar who appeals to the masses in terms of blood and soil, or in terms of the utopian *mystique* of a new humanity. Like Wordsworth in his encounter with the French Revolution, says Auden,

> Like him, we had the luck to see
> A rare discontinuity,
> Old Russia suddenly mutate
> Into a proletarian state,
> The odd phenomenon, the strange
> Event of qualitative change.
> Some dreamed, as students always can,
> It realized the potential Man,
> A higher species brought to birth
> Upon a sixth part of the earth . . .[1]

We must also include here those intellectuals who find in the march of science and particularly in the work of Freud and

[1] "New Year Letter," lines 667-676. *The Double Man* (New York: Random House, 1941), p. 37.

his followers, not only a new Renaissance of the reason and its powers, which in some true sense it is, but also a gospel.

The significant thing about all these figures and movements is that they are in various ambiguous ways related to the Christian background. Their protests are often understandable, and often grounded on a Christian criterion. Their goals as in the case of communism represent a plagiarized and distorted borrowing from Christianity. Even the anti-Christ borrows his traits from Christ, and since Nietzsche was not a real anti-Christ he continues genuine aspects of the Christian tradition which had become obscured. D. H. Lawrence is indebted to his non-conformist background for much that is best in his work. Secularized writers as different as Dreiser, Gide, Pound and Jeffers evidence the influence of their Protestant lineage in healthy ways and sometimes pay their homage to it. Robinson Jeffers' moving sonnet "To His Father" is an example of this. More than that it is a vivid document of the contrast between the lot of two generations; the younger one in wars without and within lacerated by foes the older could not know. It is to be noted that Jeffers' father was a Presbyterian minister and scholar.

> Christ was your lord and captain all your life,
> He fails the world but you he did not fail,
> He led you through all forms of grief and strife
> Intact, a man full-armed, he let prevail
> Nor outward malice nor the worse-fanged snake
> That coils in one's own brain against your calm,
> That great rich jewel well guarded for his sake
> With coronal age and death like quieting balm.
> I Father having followed other guides
> And oftener to my hurt no leader at all,
> Through years nailed up like dripping panther hides
> For trophies on a savage temple wall
> Hardly anticipate that reverend stage
> Of life, the snow-wreathed honor of extreme age.[2]

[2] *Roan Stallion, Tamar and Other Poems* (New York: Boni and Liveright), p. 225.

The acute secularization of which we speak is never easy to condemn outright in its representatives. Clear blasphemy, pornography, antinomian doctrines with regard to family and state, exaltation of sheer vitality, of powers of blood and instinct divorced from reason and spirit, appeals to folk and tribe as having no law but power, ice-cold positivistic attitudes which can lead to inhuman disregard of human life, any and all such expressions are to be assessed for what they are. It is undeniable that our age knows not only its outward conflicts and ruins but its corresponding invisible disorders. The causes of these disorders are rightly called metaphysical or demonic because they spring out of the roots of the self and the atavisms of man's social relations in which the irrational has so large a part. Psychology has its own terms for these disorders, suggesting a similar irrational morbidity or malignancy, sadism, scapegoating, masochism, the death-wish, the Christ-complex, satanism, etc. When the New Testament attributes to one group of pagan religionists or gnostics a pride in knowledge of "the depths of Satan" we can recognize what in a modern form appears as an avid antinomian exploration of forbidden experience to which the poet Rimbaud gave encouragement. Similarly Augustine's phrase, *libido sciendi,* suggests a pursuit of knowledge and experience whose unrecognized motive and goal is self-deification and intoxication.

It is at such points that it becomes necessary for the Christian to "test the spirits" whether they be of God. Here lie the cogency and value of Professor Hoxie N. Fairchild's careful analysis of the romantic movement and its background. In writers like Byron and Whitman symptoms are seen of a departure from the healthful cultural norms as well as the Christian norms of the West which have their riper fruits in more recent irrationalisms.

Caution against blanket indictment and rejection of the suspect elements in modern esthetic revolt is, however, to be registered at a number of points. An analogy from the French artistic situation in the second decade of this century is helpful. Those who recognize the stifling situation in the conventional painting of that period, the mediocrity of the schools, the regimented tyranny of the academies and judges, are today more than charitable to the scandalously violent initiators of the da-da rebellion. These painters and poets could only free their lungs and register their protest by a wholly disproportionate and antithetical revolt. Their infantilism was not wholly negative since it involved also a naive return to the elements of the esthetic life. Something like that is true in a much wider range of modern experience in the case of the acute secularization of which we are speaking.

This motive of convulsive revolt against a mountain-like burden of frustrating authority Auden ascribes to Karl Marx in the psychological terms of the "father image," and shows how the action brought illumination though this illumination was beset with excess.

> What if he erred? He flashed a light
> On facts where no one had been right.
> The father-shadow that he hated
> Weighed like an Alp; his love, frustrated,
> Negating as it was negated,
> Burst out in boils; his animus
> Outlawed him from himself, but thus,
> And only thus, perhaps, could he
> Have come to his discovery.[3]

In what follows Auden pays homage to great disturbers of tradition, including Machiavelli and Darwin, as he does in his tribute to Freud in another poem. These all are

> Great sedentary Caesars who
> Have pacified some dread tabu,
> Whose wits were able to withdraw
> The *numen* from some local law

---

[3] "New Year Letter," lines 687-695, *The Double Man, op. cit.*, pp. 37, 38.

And with a single concept brought
Some ancient rubbish heap of thought
To rational diversity . . .[4]

Those who can recognize how stifling has been the spiritual atmosphere, how stunting the moral level of many aspects of our modern culture, how conventional and Philistine many even of the sanhedrins and academies of our society, and how insensitive and regimented the authorities, these also will concede the inevitability of the extremes to which many modern secular prophets have gone from Nietzsche on. The occasional diatribes against excesses in modern poetry would have more cogency if the same critics showed themselves equally sensitive to the spuriousness of emotion and generally debilitating or toxic character of much of the best selling literature of the time.[5]

All in all, however, it is to be admitted that the writers with whom we have here been concerned have set themselves apart from the Christian tradition. Their protests and explorations can be serviceable to it. They have the merit of involving themselves in the "world" as many Christians have not, but in doing so they have so far surrendered the heritage that their work is only partially significant to those identified with it.

3. THE LIVING TRADITION

We come then to that central body in the Christian movement between the formalized and inhospitable wing on the one hand, and that identified with "acute secularization" on the other. We have here a complex Protestant tradition, including many Anglicans, whose genius is to accept involvement in the

---
[4] *Ibid.*, lines 751-758.

[5] In his volume, *Christian Discrimination*, George Every has a section on popular fiction which is very much to the point here. Among other things he says that many people "lack a permanent and mature attitude to life which could restrain the impulse to play with illusions, and help them to see through the illusory consolations of much modern romantic literature," and further, that in many popular works, "the break between fantasy and reality has been blurred and things are not in their right place. —" (pp. 3, 4).

life and new forces of the generations, but which cherishes the Christian heritage and wrestles with the task of baptizing the new experience into the faith. This boldness in interrelations with the secular movements of science, art and social change varies indeed. Many of the Protestant church bodies, even when they are not doctrinally regressive, are not exposed to modern forces or not disposed to explore them. The social and economic groups with which much of Protestantism is identified limits the awareness of its laiety and many of its ministers and theologians. It is partly for this reason that we are confronted with a very special circumstance in connection with the Protestant alternative. Many who rightly belong here and who are Protestant in background and sympathy are not active churchmen. Yet much of the most vital moral and even spiritual leadership of society comes from such groups.

We have to do here, therefore, with many sons and grandsons of Protestants who live in detachment from the religious institutions and who are reticent about their beliefs, agnostic or frankly negative. Many of our best artists, intellectuals, scientists and social pioneers belong in this group. Partly because they are not in the shelter of the religious communities they know the tensions of the time and its costs. The relativities of value and ethics, the estrangement and anxiety, the dearth of ritual and meaning, weigh upon them peculiarly. It is not surprising that it is from this group that much of our best modern art and literature comes.

The relation of this great host of modern men to the Christian faith is critically important. Most of them in this country have a Protestant background and often early Protestant training. The average man is inarticulate or unclear as to the basic reasons for his alienation from formal Christian practice. But the poets and artists among them are revealing as we shall see. Trained as they are in the esthetic traditions of many lands their religious sense cannot be satisfied in the ascetic or mediocre worship of the non-liturgical churches. On the other

THE LIVING TRADITION 189

hand, the liturgical churches may suggest only another kind of spiritual uniformity. Ralph Adams Cram was a Catholic, but Frank Lloyd Wright is a Unitarian. Similarly the intellectuals of this group are communicative. Their report often is that the churches are not drastically aware, curious, oriented to the actual realities that condition human happiness. It is not that they ask that all believers be intellectuals, but only that the churches more generally out-think the world about them as they did in other times, and that they manifest that kind of concern for learning and science which led them to found so many colleges in earlier days in this country. Likewise the secular social scientist and social worker today are articulate and can interpret their abstention from religious practice. Too often they have been rebuffed in their desire to find support among the faithful for the costly witness they must bear or the intelligent procedures to be followed.

Besides these there are innumerable secularized individuals and families who without being scornful or demanding, yet find the life of the churches, at least in their neighborhood, somewhat tepid or lacking in that vigilance and solicitude which are constant notes in the New Testament. There are others who have been seared or even corroded in family or professional conflicts, marked with nervous disability or afflicted with a sense of meaninglessness in the course of military experience or protracted economic defeat. Such may not be at home in the religious institutions because the questions they ask of life are not envisaged there.

Such aliens from the churches may often be unjust. They may lack in humility. They often are ill-informed about religion and its institutions. But their witness needs to be taken into account. In them too the Christian tradition in our society expresses itself and sometimes in very revealing and important ways.

Of these Protestants and sons of Protestants many, if not the most, have their destined spiritual home in Protestantism when it has reshaped its patterns and spirit in the course of the present cultural crisis. The reason for thinking so lies in two mutually complementary considerations. On the one hand, it is the genius of Protestantism, when it is true to its own principle, to enter into untrammeled engagement with the life of the times. On the other hand, the articulate spokesmen of the secular world today gave multiple evidence of the fact that the present crisis reopens for them the relevance if not the necessity of the Christian heritage.

4. ART AND THE PROTESTANT PRINCIPLE

The state of affairs we have so far described leads us to cast about for examples of literary expression of this central stream of the Christian movement in our time, an expression in terms neither of defensively traditional Catholicism and Protestantism nor of "acute secularization." Such literature would be revealing and prophetic of the main religious trend of the future in our society. What we are in search of would presumably be a poetry of Protestant inspiration and stamp. The term Protestant must here, however, be taken in a wide sense to include both Anglo-Catholic writers strongly conditioned by a critical and prophetic spirit and also uncommitted and non-confessional writers whose Christian expression is indirect and obscured.

In what concerns poetry the general impression today is that Protestantism lacks any significant voice. Catholicism whether in its Roman or Anglican forms has its distinguished representatives: T. S. Eliot, Claudel, and younger writers like Robert Lowell and Thomas Merton. Modern secularism has had its notable talents, whether of a neo-mystical tendency like D. H. Lawrence, W. B. Yeats, or Robinson Jeffers, or of a noncommittal humanism or naturalism like Valéry and Wallace Stevens. It is not easy to identify poets of corresponding stature who may be said to reflect a Protestant Christian position.

Vachel Lindsay might be called the last notable poet to carry a clear Protestant witness. But his work however admirable seems now to belong to a different era. We can point to the magnificent work of Robert Frost, indeed, as a real clue to the vitality of the Protestant tradition today, as well as to the work of E. A. Robinson. These two figures alone would reassure us. Yet if we are expecting to find a positive celebration of the Christian faith like that which we observe in the Catholic poets, we shall have to look further. No doubt specifically religious themes are not the main desideratum in a poet of faith. But it should sometimes make its appearance where the religious tradition is powerful. The rarity of just such uninhibited celebration of our faith in poets of Protestant background —celebration of real poetic stature—is precisely the problem. This dilemma may well point us back to the dilemma of Protestantism itself in our time. But it also raises the more general question of the relation of Protestantism to the arts.

We may phrase our problem as follows: in what particular ways does the Protestant tradition come to expression in the best contemporary poetry? What if any are the *differentiae* of the poet of Protestant background and inspiration? What special testimony is borne by such poets and in what distinctive ways do they serve or challenge the cultural situation today? We can assume that poetry of whatever spiritual background agrees on much and coincides in its general diagnosis of modern culture. Whether in poetry, fiction, drama, or criticism, there is wide agreement upon our loss of community, our loss of absolutes, our loss of ritual, our depersonalization. But in what special ways do poets of a Protestant formation reflect and challenge this situation?

We must first raise some ulterior questions as to Protestantism and the arts. It can be urged plausibly that Protestant Christianity by its very nature is not congenial to the esthetic life and not disposed to the nourishment of the arts. We may look at three observations often made.

It is alleged that the particular ascetic or iconoclastic strain in Protestantism is of a kind that tends to impoverishment and an anticultural aridity. That other-worldliness which all forms of Christianity necessarily share in some form is said in this case to take on a peculiarly sterilizing character. Here it would be necessary to scrutinize the various phases of Protestantism in time and place to decide what truth there may be in this allegation. It would be found that immediate cultural circumstances have more to do with the anticultural spirit than anything inherent in Protestantism itself.

Again, it is alleged that Protestantism has been so identified with an unimaginative and Philistine middle-class ethos that its esthetic expression is necessarily starved. The charge here is that from its very origin it has been compromised by its relationship to the pride, revolt and individualism of the modern world. Thus any even great artistic and poetic expression it may have had has been plagued by such idolatries of the culture as nationalism and mammon. Whatever Christian potency or protest survived has been stifled by the secularity which sprang from the Renaissance, the Enlightenment, and the industrial revolution. With regard to this charge it may be agreed, for instance, that Main Street religion has taken on unlovely esthetic expression from Main Street values. Yet the artistic expression of every religion is both handicapped and blessed by prevailing cultural conditions. The western culture that has both cradled the various forms of Protestantism and been fostered by them has offered both advantages and disadvantages to the arts. Moreover Protestantism is by no means inseparably linked to modern bourgeois culture, though many of its recent forms are.

A third observation is more fundamental and more valid. Protestantism by its very genius, while it inspires great cultural flowering and world-shaping moral energies, nevertheless is always critical of all cultural forms and of all temporal achievement. It is always cutting down the tree to begin again at the root. It always sees the temptation to idolatry in our human edifices, whether social or cultural or even ecclesiastical. It sees all achieved forms and traditions as under judgment and calls us back to the point of departure. Here we have, indeed, the cultural implications of "justification by faith."

Now it is true that Judaism has a similar prophetic witness. Across the centuries Judaism cries to the cultures which succeed each other, "Remember the Last Things!" Yet we must recognize that Judaism knows how to build in the temporal order, despite its homeless history. Its eschatological consciousness throws into acute relief the poignancies of the human condition, and provides the basis for a unique poetry and art. We have a recent example; in Kafka we can say that the Jew resumes his place among the supreme artists. Auden has well struck off in colloquial language the age-old experience and religious bond of Israel. The Jewess speaks to the Christian with his "light elations."

>   . . . let history be.
> Time is our trade, to be tense our gift
> Whose woe is our weight; for we are His Chosen,
> His ragged remnant with our ripe flesh
> And our hats on sent out of the room . . .
> But His People still. We'll point for him,
> Be as obvious always if He won't show.[1]

The most characteristic Jewish poetry of today is written in Hebrew and Yiddish and is unfortunately not accessible in its full force to English readers.[2]

Now it is our argument that Protestantism also has its way of

[1] *The Age of Anxiety* (New York: Random House, 1947), pp. 124-125.

[2] For contemporary and recent work in these tongues (in translation) and discussion of it see Shalom Spiegel, *Hebrew Reborn* (New York: Macmillan, 1930); *The Golden Treasury of Jewish Literature*, ed. by L. W. Schwartz; *Complete Poetic Works of H. N. Bialik*, ed. by I. Efros (Histadruth Ivrith of America, 1948).

achievement, of building, in the cultural sense. It is true that in its prophetic character it judges and rejects. *But Protestantism fertilizes.* Its esthetic expression is commonly indirect. Protestantism weds itself to the changing cultures in a daring surrender of life, and so introduces creative energies and perspectives which then make their appearance in secular form. The art and literature produced by Protestantism are always an amalgam or *tertium quid* made up of its tradition at the time and of the prevailing constellation of social and cultural forces. In Milton the Protestant faith was wedded to a moment of Renaissance humanism to produce our supreme English epic. In the romantic period the Protestant faith in its then diffused form wedded itself to the new creative energies of Europe to produce great poets—Wordsworth, Blake, Shelley, Whitman, Emerson. These were in doctrine more or less heretical, but their work represented a direct wrestling of the Christian faith with the new circumstances of the modern world. The artist of Protestant inspiration runs the risks of secularization; indeed, he is often radically secularized. But in his work the Protestant Christian tradition makes itself felt under all kinds of masks and disguises. To speak generally about our modern situation, Protestantism as a creative tradition is today in many respects like a river that has gone underground. But it gives signs of itself especially among the secularists, and even in the blasphemers.

From the Catholic point of view we have noted the objection that can here be made. Does not the Catholic poet find his material in the world? Does he not also effect a wedding between the Christian life of grace and nature? Indeed. And the Catholic poets and novelists avail themselves of nature in highly diverse ways and on the basis of diverse theological views. The last thing that one can say at least of Catholic esthetic expression is that it is monolithic! We have spoken of the extreme latitude of the Catholic religious imagination which is part of its glory—to the preoccupation of writers like Bloy, Péguy, Bernanos, Mauriac, Claudel, Graham Greene. Such latitude in Catholic writers indicates indeed an involvement in the "world." It has its dangers and corresponds in its own way to the more erratic explorations of such writers of Protestant background as André Gide and D. H. Lawrence.

But the difference, as we have seen, lies here: the Catholic poet is endowed with so massive a legacy of Christian symbol that this tends to dominate the work not only in spirit but even in theme and motif. It is the glory of Catholic poetry that the larger part of it deals with the Nativity and with the Passion. These themes are pressed upon the entirety of experience. Francis Thompson sees the sunset as a huge monstrance with the sun the host, while G. M. Hopkins addresses the Virgin as the "world-mothering air." The cosmos is appropriated to the liturgy.

The poet of a Protestant formation on the other hand, lacking the massive body of symbolism, brings to nature not so much a tradition as a leaven. Protestantism dies to live! This is often true of its esthetic fertility. Here the gospel dies as it were to rise again in works that often carry no confession or evangelical stamp, but which nonetheless glorify God by their excellence or their joy or their lucidity or their compassion. Such works may also have an admixture of the world in them; they may betray the shadows, the doubts, and the idols of the time. But they have this virtue: they arise out of a complete baptism of the Christian tradition in the actualities, the tensions, the temptations of our modern predicament. Through Protestantism the Christian faith is at first hand engaged in a desperate grappling with the great occasions of heresy in the modern world—with rationalism, with romanticism, with science, with Marx, with Nietzsche, with Freud. The resulting arts, idioms, sensibilities, rhetorics, poetics, however tortured or errorist, have the supreme merit of emerging from the place where men live today, from the central arena and battleground.[3]

5. MR. W. H. AUDEN: TOWARDS A NEW CHRISTIAN SYNTHESIS

Here is where W. H. Auden, who is a very Protestant kind of Anglo-Catholic, takes on a representative significance.[1] Eliot has also in his own way negotiated his Odyssey through the various perils, temptations, and disasters of our world. But in Auden we see modern men exposed to the risks and costs of our situation on all fronts. He takes a swarm of spears into his breast. He is initiated into our intellectual as well as our social dilemmas. And he has fought through all our issues and wrestled with our distempers without adventitious aids or extrinsic authoritarian props. His work is peculiarly representative and instructive because all these dilemmas are taken up and canvassed in his poems directly. In Eliot much lies below the surface or is taken for granted. In him, at least in the later work, we have the outcome; in Auden, the debate. Auden offers us the forum of the modern consciousness. This makes his work difficult, especially in view of its philosophical content. Both poets are moreover highly allusive. In Auden's case a rich topical allusiveness is added to the symbolical allusiveness of any modern poet. One needs to be alert to all sorts of

---

[3] It is significant that Dr. Helen C. White in her preface to the Catholic Anthology, *Drink from this Rock*, mentioned above, urges Catholic writers and poets to deal further with the role of poetry in a world of science: "I have often wondered if the great scholastic doctor who transformed Aristotle from a menace to a buttress of the faith would not have known how to meet modern science in a larger and more confident spirit than some of her contemporary followers. And I cannot imagine Dante maintaining such a complete immunity to some of the dramatic constructs of the contemporary mind as do most of the poets of *Spirit*."—Reprinted in *Return to Poetry: Critical Essays from Spirit* (New York: The Declan X. McMullen Co., Inc., 1947), p. 280.

[1] In the following discussion we have in mind especially the more recent of Auden's works: *The Double Man* (New York: Random House, 1941); *For The Time Being*, including "A Christmas Oratorio" (New York: Random House, 1944); *The Age of Anxiety* (New York: Random House, 1947). *The Collected Poetry of W. H. Auden* (New York: Random House, 1945), includes the first two works named and much of his earlier writing.

modern curiosity and science as well as to general literature to follow him. But this is what qualifies him as an interpreter. His poetry knows how to make room for the outlook of Montaigne as well as Pascal, for Nietzsche as well as Kierkegaard, for Marx and Freud as well as for Dante. Auden represents the new Christian synthesis in the making. He starts with the disarray and the sense of meaningless of the time but he gives it a Christian construction.

> We are afraid
> Of pain but more afraid of silence; for no nightmare
> Of hostile objects could be as terrible as this Void.
> This is the Abomination. This is the Wrath of God.[2]

Auden's earlier work carried no confessional labels upon it but was dense with social ethical concerns and the responsibilities of the individual as was the case with so many of the writers of the thirties. A dozen or more years given to exposure of the disorder of western life preceded his arrival in this country well before the second World War. His volume, *Another Time*, published in 1940,[3] evidences the lucidity of his analysis of the times and the extraordinary versatility of his indictments and warnings. He points out in poem XXIV that the democracies had long been inviting the Furies, luring the "crooked wing," the Terrible Presences. "We conjured them here like a lying map." For individual vices add up to public disaster. By intimate anarchies, by self-deceptions, and glossed-over violence, by personal indiscipline—"a father's rage" or "a mother's distorting mirror"—we ourselves have smoothed the way for wholesale convulsions. Not only does the tiger make easy entrance and find himself quite at home in the familiar surroundings of a heartless state, but also

> ... the ape
> Is really at home in the parish
> Of grimacing and licking.

[2] *For the Time Being*, p. 67.
[3] New York: Random House.

The course of events was to bring a rude disclosure of the character of the Almighty. In "Spain, 1937" God berates men for thinking that he was altogether such a one as themselves:

> To you I'm the
> Yes-man, the bar-companion, the easily-duped.

But events reveal his implacable aspects, and when sobered nations plead to him in panic, there is no deliverance:

> History to the defeated
> May say Alas but cannot help or pardon.

In this volume Auden rebuked democratic idealists who assigned all the fault to the fascists, and who oversimplified by announcing that the devil had broken parole and that they must go to war to chain him up again. He castigated factories "where lives are made for a temporary use, like collars or chairs." He wrote hauntingly of the refugees. He satirized Christians who escaped the real guilt by routines of cultic expiation. Recurrent in this as in his later volumes is the insight that social tyrannies in either totalitarian states or in democracies flourish on the maladies and sins of the individual. These tyrannies live on "lucrative patterns of frustration"; the masses tolerate and nourish their masters as a compensation for their own obscure hurts and cravings. When Auden pursues the basic problem of salvation to any length he turns to the insights and language of psychology. The splendid tribute, "In Memory of Sigmund Freud," found in this volume shows that at least at this time, the cure was to be sought in self-knowledge, in sunlight admitted to the deep places, in honesty, in self-pardon. Thence would come wholeness and reconciliation and man's "dark, disordered city" would be sweetened. In Freud the writer found one who

> went his way,
> Down among the Lost People like Dante, down
> To the stinking fosse where the injured
> Lead the ugly life of the rejected.

In his work published since that volume, beginning with *The Double Man*, 1941, Auden continues the use of Freudian tools in his analyses of society but a new range of reference and allusion comes into the poetry and prose drawn frequently from writings of a theological character including Pascal, Kierkegaard, Tillich and the Christian classics. In his most recent work, notably in the "Christmas Oratorio," it is evident that he has adopted not only an explicit Christian frame of reference but a Catholic formulation of it.[4] In the "Oratorio" the formulation in terms of the Word, the Child, the Miracle, is not necessarily Catholic in a dogmatic sense, and may be thought of as a borrowing for the occasion, appropriate to the particular Christian saga used. Moreover the combination of the Christian themes with all manner of psychological and philosophical elements indicates that the dogmatic elements are not taken over in any stereotyped form.

The idea of original sin which, at least in the sense of moral derangement and incapacity, marks the work of all the more notable modern writers except D. H. Lawrence and the Marxists, is presented in terms that are more Protestant than Catholic. The influence upon this writer of contemporary neo-Protestant theologians is generally recognized and the repeated use of Kierkegaard's categories radically modifies the Catholic vehicle employed. The most Catholic statement this writer has so far made is the paper contributed to the Yale Divinity School series of Beecher Lectures in the spring of 1950. As we have said above (Ch. I) he here drew a systematic line between the layman and the priest of so sharp a character as to presuppose a completely Catholic view of the church, grace and the sacraments.

On the other hand, in a paper submitted in connection with the Princeton Bicentennial conferences in 1948 he distinguished three contemporary solutions of the modern predicament of belief: (1) Greek humanism: identification with "immortal

[4] See Ch. X, section 6, below.

contemplative mind"; (2) primitive religion: modern versions of sacrifice and magic; (3) Christian humanism: acceptance of the revelation of the truth by God to man, with the consequent conversion of man's Flesh (body and mind) by the Spirit. Notable in the argument was the demonstration of the failure of secular humanism and the invocation here of Kierkegaard, Nietzsche and Freud. The first of these made it clear once and for all that the objective thinker, the scientific humanist, forgets that he is in an existential situation: he leaves out three-quarters of the problem. Nietzsche and Freud showed further that every such humanist, scientific or contemplative, is a "haunted thinker," and, moreover, that his supposed objective "truth" is only strategy and mask, i.e., rationalization.

Auden's view of the relations of poetry and religion rewards study. This writer unquestionably uses his poetic gift for didactic purposes and betrays that "interfering spirit of righteousness" which was assigned to the Puritans long ago. In his practice Auden offers us a Christian witness directed both to our social and our spiritual need. In his theory, however, he warns against confusing the poet and the prophet.[5] The temptation of poetry in our period has been to occupy the religious vacuum consequent upon modern disbelief. The poet must be more modest, says Auden. Jacques Maritain in his own way has pointed out the same danger. The older patterns of poetry have of late been enriched by the free use of symbol drawn from the unconscious. The poets have learned much as to resources for communication from the deeper life of the soul: "the contemplation of the depths" as Maritain calls it. Upon such contemplation there ensues a "release of images." The breakdown of traditions in our time invites the poet to such exploration and to the surrealist or apocalyptic expression

[5] "Criticism in a Mass Society," in *The Intent of the Critic*, ed. by Donald A. Stauffer (Princeton: Princeton University Press, 1941), pp. 127-147. Also, "Squares and Oblongs," in *Poets at Work*, Essays by Rudolf Arnheim, etc., Introduction by Charles D. Abbott (New York: Harcourt, Brace, 1948), pp. 163-181.

that is appropriate. Maritain holds that this is all to the good if the modern poet avoids the danger here of confusing such prerational experience and such oracular deliverances with grace itself or genuine religious authority.

Auden agrees here. The poet must not ascribe to himself the role of seer or prophet. If he does so he degrades himself into a magician. That is, he is manipulating, exploiting certain phenomena of the psyche or of esthetic experience for ulterior purposes. Auden speaks of him as a purveyor of "spurious emotions," and sees him really as motivated by an impious impulse to "make free with necessity." He becomes a false "healer." No, the poet must be more modest. He must look on his work as a higher kind of play, a kind of artifice, a "game of knowledge," "a bringing to consciousness (by naming them) of emotions and their hidden relationships." Auden's diatribe here is directed not only against prophets of a pagan mysticism or vitalism but also against the sway of sentimentalism in traditional poetry.

It is a Protestant instinct in him, intensified by the dialectical rigor borrowed from Kierkegaard, which breeds this caution against all the intoxications and disorders of contemporary art. But Auden overstates himself. He arraigns that whole tradition from the Greeks to the present which assigns a quasi-religious authority to the poet. He rejects Aristotle's conception of *katharsis* in connection with the function of the drama. He accuses Milton of assigning too important a function to the poet. He is especially scornful of Shelley and ridicules the latter's claim that the poets are the "unacknowledged legislators of the world." He appears to be animated by such a fear of false prophets in an age of Pied Pipers that he would abase the poets completely, or at least confine them to a kind of "intellectual play," or an intellectual-imaginative artifice.

His plea for modesty among the poets is most pungently expressed in his paper, "Squares and Oblongs," in *Poets at Work:*

The Prophet says to men: "Thus saith the Lord." The poet says firstly to God: "Lord, do I mean what you say?" And secondly to men: "Do you mean what I mean?" Agit Prop [i.e., the agitator propagandist] says to men: "You mean what I say and to hell with the Lord who, even if he exists, is rotten with liberalism, anyway." [6]

Thus Auden would dissociate the poet from all propaganda, even for the best causes.

But he vastly oversimplifies the matter. Even if a deliberate didacticism is to be excluded, yet values, presuppositions, and norms transpire in every poet and it is a matter of importance even esthetically what these are. Auden recognizes as much in other statements. Furthermore his own work shows it. He is himself the teacher, the didactic writer, sometimes in the bad sense where his plastic imagination fails, often in a persuasive and admirable way. Thus he teaches original sin and yet freedom and responsibility; he urges lucidity and honesty; he preaches social democracy; he insists on the unity of truth against all contemporary relativism; while art is not life he holds that we must recognize the interdependence of ethics, politics, science, and esthetics. He holds that *The Waste Land* (by T. S. Eliot) shows us that to be without belief is to be lost.

In his "A Christmas Oratorio" Auden celebrates the incarnation in a way that often reminds us of T. S. Eliot.

> We who must die demand a miracle.
> How could the Eternal do a temporal act,
> The Infinite become a finite fact?
> Nothing can save us that is possible:
> We who must die demand a miracle.[7]

What is distinctive is the orchestration of the different facets of the incarnation in terms of the familiar images of secularism and of the present social and psychological situation. From a

[6] P. 177.
[7] *For the Time Being*, p. 68.

theological point of view the "Meditation of Simeon" is specially interesting. The poet is careful to exclude all docetism, a danger to which the Catholic emphasis on the incarnation is always exposed. Here the Flesh is united to the Word "without magical transformation" (p. 117), and so "by Him is the perpetual recurrence of Art assured." That is, our human life remains human and our Christian art remains human. There is no false cleavage between the Flesh and the Spirit, though the former is saved by the latter. Again, writes Auden, the Word is united to the Flesh "without loss of perfection" (pp. 117, 118). This not only safeguards the finality and ultimacy of the redemption and solves the problem of the One and the Many, but so "Science is assured," "because in Him abstraction finds a passionate 'For-the-Sake-Of.' " The point here is that truth is really *given,* so that science and philosophy can know that they are not wandering in the dark. Thus also they receive a vital motivation to their tasks.

Auden then succeeds both in registering what is, in effect, a Protestant protest against false culture and false prophets, and in presenting a positive faith and morality in Anglo-Catholic terms. What makes both highly significant, however, is that in him the Christian tradition is wedded intimately to the empirical circumstances, the spiritual and intellectual climate of today. In him we see the initiation of the religious spirit into the full gamut of the modern experience: modern science, modern psychology, modern sociology, the modern sensibility and alienation. Here he enables us all better to understand ourselves—more effectively in breadth and in depth than in height, indeed. This empiricism and realism with the consequent relevance of his ,solutions we may put down to his long detachment from any binding Catholic pattern of life and symbolism.

Auden exemplifies only one of the ways in which Protestantism has artistic expression. He is the secularist who has returned to the faith and who possesses and exploits the full panoply of the modern man in his Christian utterance. But there are also poets and artists of Protestant connection whose faith is vital in their work but who have not had his wide initiation. They can speak to those within the fold but not to those without. They have not sojourned in the wilderness and their immunities have narrowed their significance. Yet like many gifted Catholic poets their songs may be all the more unsullied, not to say intelligible, in view of this handicap! Finally there are the poets without ostensible religious preoccupation who nevertheless derive from Protestantism. Many of the most significant talents of our time are to be counted here. They are the ones of whom we have spoken earlier in whom Protestantism acts as a leaven rather than a tradition. They are children of the church who have been caught up in the dilemma of the age, who are struggling at first hand with its major heresies, and whose faith is "for the time being" uncrystallized. But they carry with them, unrecognized and under disguises, the faith of their background, and in their isolated and pioneering situations contribute to the new Christian synthesis. A relevant and powerful version of Christianity for the time to come will emerge as much from the explorations of such prodigals as from the stay-at-homes of the tradition, as the case of Auden himself shows. But our special gratitude will go to those who today in the new accents of today show themselves victorious over the ills that paralyze so many, who render harmless the toxins and miasmic vapors all about us, and who so fulfill the promise of the gospel: *"They shall speak with new tongues; they shall take up serpents; and if they drink any deadly thing, it shall not hurt them; they shall lay hands on the sick, and they shall recover."*

IX

THE SHAKING OF THE FOUNDATIONS

They know not, neither do they understand;
They walk to and fro in darkness:
All the foundations of the earth are shaken.
                        Psalm 82:5

THE situation that determines the arts today is not a local or national one, but an international one, as wide as the secularized and industrialized culture which increasingly extends around the earth. Therefore the representative artists and poets today are not regional or national but international and planetary. Their world-wide character betrays itself in the words from many foreign languages used in a single poem, in the atlas character of the geographical allusions and settings, and in the deracinated and expatriate status of the artists themselves. Examples here are the *Cantos* of Ezra Pound and the poems of T. S. Eliot in both of which not only American and European, Teutonic and Latin, but also Occidental and Oriental elements appear side by side. The same thing appears in the exile theme and panorama of St.-John Perse. In Joyce's *Ulysses* and especially in his *Finnegan's Wake* this racial totality has its extreme expression. When the peculiar cultures of the various peoples are attenuated and disintegrated by similar forces they all take on a likeness to each other, and the common disintegration makes for a common consciousness. The paradox arises that peoples can understand each other in terms of a common disorder and a common language of disorder.

Again, the situation that determines the arts today is not a superficially contemporary one. The disorder is of such a general kind that the man's deeper nature is involved in it, that which he shares with all men and all times. It is not merely passing social disarrangements and ideological conflicts which disturb us. Cultural dilemmas with their roots in the long past have today their acute and public expression. This accounts for the inwardness and poignancy of our personal disorder. And, again, the representative artists and poets today are not concerned with the contemporary social problems, nor with the recent traditions of this or that land or people, but with man in his long past and with the ancient sagas and myths, rituals and arts, tumuli and cities, that document his universal story. The same writers offer themselves as illustrations. *The Waste Land* links our age with those that have gone before back to the earliest cultures, just as it links East and West. The *Cantos* pass back and forth across the centuries and have their background in early myths of metamorphosis and descent into Hades. St.-John Perse's *Anabasis* deals with man exploring and building on the verge of pre-history. *Finnegan's Wake* is planetary and racial both in the horizontal and the vertical, the special and temporal, sense.

In an essay, "T. S. Eliot as the International Hero," [1] Mr. Delmore Schwartz supports the two themes we have stated.

> Eliot's work is important in relationship to the fact that experience has become international. We have become an international people, and hence an international hero is possible. Just as the war is international, so the true causes of many of the things in our lives are world-wide, and we are able to understand the character of our lives only when we are aware of all history, of the philosophy of

[1] *Partisan Review*, Vol. XII, No. 2 (Spring, 1945), pp. 199-206. Reprinted in Leonard Unger (ed.), *T. S. Eliot: A Selected Critique* (New York: Rinehart, 1948), pp. 43-50.

history, of primitive peoples and the Russian Revolution, of ancient Egypt and the unconscious mind. Thus again it is no accident that in *The Waste Land* use is made of the *Golden Bough* and a book on the quest of the Grail.

Pound is an American in Europe too, and Pound, not Eliot, was the first to grasp the historical and international dimension of experience, as we can see in an early effort of his to explain the method of the *Cantos* and the internal structure of each *Canto*: "All times are contemporaneous," he wrote, and in the *Cantos* he attempts to deal with all history as if it were part of the present.

1. THE NEW APOCALYPSE

The breadth and depth of the modern consciousness as we have stated it enable us better to understand the character of the crisis with which we are confronted today. It is not only a political crisis (nationalism on the one hand, but a fifth column in every land dissolving age-old patriotic loyalties). It is not only a social crisis (the aspirations and revolt of the masses). It is not only a culture crisis in the sense of the dissolution of standing folkways, rituals and myths. It is even something other than a spiritual crisis, though the confusion of values and faiths is great, and it is a difficult time in which to "discern the spirits" and to say which are demonic and which represent the Spirit of God. We could also say that while we have with us a psychological crisis, evident in the widespread neurosis and psychosis and in the general psychological insecurity of extensive classes, yet this is not basic.

The crisis is deeper than any of these. It is an existential crisis. It is a crisis of man's deepest self. As Berdyaev has said, the image of man is dissolved. We have an invasion of chaos in the soul. Dr. Nathan A. Scott, Jr., has given the title *Rehearsals of Discomposure* to his studies of the modern writers, D. H. Lawrence, Kafka, Silone and Eliot. The crisis is an existential crisis, but it is all these others also. And the point is that all these other crises, social, cultural, psychological, etc., take on their peculiar character just because the existential crisis affects them all. For example, the insecurity of the proletariat or of the urban middle class would not be so fateful or so destructive if it were not compounded with this deeper crisis.

What, again, is this deeper crisis? The language used with regard to it sounds melodramatic, but points to the truth. We are all familiar with expressions of Paul Tillich. He speaks of the "sense of the abyss." He speaks of the "shaking of the foundations." Others speak of nihilism: that is, the loss of roots in modern culture, the solvent actions of positivistic science, the dehumanization of our economic order, have brought men face to face with nothingness, and so with certain experiences of vertigo, horror, nausea, estrangement. Even where the predicament is not felt at its most acute, there is a widespread sense of anxiety, and Auden speaks of the "Age of Anxiety."

It is interesting to find the many ways in which the term "apocalyptic" has been resurrected to apply to our time and its expressions. We have a school of "apocalyptic poetry." Narratives of the end of the world are written by such different figures as the Swiss novelist, Ramuz, and the Trappist poet, Thomas Merton, in his *Figures for an Apocalypse*. The three acts of Thornton Wilder's *The Skin of our Teeth* deal respectively with three crises of human survival: the ice age, the flood, and our contemporary world-wars. Many poets have rehearsed the themes of the destruction of the Cities of the Plain, Bunyan's City of Destruction, the fall of Rome to the barbarians, or the scenes of the Book of Revelation—as in Joseph Auslander's *Riders at the Gate*. The last section of *The Waste Land* speaks of

>   Falling towers
>   Jerusalem Athens Alexandria
>   Vienna London [1]

[1] *Collected Poems of T. S. Eliot: 1930-1935*, p. 88.

A similar situation to ours gave us the biblical imagery of the earth made void, the sun's light failing, the moon turned to blood, the stars falling from heaven, the conflict of spiritual agencies. Or the imagery of the flood is used, and Merton writes in one of his poems:

> Flesh cannot wrestle with the waters that are
> in the earth . . .[2]

The youngest generation of English poets, those that have emerged since 1939, include a special group that identifies itself as "The New Apocalypse." Apart from Dylan Thomas the best known names here are those of Henry Treece, Alex Comfort and J. F. Hendry. This group has published a series of anthologies, of which the first is entitled *The New Apocalypse: An Anthology of Criticism, Poems and Stories*.[3] The term apocalypse is somewhat vaguely used by these writers. They all show a strong influence of symbolism. Mr. Nicholson observes that "in its emphasis on the value of imaginative experience it is a reaction against scientific materialism."[4] But the volumes in question are above all marked by surrealistic fantasia and preoccupation with the end of time. The manifestoes of the movement indicate that the experience of war in our time, particularly the second World War, had revealed as by a flash of lightning aspects of reality which beggared the familiar methods of poetry and art. Young writers already familiar with the exploration of the subconscious and the use of myth were thus driven to a surrealist presentation of what underlies our violent and disastrous culture, but not our culture alone.

One of the interpreters of the school, J. F. Hendry, compares their characteristic imagery to "a sort of fluorescent screen on which something of the deeper structure of reality

---

[2] "Death"; *Man in the Divided Sea*, p. 127.

[3] By Dorian Cooke, J. F. Hendry, Henry Treece, D. Thomas, et al. (London: The Fortune Press, n. d.). On this group see the discussion in Francis Scarfe, *Auden and After* (London: Routledge, 1942).

[4] *Man and Literature*, p. 212.

is revealed. A germ of decay and rebirth lurks here which Apocalyptic writing attempts to photograph for the philosopher and the social scientist." [5] These writers feel their kinship with painters old and new like Hieronymus Bosch, Breughel, El Greco and Georgio de Chirico. Biblical elements are common in their work and in some cases a Christian orientation. The work of Nicholson and Dylan Thomas which we have quoted in Ch. V exemplifies some aspects of the movement.

Thus modern art and poetry are aware of this deeper crisis and make it known to us. And they are shaped by it. We have a different kind of art, at least as compared with that of the more recent past. The new art and literature take us back to William Blake's visions, to Dostoievsky's dramas of evil, to El Greco's spiritualities. Many contemporary writings and paintings remind us of the Book of Revelation. They are violent, phantasmagoric, surrealist. We have hallucinatory visions, allegories of Everyman, myths of death and transfiguration, apocalypses of Satan and Christ, demons and angels, tableaux of earthquake and catastrophe.

But the sense of apocalypse and judgment always carries with it the sense of new worlds opening. The time of crisis is a time of opportunity. "Behold, I make all things new." It is as though the membrane between man and the spiritual world had grown tissue-thin, or had even been broken, and strange new powers were at work in the world. There is an Ashanti hymn chanted at the height of their annual dance, when the orgy has finally succeeded in breaking through into the world of the spirits:

> The door of the ghosts has opened,
> The Father has come!
> The door of the ghosts has opened,
> The Father has come!

[5] *The White Horseman: prose and verse of the new apocalypse* (London: Routledge, 1941), p. 9.

THE NEW APOCALYPSE

So the pilgrimage and dark initiations of the modern soul have brought it to a dead end which proves to be a door:

> The door of the ghosts has opened.

And so we find intimations and portents of resurrection and new creation in the artists and poets. When the modern soul has gone through this stark nihilism and this drama of ultimate evil, there is reason to think that for many the Christian faith commends itself as the answer. Thus Ignazio Silone writes: "The rediscovery of a Christian heritage in the revolution of our time remains the most important gain that has been made in these last years for the conscience of our generation." And Mr. Wallace Fowlie speaking of the surprising influence today of the French Christian prophet, Charles Péguy, says: "Catastrophes were necessary—and sufficiently cosmic, in order to shatter all the forms of modern optimism—for Péguy's work to be revealed and justified." [6]

What we have said about the present crisis and its characteristic art helps us again to answer the questions that many men have with regard to traditional poetry. Is it really any wonder that writers like Masefield and Bridges, Alfred Noyes, Vachel Lindsay, Edwin Markham and a host of others do not speak to the modern soul? Is it surprising that Tennyson and Browning, Emerson and Whitman, are not for this place or for this hour? Is it any wonder that we go back rather to Herman Melville and his white whale, to Hawthorne and his symbolism of evil, to Blake, to the French symbolists, Rimbaud, Baudelaire, to John Donne, and indeed, to Dante, to Ezekiel, to the flood, the Fall of Man, and to the original myths of creation and chaos?

One of the most significant aspects of this new experience appears in the clean break with the idea of progress so characteristic of nineteenth-century thought and poetry. The idea

---

[6] *Jacob's Night*, p. 4.

of catastrophe if not of world judgment eclipses the vision of continuity. Even when the poet gathers up in his work the story of man from his earliest beginnings and marshals the saga and exploits of older empires, it is to exhibit the sameness and not the evolution of the species. The oldest myths, whether of the Fisher King or of the Fall, whether of Ulysses or of the Tower of Babel, are contemporary. Pattern is given to the welter and jungle of human society not by historical development but by myth. The locus of the soul is not in London or New York or Vienna but at the barred gate of Eden or with Odysseus on his journey, or with Kafka's hero before the court of the unaccountable judges. Just so the locus of the soul in the *Divine Comedy* is a mythological three-fold geography that takes little account of the world's times and places.

How revolutionary a perspective this is for men with our background appears when we recall the confidence in progress and the emphasis on the time process which has characterized us. Thus Reinhold Niebuhr writes:

> The dominant note in modern culture is not so much confidence in reason as faith in history. The conception of a redemptive history informs the most diverse forms of modern culture . . . though there are minor dissonances the whole chorus of modern culture learned to sing the new song of hope in remarkable harmony. The redemption of mankind, by whatever means, was assured for the future. It was, in fact, assured by the future.[7]

One must say that the writers with whom we are here concerned offer a correction in our view of history which points towards the Christian understanding. This latter, while it is teleological, thinks in terms of judgment and remnant, not general progress. However, a great deal of the secular poetry of crisis today falls back on a cyclical conception of history, native to classical mythology and primitive ritual. Yeats on

[7] *Faith and History: A Comparison of Christian and Modern Views of History* (New York: Scribners, 1949), pp. 3, 6.

the whole belongs in this camp while Pound's *Cantos* have been identified with the similarly ancient conception of universal flux.

Yeats' poem, "The Second Coming," which announces not the return of Christ but the anti-Christ at a new nativity in Bethlehem is probably the most widely quoted, even canonical, expression of the modern crisis. This poem does not, indeed, look beyond the vision of evil. First we get the overt social picture:

> Things fall part; the centre cannot hold;
> Mere anarchy is loosed upon the world,
> The blood-dimmed tide is loosed, and everywhere
> The ceremony of innocence is drowned;
> The best lack all conviction, while the worst
> Are full of passionate intensity.

Then comes the vision of the Beast which for twenty centuries has been asleep and vexed with nightmares occasioned by the Christian mystery. (Yeats sees the blood-redemption of this mystery as having a morbid and obsessive aspect which while it has quickened culture has also provoked men to frenzy and violence.)

> Surely some revelation is at hand;
> Surely the Second Coming is at hand.
> The Second Coming! Hardly are those words out
> When a vast image out of *Spiritus Mundi*
> Troubles my sight: somewhere in sands of the desert
> A shape with lion body and the head of a man,
> A gaze blank and pitiless as the sun,
> Is moving its slow thighs, while all about it
> Reel shadows of the indignant desert birds.
> The darkness drops again; but now I know
> That twenty centuries of stony sleep
> Were vexed to nightmare by a rocking cradle,
> And what rough beast, its hour come round at last,
> Slouches toward Bethlehem to be born? [8]

[8] *Collected Poems of William Butler Yeats* (New York: Macmillan, 1937), p. 215.

Note that this poem was published in 1921. One can at least see how prophetic it was in the light of the second World War. But more deeply the vision of evil, with "A gaze blank and pitiless" as the desert sun, renders something which is familiar to our generation, and which older poets like those named above did not confront. Yeats' poem is apocalyptic, and conveys the blank horror of an apocalyptic time. This is all the more significant since Yeats was not a poet who was earlier predisposed to this kind of a revelation.

What confirms our thesis is the fact that explicitly Christian writers and artists today exhibit this same catastrophic sense. Mr. Fowlie's comment on the French Catholic painter, Rouault, is striking. This painter "paints the 'last things,'" he says, as an "eschatological artist." The idea of Satan dominates but the crucifixion is at the center of all his work. Fowlie speaks of his "'dark frenzy," his "ignominy before the absolute," and his "awesome introspection."

Our point here is not that Christians should allow themselves to be swept into nightmares and pessimism, but that even Christians, if they are imaginatively aware, should recognize the wrestling with evil that is going on in the deeper culture of our time, and achieve some identification with it. Christian poets like Eliot and Auden are doing it. Christian novelists like Bernanos and Graham Greene are doing it in their medium. A Christian painter like Rouault does it in his. Christian critics like Eliot himself, Brother George Every in his volume, *Christian Discrimination,* Norman Nicholson, Fowlie and others carry the witness into philosophy and esthetics. In all such ways bridges are being built between the Christian faith and the secular mind; a powerful movement of Christian apologetic is under way; and the gospel is in confrontation with the world at profound levels.

Before we go on, however, we should attempt to meet some of the questions that will arise in the minds of many readers with regard to what we have so far said. Many are puzzled by this modern poetry. This apocalyptic crisis sounds esoteric to them. This preoccupation with evil, this talk about the "abyss" and the "age of anxiety" seems unreal, and especially to the theologically minded sounds uncomfortably like Kierkegaard and neo-orthodoxy! After all, it will be said, this kind of experience, this sense of ultimate crisis, this predicament of nihilism, is not something we actually meet among our friends, in our typical neighborhoods or Christian parishes. Such people indeed have their troubles, but most of them are normal, healthy breadwinners and housewives like their fathers and mothers of the last generation, or like their Victorian forebears, for that matter. They do not feel that the world is being dissolved, nor are they greatly haunted by nightmares. The older generation bore up under the first World War and the depression with courage, and our own generation went through the second World War similarly. Moreover, it will be urged, the art they like and that most people like is traditional art. It still speaks to them. They don't see why Keats and Shelley, Tennyson and Browning, Walt Whitman and Robert Frost, should be depreciated. And they will probably agree with the charge against current fads well stated by Archbishop Trench, who speaks of "the worship of the fleeting present, of the transient fashions of the hour in language, with contempt of that stable past which in all likelihood will be the enduring future, long after these fashions have passed away and are forgotten."

Now we wish to make it clear that we sympathize with a great deal of this protest. We are confronted with a complex cultural situation, and various experiences, various moods, and various voices have their respective justification. In particular there are groups and strata in our middle classes in this country that are relatively healthy and secure, which have not, therefore, felt the strains and stresses of the age. They live, that is, in the same climate as their fathers in important respects, and this is not said in criticism. Modern men are not all equally exposed to what is, nevertheless, a general crisis of a wholly extraordinary character. We have traditional values and traditional arts and they are not to be depreciated. But we also have a catastrophic era of change, and it will not do to speak of "fashions" in connection with its manifestations. A good many areas of our society are protected from the social and the spiritual insecurities of this crisis by buffers, protections, guard-rails. There are good buffers: inherited faiths and community forces, especially in the Christian church and in democratic traditions. There are bad buffers, where men make themselves precariously secure by fences of property or social power. But what we urge is that no such protections or privileges should or can really isolate us from the deeper insecurities of the times. Even our so-called healthy strata are affected and undermined by the changes. It is later than we think. The problem of meaninglessness, the sense of anxiety, haunt many who are perhaps not yet aware of it. Camus' novel, *The Plague,* is a parable of the subtle encroachment of a strange malady upon a society that believes itself healthy.

We should not therefore depreciate the art and the literature of the nineteenth century or of the Georgians, but we can well assign it its special relevance and limitations. Similarly with regard to the arts which reflect our crisis.

We propose now to document this crisis by further citations from contemporary poetry. Note that we are passing over writing that deals first of all with political and social matters. Many of our poets began with such concerns, but have been led deeper. Let us choose rather certain selections which exhibit what we have called the existential level or predicament. First, the sense of evil and helplessness. Second, themes of purgation.

2. *THE VISION OF EVIL*

First, then, the sense of sin, of moral and metaphysical evil, and of being helpless in its sway. It is true that many modern intellectuals believe that they do not believe in the soul, and claim that the pangs of conscience represent social prejudice or a super-ego of which we should free ourselves. Karl Shapiro, in his *Essay on Rime*,[1] notes, however, that the modern intellectual for all his sophistication, cannot keep away from the sense of guilt.

> In our neutrality
> Of spirit we cannot countenance the soul
> Or treat with it except as ectoplasm,
> That is with humor and sophistication.
> Yet curiously we note a chronic spasm
> Of guilt in rime suggesting that morality
> As the conflict of inborn good and evil
> In human nature is still a force. We play
> Semantically upon these attributes
> Which once were the omnipotent and perfect
> Prongs of the magnet of all life and death,
> And holding to this neutral course we claim
> The discovery of a science in behavior
> Our talk of which dilates on right and wrong,
> Values in point-of-view, criteria
> In taste, and criticism in everything.[2] (lines 1868-83)

But much poetry today shows that the problem of good and evil is treated as a desperate matter. We choose a confession found in an older poem of Conrad Aiken, "Tetelestai": here modern man with all his achievements acknowledges that he cannot "capture the secret of self," and is a "helpless beholder" of the war in his heart.

> I, the restless one; the circler of circles;
> Herdsman and roper of stars, who could not capture
> The secret of self; I who was tyrant to weaklings,
> Striker of children; destroyer of women; corrupter
> Of innocent dreamers, and laugher at beauty; I
> Too easily brought to tears and weakness by music,

[1] New York: Reynall and Hitchcock, 1945.
[2] Pp. 64-65.

> Baffled and broken by love, the helpless beholder
> Of the war in my heart of desire with desire, the struggle
> Of hatred with love, terror with hunger . . .[3]

It has been pointed out that men today are conscious of a special kind of despair—a lucid sense of their entanglement in evil, social and psychological. They recognize the strength of the roots of evil, and the toughness of the fibres or cables that knit the structures of habit and custom. This despair has been explored and set forth by imaginative writers with the use of Freudian tools. But T. S. Eliot has deepened the awareness of our lostness, partly by confronting it with the glories of man's spiritual past, but especially by invoking the blazing revelation of the gospel. So man cries out in "Gerontion":

> After such knowledge, what forgiveness?

The sense of being hopelessly trapped is strikingly expressed by Delmore Schwartz, the emphasis here being not on guilt but on the iron sense of impersonal fate. In the poem the speaker has been spying on a happy family scene in a comfortable home, with music by firelight and servants moving about; and he goes on:

> It is time to shake yourself! and break this
> Banal dream, and turn your head
> Where the underground is charged, where the weight
> Of the lean buildings is seen,
> Where close in the subway rush, anonymous
> In the audience, well-dressed or mean,
> So many surround you, ringing your fate,
> Caught in an anger exact as a machine![4]

"Caught in an anger exact as a machine": here is a striking expression for the sense of an automatic fate, an impersonal

---

[3] *Selected Poems* (New York: Scribners, 1938), p. 160.

[4] "Tired and Unhappy" in *In Dreams Begin Responsibilities* (Norfolk, Conn.: New Directions Press, 1938), p. 131.

THE VISION OF EVIL

hell, in which men are caught. One cannot help thinking of Paul's conception of the "wrath," or wrath of God, which for him too is a kind of impersonal process in which men are "caught" and from which they are only delivered by grace.

We can fill in this sketch of the modern sense of evil now by three quotations from Mr. W. H. Auden. Though his recent work evidences a Christian position, he has been so deeply identified with the modern temper that he is still its unique spokesman. Our citations are all taken from his volume, *The Age of Anxiety*.[5]

First, we note a passage in which, again, confession is the keynote. For all our claim to be enlightened we still pray to primitive gods; and even our worship is a kind of mumbo-jumbo, or, as he says, "galimatias," which we go through as a way of escaping from our responsibility to our neighbor:

> for plainly it is not
> To the Cross or to Clarté or to Common Sense
> Our Passions pray but to primitive totems
> As absurd as they are savage; science or no science,
> It is Bacchus or the Great Boyg or Baal-Peor,
> Fortune's Ferris-wheel or the physical sound
> Of our own names which they actually adore
> As their ground and goal. Yet the grossest of our dreams is
> No worse than our worship which for the most part
> Is so much galimatias to get out of
> Knowing our neighbor;[6]

A second passage satirizes our illusions of progress and points out that we are really dreary automatons. Here again is the theme that men have lost their spiritual freedom, and have let themselves be "caught" in an inflexible process that spells damnation.

> Led by that liar, the lukewarm Spirit
> Of the Escalator, ever timely,
> His whims their will, away from freedom

[5] New York: Random House, 1947.
[6] P. 136.

> To a locker-room life at low tension,
> Abnormal none, anonymous hosts
> Driven like Danaids by drill sergeants
> To ply well-paid repetitive tasks
> (Dowdy they'll die who have so dimly lived)
> In cozy crowds.[7]

Auden is particularly effective in blasting the superficiality and smugness of Christians, and this charge is all the more pungently put in the mouth of the Jewess, Rosetta, in the poem. The passage suggests why many modern men are due for disaster even if they have not come face to face with it. "You conventional, hearty and bumptious Christians," she says in effect, "cannot know what real desperate faith means, as we anxious Jews have to know it. You have a nice 'household god' that brings you luck, and a 'Harpist's Haven for hearty climbers' to look forward to in the next life."

> You're too late to believe. Your lie is showing,
> Your creed is creased. But have Christian luck.
> Your Jesus has wept; you may joke now,
> Be spick and span, spell out the bumptious
> Morals on monuments, mind your poise
> And take your cues, attract Who's-Who,
> Ignore What's-Not. Niceness is all and
> The rest bores . . .
>   [you] couldn't accept
> Our anxious hope with no household god or
> Harpist's Haven for hearty climbers.[8]

There are, indeed, many today who need to have their illusions punctured, but the deeper mood of today is that which we have illustrated earlier. The crisis is closely connected with the breakdown of illusions, especially with an exaggerated confidence that science and technics could meet all our needs.

[7] *Ibid.*, pp. 43-44.
[8] *Ibid.*, p. 124.

THE VISION OF EVIL

The new psychic insecurity and its consequent deepening of our experience of mystery make possible a new humility. And modern poetry and art serve a prophetic function in dramatizing this situation. William Van O'Conner in his recent volume, *Sense and Sensibility in Modern Poetry*, makes much of the theme that one of the great contributions of modern poets has been the renewal of the vision of evil, which had been banished by the dogma of absolute rationality.

One index of the sense of evil and of our world's irrevocable entanglement in evil is the recurrence of what one could call secular prayers, ejaculations for deliverance, voiced by these poets. One could make a considerable anthology of such passages, suggestive of the groping faith of our time.

Not to be omitted here is Auden's well known "Petition" which at first startles the devout reader by addressing God as "Sir" until he recalls that John Donne did the same. The petitions are in refreshingly contemporary metaphor and for that reason awaken a sense of urgency. Here is no "rehearsed response."

> Sir, no man's enemy, forgiving all
> But will his negative inversion, be prodigal:
> Send to us power and light . . .
> Prohibit sharply the rehearsed response
> And gradually correct the coward's stance . . .
> Harrow the house of the dead; look shining at
> New styles of architecture, a change of heart.[9]

From Louis MacNeice we take another petition in which again a sense of reality is found precisely in the admitted agnosticism:

> O thou my monster, Thou, my guide . . .
> O pattern of inhuman good,
> Hard critic of our thought and blood,

[9] *The Collected Poetry of W. H. Auden*, pp. 110, 111.

> By whose decree there is no zone
> Where man can live by men alone,
> Unveil thyself that all may see
> Thy fierce impersonality.[10]

One of the greatest areas of disorder and of anguish in contemporary life is that of the relation of the sexes. Mr. Schwartz has shown how frustration here recurs as a theme in T. S. Eliot's poetry.

> The difficulty of making love, that is to say, of entering into the most intimate of relationships, is not the beginning but the consequence of the whole character of modern life. That is why the apparatus of reference which (this) poet brings to bear upon failure in love involves all history ('And I Tiresias have foresuffered all') and is international.[11]

In these circumstances the distinctions between lust and love are confused and the thirst for love rightly understood is not fulfilled. It is out of this desperation that Miss Anne Ridley utters a prayer, first prefixing four lines from T. S. Eliot's "Ash Wednesday."

> "Terminate torment
> Of love unsatisfied
> The greater torment
> Of love satisfied."
>
> O Love, answer the hammering heart:
>   Only in love we live; then prove
> That quickening good, take your own part,
>   Show us that all your modes are one.[12]

In his poem, "The Last Days of Alice," Allen Tate has in

---

[10] "Prayer in Mid-Passage," *Springboard* (New York: Random House, 1945), p. 43.
[11] "T. S. Eliot as the International Hero," *op. cit.*, pp. 199-206.
[12] Anne Ridley, "Poem," *Poetry, A Magazine of Verse* (June, 1949), p. 141.

mind Alice who has passed through the looking glass, and who has thus lost her real human nature. This he sees as a figure of our own alienation:

> We too back to the world shall never pass
> Through the shattered door, a dumb shade-harried crowd . . .
>
> O God of our flesh, return us to Your wrath,
> Let us be evil could we enter in
> Your grace, and falter on the stony path! [13]

Finally a poem about Boston on a windy Sunday in March by Robert Lowell, a young New England poet who became a Roman Catholic convert. The poem is really about the garish Carnival of the world and the day of judgment. We quote the last verse with its closing cry for a new Adam:

> On Troy's last day, alas, the populous
> Shrines held carnival, and girls and boys
> Flung garlands to the wooden horse; so we
> Burrow into the lion's mouth to die.
> Lord, from the lust and dust thy will destroys
> Raise an unblemished Adam who will see
> The limbs of the tormented chestnut tree
> Tingle, and hear the March-winds lift and cry:
> "The Lord of Hosts will overshadow us." [14]

From the vision of evil to prayer for deliverance, and from the urgency of prayer to the process of purgation. Here we see that the "shaking of the foundations" opens up truly redemptive possibilities.

3. THE THEME OF PURGATION: MR. ELIOT'S THE FAMILY REUNION

In Eliot's play, *The Family Reunion*, we have a particular study of guilt and contrition. The case portrayed here is of a man

---

[13] *Poems: 1922-1947* (New York: Scribners, 1948), p. 115.
[14] "The First Sunday in Lent," *Lord Weary's Castle* (New York: Harcourt, Brace, 1944), p. 15.

who carries an intolerable burden of guilt with regard to his wife and her death. It is all the more characteristic that no actual deed of crime had clearly been committed, but hostile feelings had been cherished. Thus this character came to feel a complicity in the fatality. All men and women who have reached a certain age, can understand such a contrition bearing on family relations, particularly with regard to their parents. William Blake in his series of paintings portraying the life of Everyman and entitled "The Gates of Paradise" confirms the idea. Youth is represented as brandishing a spear against the breast of his father, who exclaims, "My son! My son!" Of course when we explore the situation of parents and children, the wrong of parents to children is disclosed also. So it is in Eliot's play, and so it is in Blake's pictures. But also the role in the tragic past of all members of the family: the brothers and sisters, and others. The mistakes and conflicts of the past are seen as infinitely sad and irremediable. Retrospect in any family recognizes the lost possibilities, what might have been, the fateful miscarriage. In the family Eliot finds a paradigm of the human situation and a motive to purgation. Emerson, in a retrospect on the lost years of his childhood and youth, speaks of how these memories are tinged with "infinite compunctions." I quote lines from *The Family Reunion*[1] which reflect the sense of remorse for the irretrievable, and men's sense of impotence in the grip of lovelessness and its penalties. Here is a profound expression of how appalled modern man can become when he comes face to face with the results of his behavior—the realization that some things cannot be changed, that the past, present and future are linked inexorably together, and that there is no help for it until grace finds a way.

> And whatever happens began in the past,
> and presses hard on the future . . .

[1] T. S. Eliot, *The Family Reunion* (New York: Harcourt, Brace, 1939).

> All are recorded.
> There is no avoiding these things
> And we know nothing of exorcism
> And whether in Argos or England
> There are certain inflexible laws
> Unalterable, in the nature of the music.
> There is nothing at all to be done about it,
> There is nothing to do about anything.[2]

In the following scene three degrees of the torments of guilt are stated. The first is "isolation—that's one hell." Next, "the numbness . . . the second hell":

> I felt, at first, that sense of separation,
> Of isolation unredeemable, irrevocable—
> It's eternal, or gives a knowledge of eternity,
> Because it feels eternal while it lasts.
>   That is one hell.
> Then the numbness came to cover it—
>   that is another—
> That is the second hell of not being
>   there,
> The degradation of being parted from
>   myself . . .
> All this last year I could not fit myself together:
>
> . . . I not a person, in a world not of persons
> But only of contaminating presences.

The third degree of torment is defined as

> A new torture
> The shadow of something behind our meagre
>   childhood
> Some origin of wretchedness.

This last points to those deeper piers and ancient buttresses of inherited evil in the family and in society which first act as

[2] Part II, Scene 1, pp. 93, 94.

a bane upon childhood; the legacy of the sins of the fathers and the forefathers.

Now this is not morbidity or a special case, but an attempt to be honest with the evil in the heart. In the closing scene of the play the leading character goes out to seek purgation and innocence through suffering. He turns himself over eagerly to the Eumenides or Furies whose mission of torment he recognizes to be for his own salvation. In Eliot's more recent play, *The Cocktail Party*,[3] the author describes the state of mind of modern men in much the same terms. One of the characters, Celia, in an interview with her counsellor, Sir Harcourt-Reilly, speaks as follows about her sense of solitude, and then of the need for atonement:

> It isn't that I *want* to be alone,
> But that everyone's alone—or so it seems to me.
> They make noises, and think they are talking to each other;
> They make faces, and think they understand each other.
> And I'm sure that they don't. Is that a delusion?[4]

Then she speaks of her "sense of sin":

> It's not the feeling of anything I've ever *done*,
> Which I might get away from, or of anything in me
> I could get rid of—but of emptiness, of failure
> Towards someone, or something, outside of myself;
> And I feel I must—atone.[5]

Men recognize more and more clearly that our private self-love and hostility are directly related to the public disorder and to the emergence of violence and tyranny on the social scene. So writes Auden, and draws the lesson.

---

[3] New York: Harcourt, Brace, 1950.
[4] P. 134.
[5] Pp. 136, 137.

> Whole phyla of resentments every day
> Give status to the wild men of the world . . .
> Our claim to own our bodies and our world
> Is our catastrophe . . .
>
> How much must be forgotten out of love,
> How much must be forgiven, even love.
>
> There must be sorrow if there can be love.[6]

We turn now for our most moving instance of this theme to a poem written during the recent war by the American poet, Marianne Moore, certainly one of the greatest poems written by an American in connection with the war. The poem is entitled, "In Distrust of Merits."[7] In this poem the writer identifies herself utterly with the atrocious costs of the struggle— the wasted lives, the agonies, cruelties and immitigable losses— and cries out against pride and blindness, against the

> small dust of the earth
> that walks so arrogantly,

against

> the blind
> man who thinks he sees,—
> Who cannot see that the enslaver is
> enslaved; the hater, harmed.

Then she is led by the appalling character of "the fighting, fighting, fighting,"

> some
> in snow, some on crags, some in quicksands,—

she is led to acknowledge that the pride is within, within herself, within all of us. There is a movement of revulsion, "in

---

[6] "Canzone," *Collected Poetry of W. H. Auden*, pp. 162, 163.
[7] *Nevertheless* (New York: Macmillan, 1944), pp. 12-14.

distrust of merits." She wistfully hopes that she may be cleansed by it.

> It cures me; or am I what
> I can't believe in?

And the poem concludes with these two stanzas.

> . . . The world's an orphans' home. Shall
> we never have peace without sorrow?
> without pleas of the dying for
> help that won't come? O
> quiet form upon the dust, I cannot
> look and yet I must. If these great patient
> dyings—all these agonies
> and woundbearings and blood shed—
> can teach us how to live, these
> dyings were not wasted.
>
> Hate-hardened heart, O heart of iron,
> Iron is iron until it is rust.
> There never was a war that was
> not inward; I must
> fight till I have conquered in myself what
> causes war, but I would not believe it.
> I inwardly did nothing.
> O Iscariotlike crime!
> Beauty is everlasting
> and dust is for a time.

The poem ends thus in a deep self-abasement, yet in an ascription of praise to that eternal beauty which we all forefeit; ends on a note of genuine purgation. Miss Moore has succeeded in penetrating all the willfulness and hardness of even good men today—that *refusal to see* which conditions our whole stalemate of social and international and private conflict. She has touched a note of tragic humility which could solve most of our problems, if men would only let themselves be taught by what they have seen and felt in our desperate time.

Let us go back to the statement of Silone quoted earlier. "The rediscovery of a Christian heritage in the revolution of our time remains the most important gain that has been made in these last years for the conscience of our generation." But if the modern world is to be aided in finding its way back to the Christian faith, the Christian church must meet the seekers half way. This means particularly that in their witness and worship the Christian people must learn to exhibit a sobriety, a chastity of mood that will show that they too, at least in imagination and sympathy, have passed through the deep places, the baptisms of suffering, that many of their contemporaries have known. This does not mean lugubriousness or solemnity; in fact, it can mean sweetness and joy. But the brassiness and complacency, the conventionality in worship, which prevail too often, shock many unbelievers, and drive them into the liturgical churches where at least they find some measure of reverence and a recognition of mystery.

Think of some of the wide groups about us who still stand outside the churches, but for whom, "the door of the ghosts has opened," and who could bring inestimable resources into the churches. There are many ex-soldiers for whom a religion if it be insipid can mean nothing. There are the countless members of broken homes, partners and children, who have suffered corrosion of heart and starvation of affection. There are the victims of the special psychological disasters which our modern urban Vanity Fair prepares for so many. There are the specially sensitive and gifted people, including artists and intellectuals, who have not been able to stand the impersonal Waste Lands of our dehumanized culture, and who have cracked up. There are the marginal groups in business life or labor or farming on whom recurrent insecurity and false values have finally left their mark. And there are the vast number of secularized men and women who have just reached the point of meaninglessness and hollowness. What we have called the existential crisis has touched all such, the vision of evil, the impulses toward catharsis. Such people, if they move toward the church, will feel themselves rebuffed unless they find there at least genuineness and sobriety; in worship, reverence; in Christian people, especially ministers, real disinterestedness and spiritual tact. If they do not find these things they will gradually evolve their own versions of religion or cult, or even their own versions of the gospel outside the traditional churches.

X

VICISSITUDES OF CHRISTIAN BELIEF

WHAT affirmations are made, what affirmations are possible, in this age of crisis, this age of anxiety in which we live? It is not, first of all, a question of doctrinal beliefs. It is the question: What do men live by today? And we rightly turn to literature and the arts in seeking an answer. The present discussion will restrict itself in two respects. We shall give our attention in the central part of the chapter to characteristic poems of two of our contemporary poets. We believe that we can generalize significantly from this selection. In the second place we shall focus on writers who would not be identified with an orthodox or dogmatic position.

1. THE DILEMMA OF FAITH

The conditions of our time make for a wide gamut of belief. Many groups have found themselves alienated from the great religious and cultural traditions. They have thus been led, negatively, to disbelief, but also, positively, to shape their own alternate faiths. It is important for us to understand the difficulties men have today with traditional patterns of belief, indeed, their difficulties in making any affirmations at all. It is also of interest to see that the exiles from tradition, the heretics if such they are, the explorers—writers who represent so many men of our modern world—these are often not so far from the great faiths of the past as may at first sight appear.

We must preface our discussion with certain observations and cautions. In the first place we should not underestimate the value of affirmations that are not expressly dogmatic or confessional. In faiths which some might be disposed to call merely esthetic or at least ambiguous, we nevertheless draw near to the hungers and aspirations of countless souls today. We live in a catastrophic period. The foundations have been shaken, and multitudes of men can find no home either for their minds or their hearts in the older religious institutions. It is a matter of poignant and grave interest to observe how they deal with the harshness of the age and the ambiguities of its loyalties.

We would also caution against the view that optimism is a fair test of art or poetry. It is true that in the greatest literature we look for great affirmation. But if we exclude all art or poetry that lacks such explicit faith we rule out a vast amount of profoundly significant work. Especially in a time like ours it is inevitable that the experience of evil will occupy a large place in the contribution of the imaginative artist. No doubt ultimately "poetry is praise" and poetry is joy, but real poetry must take up into its praise and joy the negative aspects of our experience as men.

Moreover, affirmation in art is properly implicit rather than explicit. The poet is rather an image-maker than a preacher, a celebrant than a teacher. It is true that poetry and religion are consubstantial in their origins. The poet at risk of being a magician in the bad sense cannot finally be distinguished from the seer and prophet. Yet the poet ministers to true belief and right conduct not by indoctrination or didactic, but by enabling us to *see*—in Goethe's sense of *schauen*.

Affirmation in modern works is then often only implicit. It is also, granted, often swamped in negation or even despair. This only underlines the fact that faith here is hard won. The implicit courage or affirmation is all the more significant.

Men too often want easy solutions, even in our noblest religions. But Judaism and Christianity should be able to recognize the rights of pain and dismay.

That the Victorians were protected or exempt from some of the shocks that we have had to meet explains why much of their literature has qualified appeal for us. They had their troubles like all the sons of Adam, but different kinds of troubles. The Christian affirmation of the great Victorians, as of more recent writers such as Francis Thompson, Vachel Lindsay, Masefield, appears to us now to have suffered from a limited context and experience. We have only to name contemporaries of some of them: Dostoievsky, Baudelaire, Melville, men who broke out of the framework of their age, to recognize these limitations.

Thus modern affirmation is hard won. It speaks out of intimate initiation into our cultural and spiritual crisis. This means, of course, the social crisis of world wars and economic costs. But more deeply it means the psychological strains that have accompanied the crisis: the dehumanization and lostness of the modern soul. There is something peculiarly poignant and magnificent in the spectacle of men wringing art and celebration out of these nightmares, and saying "Nevertheless" in the midst of the distempers that afflict the spirit today, and which afflict particularly the most gifted and sensitive.

We may well begin by attending to a study of our topic by a contemporary American poet, Karl Shapiro. We refer to the third section of his poem, *Essay on Rime*,[1] this section being entitled, "The Confusion in Belief."

Shapiro begins this section with a passage on Hart Crane, the strange and gifted ecstatic whose poem, *The Bridge*, is recognized as one of the few near-great achievements of our century in poetry. Crane sought in this work to project an American myth; having in mind, indeed, Walt Whitman, but

[1] New York: Reynal & Hitchcock, 1945.

using other methods and giving a larger place to the reality of evil. Crane makes no special use of the Christian tradition but seeks to build his encompassing vision out of the local myth and legend of the American scene, and the promise of technological achievement. Here is a faith, indeed, but interpreters of the work have connected its miscarriage with its thin utopianism. As one critic has suggested, Crane was strong when he leaned on Melville, weak when he leaned on Whitman. Moreover, he sought not only to build a myth but to make a religion of his art. Here he is typical of many modern poets. Unable to believe in any of our inherited faiths, and driven into a corner by the immense sway of science and rationalism, they have perforce been led to explore and exploit their subjective and irrational experience as a religious substitute.

Shapiro then turns to D. H. Lawrence. With a genuine religious vision this writer raged against the devitalized secularism and moralism of his day. He espoused an affirmative paganism more substantial than that of Crane, which may have something to do with the fact that he could survive while Crane's effort ended in suicide.

Shapiro then lists what he calls, "new and substitute beliefs," beginning with the faith in inevitable progress and its Marxian version, and following on with the Freudian phase of naturalism. But, as he says,

> By nineteen twenty the thin ice of belief
> Had cracked and given way. The figure-skater
> Of rime had sunk beneath the lake, and art
> Took on a deep and submarine aspect.
> (lines 1716-19)

This leads to a canvass of the more recent "poetry of disbelief," the early work of T. S. Eliot and the eventual anarchy of what he calls "personal systems." In these each poet wrote out his own "synthetic myth" but one in which he could not genuinely believe.

THE DILEMMA OF FAITH

> So various
> And multifoliate are our breeds of faith
> That we could furnish a herbarium
> With the American specimens alone.
> (lines 1828-31)

He then concludes with an indictment of the esoteric and impoverished character of the work of a host of moderns of the second rank.

> The frenzied poet
> Exhausted in the half-lit cage of science,
> Pretending faith and weak identity
> With his subjective soul is not the Faust
> Who stormed the door of Hell and roused the Devil.
> (lines 1852-56)

What are the causes for the difficulty of affirmation in our time? The prevailing explanation is that the older faiths are no longer meaningful. To put it in current terms: the myths are dead. By myths here are meant the older pictures of the world and of life, so long a part of our cultural and religious heritage in the West, pictures which offered an explanation of things and in which generations have found security and meaning. This means above all the Bible's story of the world, the drama basic to Milton's *Paradise Lost,* but also the interpretations of human existence offered in classical literature. These roots of our culture, these structural elements of life-affirming faith—it is said—have lost their claim upon us. The causes lie above all in the diffusion of the rationalistic, positivistic outlook since the seventeenth century. Science and its outcomes have destroyed the myths and the faiths connected with them. But a second factor bears especially on the Christian world-view. The modern man and the modern artist have found the Christian outlook ascetic and world-denying despite its message of eternal salvation. Let us now examine certain writings of two contemporary poets in their bearing on these matters.

2. MR. ALLEN TATE'S "SONNETS AT CHRISTMAS"

We turn first to Allen Tate's "Sonnets at Christmas." [1] Here we have the cogitation of a modern upon the ambiguity of the Christian faith today. The two sonnets express the difficulty of believing the Christian story and yet the need to believe it. We are reminded of Hardy's well known poem, "The Oxen." [2] There, it will be recalled, the poet, on Christmas Eve, is reminded of the pretty superstition that at midnight the cattle kneel, and he writes,

> I should go with him in the gloom,
> Hoping it might be so.

But instead of being merely wistful as Hardy is, Tate is dead serious, though after an ironical fashion. It is not possible for him, despite a sense of "crime and punishment" to be shriven.

> Therefore with idle hands and head I sit
> In late December before the fire's daze
> Punished by crimes of which I would be quit.

The trouble, he implies, is connected with our modern overemphasis on knowledge:

> . . . Man, dull critter of enormous head,
> What would he look at in the coiling sky?

That is, our kind of sophistication can see no heavenly host nor can it hear the angel's song. For us Christ is not alive but dead, and the bells of Christmas are only the tinsel bells hung in the living room, and they ring out only silence.

> But I must kneel again unto the Dead
> While Christmas bells of paper white and red,
> Figured with boys and girls spilt from a sled,
> Ring out the silence I am nourished by.

[1] *Poems, 1922-1947* (New York: Scribners, 1947), pp. 50, 51.
[2] *Collected Poems of Thomas Hardy* (New York: Macmillan, 1926), p. 439.

Notice the symbolism: the "boys and girls spilt from a sled"—pictured on the gay decorations, represent the lives of men and women spilt by death. And the poet, ironically and tragically, is nourished by silence, that is, he is not nourished at all.

As Delmore Schwartz reads the poem: "the ego of the poem is incapable of enjoying this Christmas as a day of feast partly because he is a dull critter of enormous head, an intellectual animal; partly because of the great difficulty of belief. He cannot believe, nor can he disbelieve. His difficult case is that he must kneel—to one whom he must call the Dead, with but an hour of life—he must look at the sky and he must argue his difficulty . . . It is easier to believe or to disbelieve than it is to maintain this poise between belief and disbelief which the sonnet presents. The honesty in question at the outset is fully exemplified in this difficult case."[3]

In a series called "More Sonnets at Christmas: Ten Years Later,"[4] Tate records the same dilemma. In one impulse he would free himself from being haunted and inquisitioned by a Christ who never rose:

> Ten years are time enough to be dismayed
> By mummy Christ, head crammed between his knees.[5]

But then he considers the other options open to him. Why should he not give himself entirely to an uninhibited pagan freedom, say, some reckless arrogant life of action, perhaps of a bombardier, whose fear, if any,

> Is of an enemy in remote oceans
> Unstalked by Christ: these are the better notions.

---

[3] *Southern Review*, V, 3 (Winter, 1940), p. 426.

[4] *Poems, 1922-1947*, pp. 52-55.

[5] In one of his more recent poems the "I" of the poem makes his appeal to "Venus"—as the vital principle of love—to return to the world, since Christianity is no longer potent:
> the drying God above,
> Hanged in his windy steeple,
> No longer bears for us
> The living wound of love.
> "Seasons of the Soul," *ibid.*, p. 33.

But these sonnets end in an admission that it is too late. We have been captives too long—condemned to a starved and meagre fare. Even if we emancipate ourselves at this late date we shall find that we are still helpless in the chains of habit.

> Your ghosts are Plato's Christians in the cave.
> Unfix your necks, turn to the door; the nave
> Gives back the cheated and light dividend
> So long sequestered; now, new-rich, you'll spend
> Flesh for reality inside a stone
> Whose light obstruction, like a gossamer bone,
> Dead or still living, will not break or bend.

That is, we have lived too long facing away from reality like those in Plato's allegory of the cave. If now we turn towards the light rather than the shadows—the light so long "sequestered," that is, held off—and if we seek to live the full free life that should be ours, we shall find that we are still prisoners of the cave. All sorts of intangible, gossamer-like fears and scruples and habits will still rule us.

> You will be Plato's kept philosopher,
> Albino man bleached from the mortal clay.

The secular man of today, says Tate, the man who seeks to cast off his Christian past cannot be a good pagan made of rich red earth, but only an albino whose mortal clay is bleached!

We have here an ever-recurring protest of the modern artist, not against Christianity as such necessarily, but against the impoverished forms of it that have held such wide sway in the modern world, both Protestant and Catholic. We have already noted the scorn of the Jewess, Rosetta, in Auden's *Age of Anxiety*, spoken to the Christian, condemned

> To a locker-room life at low tension . . .
> (Dowdy they'll die who have so dimly lived.) [6]

[6] New York: Random House, 1947, p. 44.

3. MR. WALLACE STEVENS' "SUNDAY MORNING"

The second illustration of the difficulties of Christian faith in our time is found in Wallace Stevens' "Sunday Morning," [1] one of the most quoted of his poems. It offers us the soliloquy of a woman having her late coffee and oranges on a sunny porch on Sunday morning. Her enjoyment of the calm scene is invaded by thoughts of "the ancient sacrifice" of Christ, and her revery deals with what we would call "the offense of the cross," the contradiction between the natural joys of men and the harshness of the Christian story and claim.

> She dreams a little, and she feels the dark
> Encroachment of that old catastrophe,
> As a calm darkens among water-lights.

And her dreaming passes

> Over the seas to silent Palestine,
> Dominion of the blood and sepulchre.

> Why should she give her bounty to the dead?
> What is divinity if it can come
> Only in silent shadows and in dreams?
> Shall she not find in comforts of the sun,
> In pungent fruit and bright-green wings, or else
> In any balm or beauty of the earth,
> Things to be cherished like the thought of heaven?

The speaker in the poem speculates as to whether we should set our hope on Paradise after the present life. But no, she is

---

[1] Reprinted from *Harmonium* by Wallace Stevens by permission of Alfred A. Knopf, Inc., copyright 1923, 1931 by Alfred A. Knopf, Inc., pp. 89-94. See the discussion of the poem in both its original and modified form in Lloyd Frankenberg, *Pleasure Dome* (Boston: Houghton, Mifflin, 1949), pp. 215-218.

content with earthly beauties.[2] After all, no old legends of Paradise or the Hesperides have "endured—As April's green endures." And yet

> She says, "But in contentment I still feel
> The need of some imperishable bliss."
> Death is the mother of beauty; hence from her,
> Alone, shall come fulfillment to our dreams
> And our desires.

Paradise itself would become insipid without death. Thus, she decides, our best hope is here on earth, and our best ritual is a chant to the sun. And the poem draws to its conclusion as follows:

> "The tomb in Palestine
> Is not the porch of spirits lingering;
> It is the grave of Jesus, where he lay."
> We live in an old chaos of the sun,
> Or old dependency of day and night,
> Or island solitude, unsponsored, free
> Of that wide water, inescapable.
> Deer walk upon our mountains, and the quail
> Whistle about us their spontaneous cries;
> Sweet berries ripen in the wilderness;

---

[2] A similar this-worldly affirmation is expressed in Ezra Pound's "Blandula, Tenulla, Vagula":
> What hast thou, O my soul, with Paradise?
> Will we not rather, when our freedom's won,
> Get us to some clear place wherein the sun
> Lets drift in on us through the olive leaves
> A liquid glory? If at Sirmio,
> My soul, I meet thee, when this life's outrun,
> Will we not find some headland consecrated
> By aery apostles of terrene delight,
> Will not our cult be founded on the waves,
> Clear sapphire, cobalt, cyanine,
> On triune azures, the impalpable
> Mirrors unstill of the eternal change?
>
> Soul if She meets us there, will any rumor
> Of havens more high and courts desirable
> Lure us beyond the cloudy peak of Riva?
Selected Poems (New York: New Directions, n. d.), p. 13.

> And, in the isolation of the sky,
> At evening, casual flocks of pigeons make
> Ambiguous undulations as they sink,
> Downward to darkness, on extended wings.

The waiving of the Christian faith here would seem to be connected with its alleged anti-naturalism, asceticism, refusal of the beauty and goodness of our creaturely life. As we have said elsewhere in connection with Yeats: "For the poets the scandal of Christ is his asceticism. The very medium of their art as poets; indeed, the very element of their experience as men, is the gamut of human living, emotions, drama. 'Man's resinous heart' and the loves, loyalties, the pride, the grief it feeds—these are the stuff of poetry and the sense of life. And the Cross lays its shadow on this; it draws away all the blood from the glowing body of existence and leaves it mutilated and charred in the hope of some thin ethereal felicity. The wine of life is changed to water. The spectrum is surrendered for an undifferentiated and commonplace white light. The 'dramatic caves' of the human heart and imagination are renounced for some wan empyrean of spiritual revery." [3] Illustration of this view is found in Yeats' colloquy with the great Catholic, Baron von Hügel, as we noted in Chapter VII. Yeats writes that his role of poet predestines him to his unbelief—only out of the lion can come forth sweetness:

> I—though heart might find relief
> Did I become a Christian man and choose for my belief
> What seems most welcome in the tomb—play a predestined part.
> Homer is my example and his unchristened heart.
> The lion and the honeycomb, what has Scripture said?
> So get you gone, Von Hügel, though with blessings on your head.[4]

[3] *The Spiritual Aspects of the New Poetry*, p. 196.
[4] "Vacillation, VIII," *Collected Poems of William Butler Yeats* (New York: Macmillan, 1937), p. 290.

The implication is that a Christian so sterilizes his heart that there is no concern left for art and the rich play, the riot and fecundity of life. It is as though the proper treasury of poetry was "the lust of the flesh, the lust of the eyes, and the pride of life."

4. THE OUTRIDERS AND THE TRADITION

Thus in the matter of Christian belief there are today major obstacles for the poet and artist, as there are for the modern man generally. We have illustrated two such obstacles. In the case of Tate, attention is given to modern man's rationalism, with its counterpart of the "uneducated heart." Man is a "dull critter with enormous head"; his intellect, his sophistication, has taken on a disproportionate role. He has become critic, observer, analyst, scientist to such an extent that a seal has been placed upon the springs of impulse, upon the myth-making and myth-believing faculties, upon the vital prodigality of the unconscious, upon the eternal child that man should always remain, upon the organic, intuitive, spontaneous sense of life which man should always have as a creature in the great web of being.

In the case of Stevens, as in that of Yeats, we see a second great obstacle to Christian affirmation: the supposed world-denial or false asceticism of Christianity. Our faith appears to say "no" to life, to be a blasphemy against the beauty and goodness of the natural order. Here, indeed, a very basic issue is raised, even when we recognize that many such charges are very superficial. The Christian cannot but admit that the poet is partly right. The Christian religion as men meet it too often justifies the criticism. What we have said about Stevens and Yeats could be said of D. H. Lawrence and others. Indeed, the rebellion against formal Christianity of older poets and prophets of the nineteeenth century here falls into line.

The best literary expressions of our secular culture can be

understood on one side as the protest of the modern soul against the starved and meagre aspects of the Christian heritage in this period. These writers, whether romantic or transcendentalist, symbolist or surrealist, from William Blake and Shelley down to Yeats and Joyce, can be understood as Christian voices, heretical, indeed, protesting against the narrowing and stifling of the Christian faith. They demand, if often on the basis of misunderstandings, and often in ways that are erroneous and even perilous, that the yea-saying impulse of the biblical faith and its moment of creative play be given their due place, and that this "yea" should be spoken not only to the spirit but also to the flesh, not only to grace but to nature. This is a necessary protest even if a dangerous one. It has a strong element of antinomianism in it. But there is a genuine kind of antinomianism in the gospel itself and in St. Paul in particular. Despite the tension occasioned by the sense of cosmic drama and catastrophic outcomes, the first Christians exhibit a simplicity and liberality of spirit (*haplotes*) and an uninhibited confidence (*parresia*) which were incompatible with moralism or insensitivity. Christianity represented a prodigious release of faith and its crowning theme was the glory of God. The great rebirths of Christianity in the midst of the years, whether in St. Francis or the Reformation, have in their various ways recognized that the chief end of man is to glorify God and enjoy Him forever. This means that the end of life is lifted above all self-centeredness and moralism into a sharing in the works of the Creator.

Much of the best witness of the modern poets, novelists and artists whom we have mentioned, including many lesser figures, represents a groping for this richer content of the Christian tradition, indeed of the Christian faith itself, and stands as a warning to the theologian and churchman. We may call such figures the outriders of the faith. They continue its explorations, its advance and its witness at a distance from the main body. If they are heretics we may yet recall the paradoxical thesis that the blood of the heretics is often the seed of the church. We should, indeed, recognize the contribution even of those that are well outside the faith. It is not the first time that providence uses the unbeliever to instruct the church. Herein is the saying fulfilled:

> And he shall convict Israel through
> the chosen Gentiles
> As he convicted Esau through the Midianites.
> *Testament of Benjamin* 10:10

It is true, moreover, that these heretics have been martyrs, secular martyrs. The struggle, persecution, loneliness of figures like Shelley, Nietzsche, D. H. Lawrence, James Joyce or of some of the modern painters like Van Gogh, represents an anguish of the modern cultural crisis, and these men have known what it costs to say "yes" to life when even the church, not to mention our Philistine dehumanized age, has said "no."

In saying these things we must, of course, be very clear that the characteristic work of these modern voices is compounded with genuine heresy, and is in various ways neo-pagan, antinomian in a bad sense, sometimes blasphemous. Thus Shelley like Santayana platonizes radically in his conception of redemption. Nietzsche, and Jeffers, presumably, confuse the poor in spirit and the meek with the slave or the craven. D. H. Lawrence is not content to recognize the sacredness of the flesh and the wisdom of the dark powers of the blood but exalts these at the expense of the full personal life. Yeats would seem to fail of the Christian perspective as appears in his cyclical conception of history and his dualism of world and spirit. But the definition of heresy is not always easy with changes in the dominant philosophies and categories. Milton was heretical in important particulars. Pascal's thought roamed across the recognized limits of his day. Especially in a time like ours when the landmarks are in disarray, our task is, indeed, always to "test the spirits," but our test will

5. THE LATER STEVENS: "CREDENCES" AND "FICTIONS"

We have spoken of reasons why modern writers find it difficult to make specific Christian affirmations. There are, of course, those who do but we are not here dealing with them. But even the others do have their affirmation. Tate and Stevens, for example,[1] both praise and celebrate man's life. Tate is concerned with that full richness of our human experience which science cannot lay hold of, and with the repossession of the religious and cultural values of his southern tradition as a way of meeting both the enigmas of life itself and the bleakness of our present culture. Like T. S. Eliot in this respect he affirms tradition in reactionary wise. Spokesman of a "fierce latinity" he is a debtor to Christian Mediterranean culture, and he values the Christian rites and symbols as expressions of that essential significance which a modern has such a hard time possessing. In his Christmas poems and in his extraordinary poem, "The Cross," he shows both how world-shaking was the coming of Christ, and what profound intimations of existence it opens up to the imagination.

Stevens' affirmation of life has been at least suggested in the citations from his "Sunday Morning." He wonderfully conveys the glorious play of the imagination in its marriage with reality. On one side of all his work there is the insistence that reality and beauty are to be found in the "flesh." Here hedonism passes over into philosophy and parallels a fundamental criticism of various forms of either idealistic or dogmatic theology. The most significant movements in theology today are those that are most audaciously incarnationist, not only with regard to our understanding of the nature of Christ but with regard

[1] Mr. Tate has more recently identified himself with an explicit Christian position. The poems cited may, however, be taken as significant for the modern crisis of faith.

to revelation generally. We are ever more aware of the dangers of "docetism," of any tendency to deny the human nature of Christ or to remove the theatre of the divine encounter outside of our concrete historical situation. We have rediscovered the naive and nonmetaphysical realism of the Bible and especially its positive view of the time process. Thus we are learning to suspect ancient or modern forms of "gnosticism" all of which wrongly transpose salvation to the realm of ideas or limit it to the experience of the "soul."

We find a pertinent analogy of this corrective recurrently in Stevens:

> Beauty is momentary in the mind—
> The fitful tracing of a portal;
> But in the flesh it is immortal.[2]

> The greatest poverty is not to live
> In a physical world.[3]

On the other hand Stevens recognizes that the mind, the imagination, the word and the myth enhance the immediate experience. It is the perpetual interplay of imagination and reality, of "fiction" and fact, which constitutes the life of the soul, and which offers us the real at a new level.

Another point at which this poet's thought has its analogies with contemporary theological reconstruction appears when he writes:

> The death of Satan was a tragedy
> For the imagination [4]

The passage in which this occurs is, assuredly, far removed from a theological disquisition, but the poem as a whole, "Esthétique du Mal," deals with evil and with war. The myth

[2] "Peter Quince at the Clavier," reprinted from *Harmonium* by Wallace Stevens by permission of Alfred A. Knopf, Inc., copyright 1923, 1941 by Alfred A. Knopf, Inc., p. 134.
[3] "Esthétique du Mal," reprinted from *Transport to Summer* by permission of Alfred A. Knopf, Inc., copyright 1942, 1947 by Wallace Stevens, p. 52.
[4] "Esthétique du Mal," *ibid.*, p. 45.

THE LATER STEVENS

of Satan is important because it enables us to admit and not suppress a part of reality, and then to call it all, nevertheless, good. But the denial of Satan furthermore betokens the loss of sensibility.

> How cold the vacancy
> When the phantoms are gone and the shaken realist
> First sees reality.[5]

It is true that the poet must take up the theme of evil into his song:

> Life is a bitter aspic. We are not
> At the center of a diamond.[6]

But the new chant will exhibit all of truth's favors.

Section X of this poem is very revealing on a number of religious issues. We shall cite the entire section and add a rough paraphrase and comment:

> He had studied the nostalgias. In these
> He sought the most grossly maternal, the creature
> Who most fecundly assuaged him, the softest
> Woman with a vague moustache and not the mauve
> *Maman*. His anima liked its animal
> And liked it unsubjugated, so that home
> Was a return to birth, a being born
> Again in the savagest severity,
> Desiring fiercely, the child of a mother fierce
> In his body, fiercer in his mind, merciless
> To accomplish the truth in his intelligence.
> It is true there were other mothers, singular
> In form, lovers of heaven and earth, she-wolves
> And forest tigresses and women mixed
> With the sea. These were fantastic. There were homes
> Like things submerged with their englutted sounds,
> That were never wholly still. The softest woman,
> Because she is as she was, reality,

[5] *Ibid.*, p. 46.
[6] *Ibid.*, p. 48.

> The gross, the fecund, proved him against the touch
> Of impersonal pain. Reality explained.
> It was the last nostalgia: that he
> Should understand. That he might suffer or that
> He might die was the innocence of living, if life
> Itself was innocent. To say that it was
> Disentangled him from sleek ensolacings.[7]

The poet has studied the "nostalgias," i.e., those traditional, well-beloved myths and gods of the past. Among these he passed over the sentimental ones which disguise the tonic reality of evil and suffering (cf. sections III-V). Yet reality has a maternal gentleness and it is in terms of the woman that he conceives it. But again not as an indulgent "Maman" but a mother conceived in terms of "savagest severity" both as regards his body and his intelligence. It is true that myth and religion offer archaic goddesses, whether Cybeles or Madonnas, but these are "fantastic" and not at hand. Reality itself is both tender and fierce; "the softest woman," yet gross and fecund. But even here the last nostalgia that we must deny ourselves is the presumption that we can reach final explanation. But that life is innocent, i.e., that there is no malice in the gods (see "Auroras of Autumn" below), is only fully grasped when we accept suffering and death as part of our proving and an aspect of the "mother." Thus we are disabused of false self-pities and sentimentalities.

In this whole volume, *Transport to Summer*,[8] we find a freer approach to ultimate matters, always, indeed, in terms of the poet's "fictions." In "Credences of Summer," the plenitude of the season has that in it which

> must comfort the heart's core against
> Its false disasters—these fathers standing round,
> These mothers touching, speaking, being near,
> These lovers waiting in the soft dry grass.[9]

---

[7] *Transport to Summer*, pp. 47, 48.
[8] New York: Knopf, 1947.
[9] *Op. cit.*, p. 105.

THE LATER STEVENS 249

Here the conviction grows that

> The utmost must be good and is
> And is our fortune and honey hived in the trees
> And mingling of colors at a festival.[10]

The term "certainty" enters in connection with the vision of reality, like a mountain of truth, proffered by the season.

> But it is not
>
> A hermit's truth nor symbol in hermitage.
> It is the visible rock, the audible,
> The brilliant mercy of a sure repose,
> On this present ground, the vividest repose
> Things certain sustaining us in certainty.[11]

Such affirmation is superbly expressed in an even more recent poem, "The Auroras of Autumn,"[12] in which Stevens meditates the aurora borealis. Here even when the "transport" of summer is past and winter is at hand an abiding plenitude offers its sign from beyond the earth. A man, he says,

> opens the door of his house
>
> On flames. The scholar of one candle sees
> An Arctic effulgence flaring on the frame
> Of everything he is. And he feels afraid.

Is there, he asks, "an imagination that sits enthroned" behind all that is—"as crown and diamond cabala?" The reality behind the Northern Lights, the original Beauty, the pure principle of Innocence, is not an illusion. For

> it exists,
> It exists, it is visible, it is, it is.

[10] *Ibid.*, p. 107.
[11] *Ibid.*, pp. 108, 109.
[12] *The Auroras of Autumn*, New York: Alfred A. Knopf, Inc., 1950.

> So, then, these lights are not a spell of light,
> A saying out of a cloud, but innocence,
> An innocence of the earth and no false sign
>
> Or symbol of malice. That we partake thereof,
> Lie down like children in this holiness,
> As if, awake, we lay in the quiet of sleep,
>
> As if the innocent mother song in the dark
> Of the room and on an accordion, half heard
> Created the time and place in which we breathed.

It is true, Stevens acknowledges, that "this imagination that sits enthroned" brings us all and the planets and suns to death. Yet

> these heavens adorn
> And proclaim it . . .
> by way of majesty
> In the sky, as crown and diamond cabala.[13]

It is illegitimate if not impertinent to press theological tests too far in connection with poetry of this kind. But this bears also upon the facile assignment of hedonism to Mr. Stevens by certain critics. He is exploring experience in his own terms and in his own medium.[14] The situation of our religious tradition today for many is so inchoate that even many theologians find it best to wrestle with the problems of life on the new ground of naturalism; how much more the artist. This does not mean that the religious heritage is excluded from their

---

[13] We cannot refrain from citing a passage on the aurora borealis from the *Journals* of Gerard Manley Hopkins which offers a different reading of similar perceptions: "This busy working of nature wholly independent of the earth and seeming to go on in a strain of time not reckoned by our reckoning of days and years but simpler and as if correcting the preoccupations of the world by being preoccupied with and appealing to and dated to the day of judgment, was like a new witness to God and filled me with delightful fears." *Journal* 135. Cited by M. B. McNamee, S. J., in *Immortal Diamond*, pp. 228, 229.

[14] The two following papers by Stevens illuminate his understanding of his art: "The Noble Rider and the Sound of Words," in Allen Tate (ed.) *The Language of Poetry* (Princeton: Princeton University Press, 1942), pp. 91-125; and "Imagination as Value," in D. A. Robertson, Jr. (ed.) *English Institute Essays, 1948* (New York: Columbia University Press, 1949), pp. 3-25.

materials or reckonings. The agreement or disagreement of such explorations with the Christian heritage has to be sought in terms of correspondences and parallels not in terms of the established symbols of the faith. On such a basis it seems proper to note a movement in Stevens from the purview of his work in *Harmonium* (including "Sunday Morning") published in 1923, and the quite recent poems we have here been considering. There is a larger concern with evil in all its aspects, and with ultimates. Affirmation finds more general expression in this context. The perpetual consideration of the myth or the "fiction," indeed, "the supreme fiction," has its religious bearings. Substitute "dogma" for "fiction" in his "Notes Towards a Supreme Fiction," and, here again by analogy we are on Protestant ground when he insists in his second section, "It must change." In what sense it must change is to be sure a crucial matter. But this poet's metaphysic does not, in any case, appear to be one of sheer flux.

6. RECOVERY OF THE TRADITION: MR. AUDEN'S "CHRISTMAS ORATORIO"

The work of Stevens is, in many respects, a special case. His perennial interest has been in the reciprocal relation of reality and the imagination. In this context the central symbols of the Christian faith are not immediately indispensable. It is otherwise with poets acutely exercised by the ethical life. It is difficult today for such poets to find adequate symbols for our personal and social disorder and their ultimate significance apart from the religious terminology of the past. The Jewish-Christian faith, particularly, arose out of revelations occasioned by moral need, though man's relation to nature and the life of reason were involved.

Thus the secular poet of today preoccupied by ethics as well as the general problem of meaning, tends to recur to the biblical tradition. We may take for example of this a poem of Mr.

Delmore Schwartz, whose vision of an impersonal social bondage we have already cited:

> Caught in an anger exact as a machine.[1]

The total work of this author indicates how much he is at home in the sophisticated if not disabused outlook of many moderns. But these circles of artists, critics and poets in their own detached way are often as much preoccupied by the moral and religious dimensions of life as those who are confessionally inclined. The poem deals with the state of mind of the apostles after the crucifixion and is entitled, "Starlight Like Intuition Pierced the Twelve." It would be difficult to name a devotional poem by any of the notable Christian poets of our period that excels it for its evocation of what the crucified and risen Christ meant to his followers. We quote only the fifth and the last two stanzas.

> "And I will never be what once I was,"
> Said one for long as single as a knife,
> "And we will never be as once we were;
> We have died once, this is a second life."
> "My mind is spilled in moral chaos," one
> Righteous as Job exclaimed, "now infinite
> Suspicion of my heart stems what I will,
> —No matter what I choose, he stares at it!"
>
> "And I will always stammer, since he spoke,"
> One, who had been most eloquent said, stammering.
> "I looked too long at the sun; like too much light,
> Too much of goodness is a boomerang,"
> Laughed the eleventh of the troop. "I must
> Try what he tried: I saw the infinite
> Who walked the lake and raised the hopeless dead:
> No matter what the feat, he has accomplished it!"
>
> So spoke the twelfth; and then the twelve is chorus:
> "Unspeakable unnatural goodness is
> Risen and shines, and never will ignore us;
> He glows forever in all consciousness;

---

[1] See above, Ch. IX, p. 218.

Forgiveness, love, and hope possess the pit,
And bring our endless guilt, like shadow's bars:
No matter what we do, he stares at it!
What pity then deny? what debt defer?
We know he looks at us like all the stars,
And we shall never be as once we were,
This life will never be what once it was!" [2]

The movement of W. H. Auden's work towards an explicit Christian statement may be taken as significant for the direction if not the goal of much of the wrestling with the modern situation. As few others Auden has been in position to register the intellectual as well as the spiritual predicaments of the time, both because of the alertness of his intelligence and of the social conscience which characterized his circle. His writing for a considerable period reflected not only the dehumanization and anguish of modern men but also their unbelief.

In his "Christmas Oratorio" [3] we can observe not only these moods but their transmutation into faith, and so have a disclosure of both sides of the same coin. It is one theme of this work that the initiation into estrangement and the exploration of the mistaken courses must proceed to their limit before the way out presents itself.

> For the garden is the only place there is, but you will not find it
> Until you have looked for it everywhere and found nowhere that it is not a desert.[4]

---

[2] *The Kenyon Review*, Summer, 1944, pp. 383-385. Mr. Schwartz's use of this theme is illuminated by the following sentence with regard to *The Waste Land* from his essay, "T. S. Eliot as the International Hero" (Partisan Review, Vol. XII, No. 2 (Spring, 1945): "In modern life, human beings are whirled beyond the circuit of the constellations: their intimate plight is seen in connection or relation with the anguish of the Apostles after Calvary, the murder of Agamemnon, the insanity of Ophelia and children who chant that London bridge is falling down."

[3] *The Collected Poetry of W. H. Auden* (New York: Random House, 1945), pp. 407 ff.

[4] *Ibid.*, p. 412. Cf. H. N. Fairchild, "But the claims of historic Christianity will be resisted so long as there remains the slightest hope of devising a substitute-religion which will proclaim man's ability to redeem himself." *Religious Trends in English Poetry*, Vol. III, p. 512.

What comes with the necessary "miracle" is not a different world but the same world in a different light.

Of particular interest here is the way Auden deals with the two issues our discussion has raised: the tyranny of intellect and the dilemma between affirmation and negation of the natural order. The "Christmas Oratorio" follows the episodes of the nativity narratives in the gospels and orchestrates their implications by means of discourses placed in the mouths of the participants in the familiar scenes and of narrators, choruses and other additions to the cast.

On the eve of the annunciation, a moment at which the secular world always stands, the Four Faculties of man, Intuition, Feeling, Sensation and Thought—corresponding to the four elements in Blake's "Gates of Paradise": earth, water, air and fire—are represented as sundered from each other since the fall of man and, therefore, in their separate anarchic self-assertion, as false guides. The condition of Thought is presented as follows; and here we may bear in mind the inhibition of imagination and faith by intellect in Tate's "Sonnets at Christmas." It is the emptiness of intellect and therefore the vacuity of the life of the autonomous mind that Auden emphasizes. "Thought" speaks:

> ... where I was,
> The haunting ghosts were figures with no ground,
> Areas of wide omission and vast regions
> Of passive colour; higher than any squeak,
> One note went on forever; an embarrassed sum
> Stuck on the stutter of a decimal,
> And points almost coincident already
> Approached so slowly they could never meet.
> There nothing could be stated or constructed:
> To be was an archaic nuisance.[5]

What the incarnation must mean to sophistication is stated by "The Star of the Nativity":

[5] *Ibid.*, pp. 417, 418.

> I am that star most dreaded by the wise,
> For they are drawn against their will to me,
> Yet read in my procession through the skies
> The doom of orthodox sophrosyne . . .
>
> All those who follow me are led
> Onto that Glassy Mountain where are no
> Footholds for logic, to that Bridge of Dread
> Where knowledge but increases vertigo . . .[6]

But the "Oratorio" also deals with the issues of sense and imagination, the renewal of innocence in man's enjoyment of the natural order, thus excluding all false asceticism. The "romantics," caught in an unredeemed "Time and Space" which therefore change Love into voluptuousness, intercede for each other:

> Joseph, Mary, pray for those
> Misled by moonlight and the rose,
> For all in our perplexity . . .
> Pray for us, enchanted with
> The green Bohemia of that myth
> Where knowledge of the flesh can take
> The guilt of being born away,
> Simultaneous passions make
> One eternal chastity:
> Pray for us romantics, pray.[7]

The answer is found in the acclamation of the Wise Men at the manger:

> O Living Love replacing phantasy,
> O Joy of life revealed in Love's creation;
> Our mood of longing turns to indication:
> Space is the Whom our loves are needed by,
> Time is our choice of How to love and Why.[8]

---

[6] *Ibid.*, pp. 428, 429.
[7] *Ibid.*, p. 426.
[8] *Ibid.*, p. 447.

In the words of Simeon the two deliverances are summed up:

> Because in Him the Word is united to the Flesh without loss of perfection, Reason is redeemed from incestuous fixation on her own Logic, for the One and the Many are simultaneously revealed as real . . .

> Because in Him the Flesh is united to the Word without magical transformation, Imagination is redeemed from promiscuous fornication with her own images . . .[9]

Thus the warring faculties of man are restored to a harmonious unity by the incarnation.

We may draw three brief conclusions from the evidence adduced. First, it is true that the larger part of the most significant poetry of today is ambiguous or heretical if tested by our Christian tradition. But secondly, such productions are offering a necessary criticism, correction and protest. Thirdly, such productions when scrutinized more deeply surprise us, for we discover how far they are, after all, rooted in our religious tradition, witness to it, and in some cases move towards its fuller recovery.

[9] *Ibid.*, pp. 452, 453.

XI

THE SURPRISES OF GRACE

"Grace is insidious, it twists and is full of surprises. . . . When it doesn't come from the right it comes from the left. . . . When it doesn't come from above it comes from below; and when it doesn't come from the center it comes from the circumference."

Charles Péguy, *Clio* [1]

DIAGNOSIS of our time in terms of its imaginative literature allows us to speak rather of directions than of solutions or conclusions. For the cultural crisis is still in its acute phase, reflecting itself in a continued medley of tongues and incoherence of artistic expression. At most, perhaps,

> by attending with intense and detached interest to what the imagination (at all levels) presents to us, we may hope to catch at times a hint concerning the myth that is forming at the heart of our world.[2]

Our period, that is, is one of gestation, and on a world scale. What political or social forms are emerging are finally of less significance than the new spiritual orientation. Such an "emergent" involves a new unifying picture of man and the world, what the writer quoted in common with many today speaks

[1] Cited in Halévy *Charles Péguy and Les Cahiers de la Quinzaine*, p. 184.
[2] Miss Louise Bogan, cited in W. V. O'Connor, *op. cit.*, p. 13.

of as a new myth. This term "myth" (or "new myth") is, indeed, ambiguous and will rightly be suspect to those who assign ultimacy to the decisive historical events about which the Christian faith has articulated itself. But this term has at least the merit of suggesting that the heart of our problem today lies deeper than the level of science and social engineering. It also implies the congeniality of the arts to the solution of the problem. Even if we prefer to speak of a reconception of the Christian myth or faith rather than of the shaping of a new myth, the role of the creative spiritual imagination is necessarily in view. For the gestation and communication of ultimate symbols belongs to its domain.

When Berdyaev describes the age on whose threshold we stand as a "new middle age," he means an age in which man's intuitive and myth-making powers take precedence. When he identifies it with the Night in contrast with the last three centuries identified as the Day he means that it will be an age in which the powers of faith and the imagination will have again a dominant role. He draws on painting and poetry for illustration and assigns them a major role in the diffusion of the new awareness.[3] Paul Tillich similarly in his writings dealing with cultural diagnosis assigns a major significance to modern artistic manifestations.[4]

"The myth that is forming at the heart of our world" certainly bears a relation to the Christian faith. That is, we may link this augury of Miss Bogan with Silone's observation to which we have several times referred:

> The rediscovery of a Christian heritage in the revolution of our time remains the most important gain that has been made in these last years for the conscience of our generation.

[3] *The End of Our Time* (New York, 1933, translation of *Un nouveau moyen age*, Paris, 1933).
[4] *The Religious Situation* (New York: Holt, 1932), pp. 53-70; also Section II "Religion and Culture," passim, in *The Protestant Era* (Chicago: University of Chicago Press, 1948).

Silone's statement does not necessarily envisage actual Christian confession on the part of our generation. It announces, however, that the Christian faith has again become relevant and inescapable for men initiated into the modern experience. They are now in a position to recognize that it speaks to dilemmas for which they must have an answer; it speaks to their condition. Thus the new "myth" or vehicle of world-interpretation now evolving will at least take shape out of a renewed wrestling with the Christian tradition. Evidence for this we have noted in our earlier chapters.

Mr. T. S. Eliot is no doubt right in foreseeing a long period of rival faiths and ideologies in the West, many of them not identifiable with Christian belief. The conditions of our life will, however, offer a severe testing of aberrant or shallow faiths. Only a constructive "myth" incorporating the enduring elements of the Hebraic-Christian tradition with their sanctions of personal and ethical values, can survive in the destructive fires of today and, indeed, flourish upon them. But among the elements of our society marked for destruction will surely be found varying aspects of that tradition itself.

1. *SECULAR THEOLOGY AND WITNESS*

The most remarkable feature with regard to the situation of the Christian heritage today is that its custody has to a considerable degree passed over into the keeping of secularized groups and forces. The disarray of institutional religion and the isolation of its more conservative bodies from modern life have left the gospel if not homeless at least in a highly ambiguous position. This has involved the "world" in a peculiar responsibility for the faith and in a process of travail with the faith, in considerable measure apart from the guidance of the church. In secular movements of thought, but especially in the arts and in imaginative literature, the vicissitudes of this struggle are disclosed.

We should, no doubt, recognize that the terms secular and

secularism are used in various senses. Secularism in the most negative sense has been defined as "believing and behaving as though man were an end in himself, as though humanity existed in its own right and for the sole purpose of its own power and glory." This spirit, evidently, where it exists or is consciously formulated, is antithetical to the gospel and even to the broader spiritual traditions of the West. To call our culture secular in this sense is to over-simplify. The fact is that the term is too ambiguous to use as a general category. We prefer to use the term secular in a more general sense and as it is more commonly used. Here it means the way of life, the perspective, the categories of thought and value of that great part of the modern world which has separated itself from traditional religion. Secularism in this sense too is ambiguous. It may mean humanistic self-sufficiency. It may also mean the retention of Christian faith and values in disguised forms. In both senses secularism is found in the religious institutions themselves. Secularism is not necessarily apostasy, declared or tacit. It represents rather a period of dilemma in Christendom occasioned by the modern situation leading to a new formulation and synthesis of the faith.

The church, indeed, bears the clearest witness to the gospel in its testimony and sacraments, but with an uncomfortable awareness that contact and relevance have been forfeited. Another way to say this is that the power of the keys has been shaken. It is no doubt true that the redeemed community, the Body of Christ, retains always in its deepest life, by the Holy Spirit, the authority which inheres in the gospel. But there are times in which the church is called to repentance and in which judgment begins at the house of God. In such times the visible church is or should be chastened in its claims and hesitant in its exercise of the authority to bind and to loose. And in such times it should hear what the spirit says to the churches, speaking through the laity and the disaffected, and even through the apostates and the Gentiles.

Today both the church and the world are under judgment. The future lies with two remnants, a remnant from the church and a remnant from the world. These two remnants are today converging to shape the Christianity of the future. The discarded elements on either side will perish in the catastrophes of the period as some already have, or will remain as devitalized survivals of the past.

The renewal of a tradition is perhaps always inseparable from a period of catastrophe. Life, as Karl Barth has said, emerges at the point of mortification. In a paradoxical way Yeats has stated the same truth.

> Test act, morality, custom, thought in Thermopylae. Love war because of its horrors, that belief may be changed. We desire belief and lack it. Belief comes from shock which is not desired. Belief is renewed continually in the ordeal of death.[1]

Our canvass of modern poetry has documented the responses of the secular world today to the disasters of our time. Even where there has been no explicit movement towards Christian commitment we are aware of a wrestling with the Christian heritage and the assertion of attitudes inseparable from it. An immense spiritual ferment declares itself in imaginative literature, consequent upon the dislocations of culture and tradition and an epoch of violence. These conditions have deepened the dilemmas familiar to nineteenth-century society and have resulted in the extraordinary fact that all the greatest creative works of our time are indubitably theological in character. The modern writer and artist have a "vocation to tragedy." For the most part the tragedy is dealt with as an occasion to insight rather than to cynicism.

The most reassuring feature in the work of the more notable writers, but also of many less gifted ones passed over in our

[1] Cited in M. Channing-Pearce, *The Terrible Crystal* (New York: Oxford University Press, 1941), p. vii.

survey, is the joint note of compassion and responsibility. With the social costs of peace, insecurity, unemployment, homelessness; with the visitations of civil strife and world wars—notable with the loyalist cause in Spain; with the psychological attrition and spiritual bleakness of private man; with all these human needs the writers in question have in one way or another had communion typified by their "ancestor" Wilfrid Owen who gave his life in the first World War, and who defined the character of poetry of such an age: "the poetry is the pity." They have thus been on the side of pity if not always of orthodoxy. Since this compassionate identification has been so largely free of sentimentality, their immediacy of experience and integrity of attitude has commonly safeguarded their ultimate direction even apart from theological commitment. It can be said of them, as Auden has written of Freud in lines we have already quoted:

> he went his way,
> Down among the Lost People like Dante, down
> To the stinking fosse where the injured
> Lead the ugly life of the rejected.[2]

Furthermore, these poets by their identification with the wider desolations and their sojourn "at the bottom of the night," have shown the way at least to a secular praise which needs but little to pass over into religious terms. Here again we can turn to the same poet, in his tribute to Yeats.

> Intellectual disgrace
> Stares from every human face,
> And the seas of pity lie
> Locked and frozen in each eye.
>
> Follow, poet, follow right
> To the bottom of the night,
> With your unconstraining voice
> Still persuade us to rejoice;

[2] *The Collected Poetry of W. H. Auden* (New York: Random House, 1945), p. 165.

> With the farming of a verse
> Make a vineyard of the curse . . .[3]

Much of the scandal involved in the role of the modern artist arises precisely out of his refusal to separate himself from the arena of today's struggle and from those involved in it. Partly to safeguard this immediacy he has shunned commitment to existing religious patterns. The rejection of familiar art forms has had a similar motivation. Traditional artistic sensibility and expression inhibit full immersion in experience. The modern artist has needed to be alert lest accepted traditions of either art or religion should beguile him away from actualities.

Both aspects apply in the case of James Joyce of whom Mr. Harry Levin says: "He did not want to lose the common reality, no matter how it offended him." No doubt in repudiating the Catholic Church and the set patterns of Irish family and society Joyce deprived himself of genuine and nourishing relations. Art inevitably becomes an exile today when it refuses the banal, the conventional and the debilitating. No doubt impulses of arrogance enter in as an alloy in such rebellion, and responsibility is tainted with pride. Nevertheless there are passages in *A Portrait of the Artist As a Young Man* which show that the young Joyce craved to find true spiritual authority in the priesthood and was disappointed. The portrait of a Jesuit priest is revealing.

> His very body had waxed old in lowly service of the Lord . . . and yet had remained ungraced by aught of saintly or of prelatic beauty. Nay his very soul had waxed old in that service without growing towards light and beauty or spreading abroad a sweet odour of her sanctity . . . Like Ignatius he was lame but in his eyes burned no spark of Ignatius' enthusiasm. Even the legendary craft of the company, a craft subtler and more secret

[3] *Ibid.*, p. 51.

than its fabled books of secret subtle wisdom, had not fired his soul with the energy of apostleship . . .[4]

In abjuring Ireland as commonly cherished Joyce like Yeats entered into the wider life of mankind and so became a greater Irishman and rendered greater services to Ireland. In his tragic break with his mother and the Catholic pieties of his family, he launched himself out on the deep in search of a new brotherhood and a new faith. In the agonizing ambiguities of loyalty in our time and in the exceptional cleavage between the older and younger generation we have in Joyce's case a remote analogy of him who when he was sought out in Galilee by his family replied: "Who are my mother and my brothers?" But Joyce's exile likewise maintained his solidarity with man in a deeper sense. "I go," he said, "to forge in the smithy of my soul the uncreated conscience of the race." And it is recognized today that the global or planetary consciousness of man is a common theme of our leading contemporary writers, one whose significance either spiritual or political cannot be exaggerated, and that Joyce has been its greatest exponent.

An analogous case is that of Charles Péguy. Péguy was all but obsessed with the lot of the poor and the fate of the unchurched. He could not reconcile himself to the church's teaching with regard to perdition and the fate of the unbaptized, especially of the Jew. He dwelt insistently upon the motives of Jesus in risking his soul among the publicans and sinners. In his *Mystery of the Charity of Joan of Arc* the compassionate shepherdess disputes vehemently the church's teaching with regard to the damnation of the unbaptized and the unbelieving. Halévy, in his life of the poet connects Péguy's life-long detachment from the Catholic Church and its sacraments with his passion to identify himself with the

---

[4] New York: The New American Library: Penguin Signet Books, 1948, pp. 143, 144; See the discussion of Joyce's break with the church in George Every, *Poetry and Personal Responsibility* (London: S. C. M. Press, 1949), pp. 31-34.

unchurched. Like the Joan of his poem, says Halévy, he did not want to be separated by Catholicism from those who needed saving. And like Joan he risked his soul with the sword.[5]

The renewal of Christianity today comes in various ways and in various disguises. Sometimes it comes with the quickening of Catholic church life and sometimes with those who rebel against it. Sometimes it comes with the quickening of the Protestant denominations and sometimes with those who repudiate them. As Péguy says of grace:

> When it doesn't come from the right it comes from the left. When it doesn't come straight it comes bent, and when it doesn't come bent it comes broken. When it doesn't come from above it comes from below; and when it doesn't come from the center it comes from the circumference. When it doesn't come like a bubbling spring it can if it like come like a trickle of water oozing from under a Loire dyke.[6]

We find a corroboration of this theme in what a Jewish writer has to say with regard to the significance of

> the new thinking going on in Jewish intellectual circles today, largely outside the sphere of the synagogue though not unfriendly to it. Much of this thinking seems to be pervaded with a deep religious concern, with a genuine anxiety to find a saving faith, a total existential commitment in terms of which one's life may be related significantly to ultimate reality. Unless the official synagogue proves utterly insensitive to this ferment, there is every probability that these newly awakening elements in American Jewry . . . will ultimately find their place within it. And it is hardly likely that this "return" will be without effect, even institutionally.[7]

[5] Halévy, op. cit., p. 183.
[6] Ibid., p. 184.
[7] Will Herberg, "Secularism in Church and Synagogue," Christianity and Crisis, Vol. X, No. 8 (May 15, 1950), p. 60.

We have said that the custody of the Christian heritage has in some real degree passed over into the keeping of secularized groups. The tradition is powerfully operative and indirectly articulate in figures not committed to the religious institutions. Not only are their actual writings indicative of the struggle but their personal lives. In these we see dramatized the cultural and spiritual conflicts and temptations of the time. Expatriation, exile, apostasy, conversion, instability, suicide—yes, even seduction for shorter or longer periods by one or other of the great rival ideologies of the hour such as fascism or communism; in such varied roles the lives and fates of these artists become revelatory, become signs of the great forces engaged.

Even where the Christian heritage is not involved in any overt way the artist is characteristically a voice against the dehumanizations all about us, whether of intellect, of technology, of social routines or of mass dogmas. He represents "the blessed rage for order" (Stevens), recovery of "the antique courtesy of your myths" and of "the living wound of love" (Tate), the building of "the Just City now" and the replacing of phantasy by Living Love (Auden), the "Nevertheless" affirmed against disaster, and the freedom acquired through "relinquishing what one would keep" (Marianne Moore), the protest against *Usura Contra Natura* (Pound), against "the waste sad time stretching before and after" (Eliot), and against the "anger" in which man is caught "exact as a machine" (Schwartz).

We cannot of course connect all the creative impulses in the arts today with Christianity or even with what could be called healthful religious renewal. But what is highly curious and worthy of close scrutiny is the quasi-religious character of these impulses. This is paradoxical if we fix our attention upon the general loss of ritual in modern life and if we recall the wide sway of realistic naturalism in the very recent past. Yet it remains true that today, perhaps by way of compensation, the artist takes on the role of the seer and art tends toward religious ceremony, especially in the wide use of myth. Ours has been called "an age of magicians." The masses appear to crave religious satisfaction and they are ready to hail miracles, create legends, revive myths.

This is an ambiguous and dangerous situation, certainly. The best poets and artists are those who canalize these impulses in the direction of order and control. Here the compassion and responsibility of which we have spoken, and the links with older Christian tradition, conduce towards a healthful symbolism and celebration.

One aspect of this situation is the tendency at least after an interval to surround the notable talents with a kind of religious aura. This has its partial explanation in the fact that these figures inevitably find themselves the foci of the explosive forces that are engaged today in revolt and conflict. So they become revelatory, become signs and paradigms of the general situation. One can see the process in figures of the recent past. The drama of their lives takes on a legendary or even mythical character. This is certainly true of Rimbaud. Something of the same kind can be said of D. H. Lawrence and Hart Crane, as indeed of Léon Bloy and Péguy. The process is evident also in the cases of modern imaginative men of action like Lauro de Bosis, martyr of the resistance in Italy to Mussolini, and Lawrence of Arabia. Secularism today has its own demands of cult and canonization.

We can only properly understand the situation in the light of the following considerations. In more "normal" times it is in the religious community, in Christendom in the older sense that prophets arise, that spiritual issues and conflicts declare themselves, that the Holy Spirit thrusts forth its witnesses, reformers, saints and martyrs. It is within a Christian society that the dilemmas of culture have their dramatic expression in crusade and schism and that fountains of quickened spiritual life are opened up for culture as a whole. But in an abnormal situation like ours these operations of the Spirit perforce take place in quasi-secular terms in a Christendom that is not indeed "pagan" but which is detached from the institutions and their orthodoxies. The spiritual alternatives and conflicts of the age have therefore a secularized expression and are fought out in the secular arena. The protagonists of traditional values, the witnesses of the older covenants and charters of our common life, the saints in the sense of the dedicated and disciplined individuals who assume the costs of non-conformity, the martyrs of scapegoats of the general crisis: all these are found in secular guise, unordained except by the authenticity of their utterance.

In an inchoate but still fundamentally Christian culture the fountains of spiritual renewal inevitably break forth often outside the churches in uncanonical witness, prayer and celebration. The outriders of the tradition carry a considerable part of the task of the defense of the faith and its renewal. Even within the church such a figure as Léon Bloy represents so creative and radical a witness that it bursts the frame of canonical piety in a way embarrassing to the institution. For it draws its power from cultural pressures of which the spiritual life of the church is not cognizant.

The prophets, then, are not always found in the church alone. This holds also with respect to prediction. Of the French political thinker Sorel it is said by Halévy: "Those who listened to him forty years ago owe it to him that a changing world did not take them by surprise." The same thing has been said over and over with regard to the new movement in the arts which in Europe anticipated the acute phase of the contemporary crisis. Rabelais observed that destiny pushes out ahead those who recognize the direction it is taking but has to drag after it the inert mass of the unperceptive. A more recent wit remarked, not without malice, that if Wall Street investors knew their business they would keep their eyes on the modern poetry magazines and exhibitions of contemporary art.

2. THE DARK DOVE: GRACE IN CATASTROPHE

The theme of judgment is no doubt the profoundest in contemporary poetry. We have given attention to the apocalyptic note in much of the literature. The vision of catastrophe almost inevitably involves a moral dimension. "Each man's work will become manifest: for the Day will disclose it, because it will be revealed with fire." Disaster is construed in terms of divine judgment and the impulse to purgation, individual and social, follows. The world, says T. S. Eliot,

> is trying the experiment of attempting to form a civilized but non-Christian mentality. The experiment will fail.

Meanwhile, he continues, it is the task of Christians

> to redeem the time so that the Faith may be preserved through the dark ages before us: to renew and rebuild civilization to save the world from suicide.

Here is the doctrine of the saving remnant. Much of the world goes into the discard according to the pattern recognized by the prophets of the Old Testament in connection with Israel itself. But a remnant preserves the heritage of the past and mitigates the disaster. We can agree with this sombre view applied to our own time. But we would insist that the Christians in question will find an ally in a corresponding remnant in the "world" itself. Just as judgment is at work both in the world and the church so grace is operative in both.

The consciousness of disaster and so of judgment today has been most appallingly felt and most powerfully expressed in connection with two areas of experience, one in peace and the other in war. In these special areas it is the sense of the total absence of God which constitutes the height of the horror. The first area is that of meaninglessness and lostness in the modern city. It is compounded of the haunting anxiety, the fierce impersonality, the lack of love, the frigid indifference of stranger to stranger. It is this experience of the "unreal city" and the throngs "undone" which runs through so much of Eliot's work. This experience in peace corrodes and lacerates, indeed destroys, innumerable men just as war does in its different theatre. As Karl Barth says, paraphrasing a passage on the judgment of God in the Epistle to the Romans:

> Here is the final vacuity and disintegration. Chaos has found itself and anything may happen. The atoms whirl, the struggle for existence rages. Even reason itself becomes wholly irrational. Ideas of duty and of fellowship become wholly unstable. The world is full of personal caprice and social unrighteousness—this is not a picture merely of Rome under the Caesars. . . . Our ungodliness and unrighteousness stand under the wrath of God. His judgment now becomes judgment and nothing more.[1]

But this experience not only disintegrates; it likewise serves as the final terror and shock to initiate impulses towards salvation. Grace operates in and through catastrophe.

The second area is that of war, and it was especially in the great raids on London that the horror of the modern lot was most acutely felt. This also finds its expression in T. S. Eliot. Just as in the first of the *Four Quartets,* "Burnt Norton," we have one of the most vivid pictures of the emptiness and the "tumid apathy" of the city and of its "strained time-ridden faces," so in the fourth, "Little Gidding," we have in section II a glimpse of the author's experience as an air-raid warden, and a meditation on the "incandescent terror" of the raids construed in terms of Dante's *Inferno.* In the early dawn after a night of destruction symbolized by "the dark dove," i.e., as a baptism of fire but a refining fire of judgment, the speaker

[1] *The Epistle to the Romans* (London: Humphrey Milford, 1933), pp. 53, 54.

encounters a figure from the world of the dead who describes the ordeal of the spirit.

> In the uncertain hour before the morning
>   Near the ending of interminable night
>   At the recurrent end of the unending
> After the dark dove with the flickering tongue
>   Had passed below the horizon of his homing
>   While the dead leaves still rattled on like tin
> Over the asphalt where no other sound was
>   Between three districts whence the smoke
>   arose
>   I met one walking. . . .

This phantom summons the speaker to purification especially by a harsh portrayal of old age and its remorse for what cannot be changed.

> 'And, last, the rending pain of re-enactment
>   Of all that you have done, and been; the shame
>   Of motives late revealed, and the awareness
> Of things ill done and done to others' harm
>   Which once you took for exercise of virtue.
>   Then fools' approval stings, and honor stains.
> From wrong to wrong the exasperated spirit
>   Proceeds, unless restored by that refining fire
>   Where you must move in measure, like a dancer.'
> The day was breaking. In the disfigured street
>   He left me, with a kind of valediction,
>   And faded on the blowing of the horn.[2]

We recognize the theme of purgation and the willing acceptance of its torments already noted in connection with *The Family Reunion* and *The Cocktail Party*. In section IV of "Little Gidding" the meditation of Section II is given perfect expression, and is carried on to the most difficult insight that love operates through the blastings and terror of the raids.

---

[2] *Four Quartets* (New York: Harcourt, Brace, 1943), pp. 33-35.

> The dove descending breaks the air
> With flame of incandescent terror
> Of which the tongues declare
> The one discharge from sin and error.
> The only hope, or else despair
> > Lies in the choice of pyre or pyre—
> > To be redeemed from fire by fire.
>
> Who then devised the torment? Love.
> Love is the unfamiliar Name
> Behind the hands that wove
> The intolerable shirt of flame
> Which human power cannot remove.
> > We only live, only suspire
> > Consumed by either fire or fire.[3]

The London raids are again the subject of one of the most powerful poems to have come out of the second World War, "Still Falls the Rain (The Raids, 1940. Night and Dawn)," by Edith Sitwell. This poem is to be put beside Marianne Moore's "In Distrust of Merits," cited at length in Chapter IX. In both, the ordeal of war points towards purgation, as is true of Mr. Eliot's more allusive use of the raids in "Little Gidding."

> STILL falls the Rain—
> Dark as the world of man, black as our loss—
> Blind as the nineteen hundred and forty nails
> Upon the Cross.
>
> Still falls the Rain
> With a sound like the pulse of the heart that is changed
>   to the hammer-beat
> In the Potter's Field, and the sound of the impious feet

---

[3] *Ibid.*, pp. 37, 38. As M. C. Bradbrook says, this section of the poem "is an apocalyptic vision in which the descent of the Spirit in tongues of flame is blazoned upon a field of fire which is at once burning London, the shirt of flame and deifying funeral pyre of a dying Herakles, and the purgatorial fire of Arnaut Daniel." "Little Gidding," *Theology*, Vol. XLVI, No. 273 March, 1943), p. 61.

On the Tomb:
>   Still falls the Rain
> In the Field of Blood where the small hopes breed and
>   the human brain
> Nurtures its greed, that worm with the brow of Cain.
>
> Still falls the Rain
> At the feet of the Starved Man hung upon the Cross.
> Christ that each day, each night, nails there,
>   have mercy on us—
> On Dives and on Lazarus:
> Under the Rain the sore and the gold are as one.
>
> Still falls the Rain—
> Still falls the Blood from the Starved Man's wounded Side:
> He bears in His Heart all wounds,—those of the light
>   that died,
> The last faint spark
> In the self-murdered heart, the wounds of the sad
>   uncomprehending dark,
> The wounds of the baited bear,—
> The blind and weeping bear whom the keepers beat
> On his helpless flesh . . . the tears of the hunted hare.
>
> Still falls the Rain—
> Then—O Ile leape up to my God: who pulles me doune—
> See, see where Christ's blood streames in the firmament:
> It flows from the Brow we nailed upon the tree
> Deep to the dying, to the thirsting heart
> That holds the fires of the world,—dark-smirched with pain
> As Caesar's laurel crown.
>
> Then sounds the voice of One who like the heart of man
> Was once a child who among beasts has lain—
> 'Still do I love, still shed my innocent light, my Blood,
>   for thee.' [4]

[4] *The Song of the Cold* (London: Macmillan, 1945), pp. 15, 16. C. M. Bowra writes of this peom: "Its victims are no longer the men and women of London but mankind symbolized in a single divine figure who suffers the weaknesses and woes not merely of humanity both rich and poor but of hunted and tortured animals. The appalling bloodshed becomes nobler by its association with this divine figure, and the notion of purification through suffering takes a new and terrible form. The picture which emerges with so tragic a grandeur fits the enormous issues which such a situation raises. . . . *The Background of Modern Poetry: An Inaugural Lecture* (Oxford: Clarendon Press, 1946), p. 13.

The experience of judgment, indeed of the annihilation of man, which has its most powerful literary transcriptions in connection with modern city life and with war, leads thus at its deeper levels towards Christian themes of purgation and renewal as in Lincoln's second inaugural address. Here we may note a covert and insidious grace at work, remote often from ecclesiastical channels. But it is far too simple for Christians to say in a moralistic and patronizing way that a godless world is learning its lesson through retribution and suffering. The regenerative forces that can be observed in the modern crisis arise often in secularism itself, and in those healthful traditions in it which have long opposed the maladies of the modern age. Grace has all along been at work in the world as well as in the church. Moreover, any "return" of an alienated world to the Christian faith waits upon a renewal of that faith and a purging of the church itself.

3. GRACE AND DISPOSSESSION IN ELIOT'S FOUR QUARTETS

The regenerative impulse toward purgation and dispossession in our crisis should not be understood as a total rejection of the values of our modern humanistic period. It should not involve a denial of the values of the French revolutionary tradition, for example, or of those of the democratic way of life, properly understood, or of the great legacy of science. Contrition must not pass over into masochism as it tended to do in France after the collapse of 1940.

Here a question arises as to the appeal to expiation in much of T. S. Eliot's later writing. In his work from "Ash Wednesday" through the *Four Quartets,* including his plays, we have an incomparable and valid presentation of that moment in the religious life which involves contrition, purification, dispossession. This theme, however, is so accented and so isolated from other more positive motifs of piety that an excessively negative and ascetic principle appears to be determinative.

GRACE AND DISPOSSESSION IN ELIOT

In a day of judgment like our own this theme may have large justification. But even a fulminating Jeremiah and a haggard Dante offer their summons to repentance in a wider context of passionate cultural affirmation and diversified religious mood.

Mr. Eliot's prose treatment of problems of culture and education, taken in connection with his poetry, tends to confirm us in the suspicion that his great theme of purgation involves too negative a view of the operation of grace in the secular life. Salvation is experienced only in rejection, rejection not only of the world in its evil aspect but of creaturely existence itself. Due care is needed in registering such a demurral. Thus in the third section of "Burnt Norton" dispossession is to be understood in terms of the discipline of the Christian mystic as a temporary exercise in purification. This discipline requires descent into a

> World not world, but that which is not world,
> Internal darkness, deprivation
> And destitution of all property,
> Dessication of the world of sense,
> Evacuation of the world of fancy,
> Inoperancy of the world of spirit.[1]

But in the conclusion of this quartet love as the goal of the search is set over against desire as something unmoving and timeless which does not really enter into the movement and time of our life.

> Desire itself is movement
> Not in itself desirable;
> Love is itself unmoving,
> Only the cause and end of movement,
> Timeless, and undesiring
> Except in the aspect of time
> Caught in the form of limitation
> Between un-being and being.[2]

[1] *Op. cit.*, p. 6.
[2] *Ibid.*, p. 8.

Those familiar with the theological discussion of *agape* and *eros* will recognize that Eliot sides with Nygren's exclusive dialectic.

Thus, despite fluctuations, time here, as in *Murder in the Cathedral,* is on the whole viewed negatively. It is not just the "waste sad time," misused and corrupted, which is evil but time itself. It is only when time is intersected by revelation—"The point of intersection of the timeless with time,"— where we have a moment "outside of time," that meaning or grace is acknowledged. In other words Eliot employs an extreme Kierkegaardian antithesis, though he may combine it with an analogous depreciation of time as over against eternity or being from the language of the mystics or of the *Bhagavad-Gita.* Here the experience of that reality of which "human kind cannot bear very much," the experience of the eternal moment, is in effect the sole good and the chief end of life from the religious viewpoint. Of that moment we have only adumbrations:

> The hint half-guessed, the gift half-understood,
>   is Incarnation.

It is continually evoked in the poems as a memory or an aspiration under the figure of the rose-garden and the children, or of "the still point of the turning world."

It is to be granted that the experience of men in time is not always viewed as wholly meaningless or evil. There are passages in the *Quartets* where it is recognized, as in Ecclesiastes, that

> There is a time for the evening under starlight,
> A time for the evening under lamplight
> (The evening with the photograph album).[3]

There are also passages in which the forms of the arts, the Chinese jar, or the patterns of ceremonial tradition, the dance,

---

[3] East Coker, V, *ibid.,* p. 17.

convey to us in time the timeless pattern. But such are outweighed by passages in which the past and future are only

> movement
> Of that which is only moved
> And has in it no source of movement—
> Driven by daemonic, chthonic
> Powers.[4]

The two possible solutions of meaninglessness proposed in *The Cocktail Party* bear on this. The only real way of salvation is that of complete renunciation of the world as exemplified in the religious vocation of the character Celia, pointing in this case to martyrdom. On the other hand, the two Chamberlaynes, Edward and Lavinia, remain in the world, but only a negative value is assigned to their disciplinary ordeal of mediocrity. As Eliot says in "The Dry Salvages" of that higher way:

> For most of us, this is the aim
> Never here to be realized;
> Who are only undefeated
> Because we have gone on trying.[5]

Is there no middle ground? Or rather, is not the way of victorious renunciation practicable in the world? There would seem to be here a systematic, not to say dogmatic, prejudgment which in effect excludes the full operation of grace in the secular life. Eliot follows a thorough-going Catholic distinction of natural and supernatural, and sometimes compounds it with a Kierkegaardian conception of "the moment" which further evacuates time of real meaning. Even Catholic theology has its way of avoiding Eliot's position here. Protestant theology (apart from the dialectical tradition reaching from Kierkegaard to Barth) would make it clearer on the one hand that it is

[4] The Dry Salvages, V, *ibid.*, p. 28.
[5] Section V; *ibid.*, p. 28.

sin which is evil and not existence itself, and on the other that grace can operate as fully in the secular life as in the life of the religious: i.e., as fully in the case of the Chamberlaynes as in those of Celia or Becket.

We find our judgment supported here by Dr. Nathan A. Scott, Jr. who feels that a dramatic fault in *The Cocktail Party* is connected with "a certain doctrinal incompleteness in Eliot's grasp of the Christian concept at issue" in what concerns "vocation." [6] Citing Mr. Lionel Trilling who says apropos of the "way" assigned to the Chamberlaynes: "few of us will want to say much for the life of the common routine, the life without an eagle, yet we know we can say more than this," [7] Dr. Scott writes:

> Mr. Trilling voices here, I believe, what must surely be felt by many of us: namely, an irrepressible conviction of the relative unattractiveness of the portion allowed by the poet to those who "build the hearth" as against that allowed to "those who go upon a journey." And I should like now to suggest that his failure to evoke from us at this point, as an artist, an act of imaginative assent may possibly be the result of his having neglected, on the theological level, to examine the eschatological dimension of the Christian notion of "vocation." . . . But, though Eliot's handling of Celia and her "way" embraces this eschatological aspect, there is no similar suggestion of it in his handling of the nonheroic Chamberlaynes (which provides the more crucial test of his theological wisdom). In the life allotted Edward and Lavinia, there is no vertical dimension, there are no "moments of glory," and so we reject it as something too thin and gray to be either esthetically or spiritually quite valid.[8]

[6] "T. S. Eliot's *The Cocktail Party*: Of Redemption and Vocation," *Religion in Life*, Vol. XX, No. 2 (Spring, 1951), pp. 274-285.

[7] "Wordsworth and the Iron Time," *The Kenyon Review*, Vol. VII, No. 3, pp. 493-494.

[8] *Op. cit.*, pp. 284-285.

Our observations here confirm the theme of our earlier chapters on Catholic poetry and on G. M. Hopkins (Chs. VI and VII). The Christian heritage in its Catholic frame has too formal a character to enter into full encounter with modern experience. It is a subsidiary point that the Catholic artist labors under a special handicap because of the increasingly esoteric character of his symbolism. The artist of Protestant background, even if he works in detachment for the time being from the religious institution, is able to employ a flexible and transmuted Christian symbolism, and so enter into a more profound conversation with men of today in their peculiar dilemmas.

Nevertheless grace operates today through Catholic witness as well as Protestant, and through uncanonical as well as orthodox channels. We may take our concluding statement from Charles Péguy, a writer whose Catholic connection was irregular precisely because, as we have seen, he felt himself under bond to the unchurched multitudes and conscripted to those causes and struggles of the modern world with which the institution could not adequately identify itself:

> Grace is insidious, it twists and is full of surprises. . . . Certainly the modern world has done all it can to proscribe Christianity, to rid itself of all substance, every atom and every trace of Christianity. But if I catch sight of an invincible, insubmersible, incomprehensible Christianity creeping out again from below, creeping in from the surroundings, creeping in from all around, am I to miss my chance of hailing it just because I was not up to calculating where it would come from? . . . Where is it written that God will abandon man in sin? . . . This people will finish a way they never began. This age, this world, this people will get there along a road they never set out on. And many moreover and thus will take upon themselves and find themselves together in the sacramental forms.[9]

[9] "Clio," cited in Daniel Halévy, *op. cit.*, pp. 184, 185.

THE BROSS FOUNDATION

IN 1879, the late William Bross of Chicago, lieutenant-governor of Illinois from 1866-70, desiring to have a permanent memorial of his son, Nathaniel Bross, who had died in 1856, entered into an agreement with the "Trustees of Lake Forest University" whereby there was finally transferred to the Trustees a large sum of money, the income of which was to accumulate in perpetuity for successive periods of ten years, the accumulations of one decade to be spent in the following decade, for the purpose of stimulating the production of the best books or treatises "on the connection, relation, and mutual bearing on any practical science, or the history of our race, or the facts in any department of knowledge, with and upon the Christian Religion."

In his deed of gift the founder had in view "the religion of the Bible, composed of the Old and New Testaments of our Lord and Saviour Jesus Christ, as commonly received in the Presbyterian and other evangelical churches." His object was "to call out the best efforts of the highest talent and the ripest scholarship of the world, to illustrate from science or any department of knowledge, and to demonstrate, the divine origin and the authority of the Christian Scriptures; and, further, to show how both science and revelation coincide, and to prove the existence, the providence, or any or all of the attributes of the only living and true God infinite, eternal and unchangeable in His being, wisdom, power, holiness, justice, goodness, and truth."

In 1900, at the end of the first decade of accumulations from the Bross Fund, the Trustees began to carry out the provisions of the Trust Agreement. It was determined that the series of books published by the Foundation should be called the Bross Library. Mr. Bross had specified that Volume I of the series should be *Evidences of Christianity*, by Mark Hopkins, who was his revered teacher at Williams College and to whom he went for advice in planning the Foundation. Accordingly, the copyright of this book was secured and it was published in a presentation edition as Volume I. Succeeding volumes of the series were procured by the two methods prescribed in the Trust Agreement: (1) by conducting competitions and (2) by publishing lectures delivered under the auspices of the Foundation.

Five competitions have been held to date, the award in each of the first three being six thousand dollars.

In the first competition, completed in 1905, the prize was awarded to the Reverend James Orr, D.D., Professor of Apologetics and Systematic Theology in the United Free Church College, Glasgow, Scotland, for his treatise on *The Problem of the Old Testament*. This book was published in 1906 as Volume III of the Bross Library. The prize in the second competition was awarded in 1915 to the Reverend Thomas James Thorburn, D.D., L.L.D., Hastings, England, for his book entitled, *The Mythical Interpretation of the Gospels*, Volume VII of the Bross Library. The third competition was won by Douglas Clyde Macintosh, Ph.D., Dwight Professor of Theology, Yale University, New Haven, Connecticut, in 1925, with his book entitled *The Reasonableness of Christianity*, which became Volume XIII of the series. The fifteen thousand dollar prize of the Fiftieth Anniversary Competition was awarded in 1940 to Harris Franklin Rall, Ph.D., Professor of Christian Doctrine, Garrett Biblical Institute, Evanston, Illinois, for his *Christianity: An Inquiry Into Its Nature and Truth*, Volume XV of the series. The seven thousand five hundred dollar prize in the 1950 competition was awarded to the author of the present volume, Dr. Amos Niven Wilder, Chairman of the Department of New Testament and Early Christian Literature, Chicago Theological Seminary and Federated Theological Faculty, University of Chicago.

All the competitions have been announced three or four years in advance in order that prospective entrants would have ample time to prepare books for submission. Also, the administrators of the Foundation have sought to advertise them as widely as possible. Recognized religious leaders and scholars have served as judges in the competitions, and to insure an objective judgment the names of the writers have been withheld from them. These contests have without doubt helped to realize the aims of William Bross to reward more generously those who make significant contributions to man's religious and intellectual progress and to stimulate men to greater achievements.

Ten volumes of the Bross Library consist of lectures delivered at Lake Forest University. The first course sponsored by the Foundation on *Obligatory Morality*, delivered in May, 1903, by the Reverend Francis Landey Patton, D.D., L.L.D., President of Princeton Theological Seminary, was not published. Volume II of the Bross Library, published in 1905, contains a course of lectures on *The Bible: Its Origin and Nature*, delivered in May, 1904, by the Reverend Marcus Dods, D.D., Professor of Exegetical Theology in New College, Edinburgh. The third course of lectures, *The Bible of Nature*, delivered in September and October, 1907, by J. Arthur Thomson, M.A., Regius Professor of Natural History in the University of Aberdeen, was published in 1908 as Volume IV. The fourth course, *The Religions of Modern Syria and Palestine*, delivered in November and December of 1908 by Frederick Jones Bliss, Ph.D., of Beirut, Syria, comprises Volume V. In Volume VI was published the fifth series of lectures, *The Sources of Religious Insight*, delivered in November, 1911, by Professor Josiah Royce, Ph.D., of Harvard University. The next course of lectures, *The Will to Freedom*, given in May, 1915, by the Reverend John Neville Figgis, D.D., LL.D., of the House of Resurrection, Mirfield, England, formed Volume VIII of the Bross Library. A course of lectures entitled, *Faith Justified by Progress*, delivered in 1916 by Henry Wilkes Wright, Professor of Philosophy in Lake Forest College, was published as Volume IX.

Bible and Spade, a series of lectures delivered in 1921 by the Reverend John P. Peters, Ph.D., of Sewanee, Tennessee, makes up Volume X. Volume XI, *Christianity and Problems of Today*, consists of a group of lectures given by several men on the occasion of the inauguration of Herbert McComb Moore, D.D., as President of Lake Forest College. The lectures of M. Bross Thomas, D.D., Professor Emeritus of Biblical Literature at Lake Forest College, on *The Biblical Idea of God*, were delivered in 1923 and published as Volume XII. *England's First Library*, a series of lectures delivered in 1929 by the Reverend James G. K. McClure, President Emeritus of The Presbyterian Theological Seminary, Chicago, Illinois, was published as Volume XIV under the title, *The Supreme Book of Mankind*.

Besides providing for the production of books, William Bross was concerned with their distribution. Moved by the desire to make them available to a large number of people, he specified that the copyright of all books obtained by competition or presented as lectures should be transferred to the Foundation. He limited the royalties from their publication to a small amount so that they could be sold at a cheaper price than is customary for books of a similar nature. Also, in order that they might be read by people who could not afford to buy books, he requested that they be distributed by the Foundation to selected libraries where they would be free to all who asked for them.

William Bross hoped that the foundation which he designed as a memorial to his son would be an instrument for the spiritual enrichment of life. In the minds of those who know the Bross Library there can be no doubt that his hope has come to fruition.

ERNEST A. JOHNSON,
President of Lake Forest College

Lake Forest, Illinois

INDEX

References in heavy type indicate quotation or discussion

Barth, K., 67,' 261, **270**
Baudelaire, 11, 233
Baxter, Richard, 8
Berdyaev, N., **258**
Bernanos, 130, **145f.**, 195, 214
Bialik, H. N., 193 f.n.
Bishop, J. P., **123**
Blake, William, 29, 96, 100, 210, 243
Bloy, L., **130f.**, **268**
Boccaccio, 3
Bogan, Louise, **257**
Bowra, C. M., **273** f.n.
Bremond, H., **11f.**, 16 f.n., **20** f.n.
Bridges, R., 9, 12, 95, 148, 150, **159**
Brooke, R., 84, 91
Brooks, Gwendolyn, **64f.**
Browning, R., 157
Bunker, John, **61**
Burns, C. A., 168

Cabot, Richard, 5
Calvin, **32f.**, 39
Camus, 216
Carmen, Bliss, **95**
Channing-Pearce, 161 f.n., 261 f.n.
Claudel, 145, 190
Cram, R. A., 189
Crane, Hart, 5, 11 f.n., **233f.**
Crouch, Joseph, 81 f.n.
Curti, M., 31 f.n.

Dante, **40**, 212
de Bosis, L., 267
Dickens, 157

Dixon, R. W., 149f., 168, **170**
Donne, J., 8, 26, 47
Dostoievsky, 210, 233
Doughty, 157

Eberhart, R., **148**
El Greco, 210
Eliot, T. S., 104, **177**, **206f.**, **218**, 222, 259, **269**, The Waste Land: **22**, 202, 206, **208**; The Four Quartets: **53**, **270-272**, 274; The Family Reunion: **223-226**; The Cocktail Party: **226**, 277
Emerson, 30, **34-37**
Every, George, **81**, 83 f.n., **187** f.n., 214

Fairchild, H. N., **38-43**, 185, 253 f.n.
Fearing, K., **57f.**
Fichte, **60**
Flanagan, J. B., **152**
Forster, E. M., **151**
Fowlie, Wallace, 130 f.n., **131f.**, 211, 214
Frankenberg, L., 239 f.n.
Freud, S., 48f., **186f.**, **197f.**, 200, 262
Fromm, E., 25
Frost, Robert, 69f., **92f.**, 97, 191

Gabriel, R., 31 f.n.
Gardner, E. G., 128
Gauguin, **63**, 97
Gibran, K., 84
Gide, André, 19, **137**, 157, 184

Gray, Thomas, **99**
Green, Julian, **113f.**, 133, 135, 214
Greene, Graham, 145, 195

Halévy, Daniel, 130 f.n., **133f.**, **264f.**
Hardy, T., **236**
Hawthorne, N., 30, 34, 211
Hazelton, R., **83**
Heard, G., 63
Hendry, J. F., **209f.**
Henley, W. E., 77
Heppenstall, R., 130 f.n., **145ff.**
Herberg, W., **265**
Herbert, George, 8, 80, 157
Herford, C. H., **121, 125**
Hillyer, R., 71
Hodgson, R., 103
Hopkins, G. M., 12, 73, **125f., 148-175,** 195, **250** f.n.
Hulme, T. E., 21
Huxley, Aldous, **56,** 63

Jacob, Max, 138
Jarrell, R., **47f.**
Jeffers, R., 63, 110, 183, **184,** 244
Johnson, Samuel, **14f.**
Jones, H. M., **30-32**
Jones, Rufus, 93
Joyce, James, **19,** 205, 243f., **263f.**

Kafka, F., 55, **56f.,** 193, 212
Keats, J., 16
Keble, 8
Kierkegaard, 12, 161, 199f.
Kingsley, C., 84
Kipling, R., 77, 91
Koestler, A., 62
Koyré, A., **23f.**
Kunitz, S., **54**

Lautréamont, 137
Lawrence, D. H., 9, 19, 35, **63, 104,** 183f., 234, 244
Lawrence, T. E., **267**
Leavis, F. R., **156**

Lenin, 10
Leonard, W. E., 93 f.n.
Lewis, C. Day, **157f.**
Lindsay, V., 73, 77, **151**
Locke, John, 33
Lowell, Robert, 73, **138-141, 223**
Lowes, J. L., **9**
Loyola, F., **171f., 175**

MacDonald, D. B., **4**
MacIver, R. H., 53
MacLeish, A., **61, 91, 105f., 110**
McNamee, M. B., 250 f.n.
MacNeice, L., **221f.**
Mallarmé, 16
Mann, T., 50, 56f.
Mannheim, K., 51
Maritain, Jacques, 3, **11, 131, 137, 166, 200f.**
Maritain, Raissa, 130 f.n.
Marx, K., **186**
Masters, E. L., 77
Matthiessen, F. O., 31 f.n., **33-35,** 78
Mauriac, F., 145f., 195
Melville, H., 30, 34, **35,** 211, 233
Merton, Thomas, **13,** 115, **141-143,** 208, **209**
Miller, Perry, 31 f.n.
Milton, J., 9, 21, **25-27,** 53, 85, **152,** 201
Moore, Marianne, **82, 227f., 266**
Murdock, K. B., **8,** 9 f.n., **79f.**

Newman, J. H., 153
Nicholson, N., **98-100,** 209
Niebuhr, Reinhold, **212**
Nietzsche, 34f., **49f.,** 62, 200, 244
Norton, C. E., 35
Noyes, A., 84

O'Connor, W. V., 16 f.n., 221
Oldham, J., 50
Owen, Wilfred, 91, 262

INDEX

Pach, W., **152**
Pascal, 197, 244
Patmore, C., 149
Péguy, C., **130-137**, 146, 211, **257**, **264f.**, **279**
Perry, R. B., **31**, **32**
Perse, St.-John, 5, **103-111**, 205f.
Phare, E. E., **14f.**, 150 f.n., 158
Picasso, 176
Pick, J., 168, **171-173**
Planck, M., 50
Plato, 10
Poe, E. A., 16
Pound, E., 52, 105, 184, 205f., **207**, 213, **240**, 266
Psalter, 15, 83

Raphael, **113f.**
Read, Herbert, **78**
Ridley, Anne, **222**
Rimbaud, 5, 11, 137, 156
Robinson, E. A., 70, 191
Rodman, S., **139**
Rouault, G., **130-132**, 214
Rukeyser, M., **61**
Ruggles, E., 150
Rylaarsdam, J. C., 6 f.n.

Sackville-West, V., **89-97**
Sandburg, C., 69, 77
Santayana, 3 f.n., 244
Sayers, D., **10**
Schwartz, D., **206f.**, **218**, **222**, **237**, **252f.**
Scott, N. A., 207, **278**
Scotus, D., **160**, 172
Shapiro, K., 11 f.n., **217**, **233-235**
Shelley, 29, **121f.**, 201, 243f.
Sherman, S. P., **36f.**
Siegfried, André, **31f.**

Silone, I., **211**, 258
Sitwell, Edith, **272-273**
Sorel, 268
Sperry, W. L., 31
Spiegel, S., 193 f.n.
Stevens, Wallace, 74, 190, **239-241**, **245-251**, 266
St.-John Perse, see Perse
St. Paul, 45
Stravinski, 176
Sweeney, J. L., **101**

Tagore, R., 84, 103
Tate, Allen, 138, **140**, **222f.**, **236-238**, **245**, 266
Tennyson, 91
Thomas, Dylan, 55, **100-102**, 209
Thompson, F., 95, **114-125**, **142f.**
Thoreau, H. D., 34
Tillich, P., 208, 258
Treece, H., 209
Trilling, L., 42, **278**

Valéry, P., **16**, **19f.**, **110f.**, 190
Van Gogh, 97f., 244
von Hügel, F., 169
Vergil, 94

White, Helen C., 196 f.n.
Whitman, Walt, 30, 34f., **37f.**, **157f.**, 185
Wilder, T., 208
Willey, Basil, 28
Winters, Yvor, 11 f.n., 36
Wordsworth, W., 9, **28-30**, 85, 97f., 103
Wright, F. L., 189

Yeats, W. B., 9, 19, **52**, 84, 121, 169, **213f.**, **241f.**, 244, **261f.**

www.ingramcontent.com/pod-product-compliance
Lightning Source LLC
Chambersburg PA
CBHW071233230426
43668CB00011B/1421